300

Szas/48

Literary Advertising and the Shaping of British Romanticism

Literary Advertising and the Shaping of British Romanticism

NICHOLAS MASON

The Johns Hopkins University Press
Baltimore

© 2013 The Johns Hopkins University Press
All rights reserved. Published 2013
Printed in the United States of America on acid-free paper
2 4 6 8 9 7 5 3 1

The Johns Hopkins University Press
2715 North Charles Street
Baltimore, Maryland 21218-4363
www.press.jhu.edu

Mason, Nicholas, 1970–
Literary advertising and the shaping of British romanticism / Nicholas Mason.
pages cm. Includes bibliographical references and index.
ISBN-13: 978-1-4214-0998-6 (hardcover : alk. paper)
ISBN-13: 978-1-4214-1071-5 (electronic) ISBN-10: 1-4214-0998-4 (hardcover : alk. paper) ISBN-10: 1-4214-1071-0 (electronic)
1. Literature publishing—Great Britain—History—18th century. 2. Literature publishing—Great Britain—History—19th century. 3. Authors and publishers—Great Britain—History—18th century. 4. Authors and publishers—Great Britain—History—19th century. 5. Advertising—Great Britain—History—18th century. 6. Advertising—Great Britain—History—19th century. 7. Romanticism—Great Britain. I. Title.
Z326.M37 2013   070.50941090'033—dc23
2012045506

A catalog record for this book is available from the British Library.

Special discounts are available for bulk purchases of this book. For more information, please contact Special Sales at 410-516-6936 or specialsales@press.jhu.edu.

The Johns Hopkins University Press uses environmentally friendly book materials, including recycled text paper that is composed of at least 30 percent post-consumer waste, whenever possible.

Contents

Acknowledgments vii

INTRODUCTION Entangled Histories 1

CHAPTER 1 Advertising in the Romantic Century 11

CHAPTER 2 The Progress of Puffery 23

CHAPTER 3 Building Brand Byron 50

CHAPTER 4 L.E.L., Bandwagon Marketing, and the Rise of Visual Culture 81

CHAPTER 5 Puffery and the "Death" of Literature in Late-Romantic Britain 118

CONCLUSION The Art of Advertising 143

Notes 151
Bibliography 167
Index 193

Acknowledgments

This book began in the late 1990s and has benefited, I hope, from the long gestation period that has followed. Much of my early thinking on the connections between literary and advertising history grew out of exchanges with Helen Cooper, Heidi Hutner, Ira Livingston, Cliff Siskin, and Michael Sprinker. Cliff and Michael, in particular, gave crucial guidance, helping me formulate some of my key research questions and consistently offering detailed, incisive feedback. Cliff has long been the model mentor—at once exacting, supportive, and unfailingly generous. Michael shared his insights and knowledge until literally his last hours. I frequently share with my students his final, entirely characteristic, bit of feedback: "This is by far the best thing I have seen on this subject . . . from you."

Since coming to Brigham Young University in 1999, I have benefited from a stimulating teaching environment, the resources and time to expand and rethink this book, and a remarkably large and intellectually diverse set of colleagues with interests in eighteenth- and nineteenth-century British literature. Among those at BYU who deserve particular thanks for reading and commenting on sections of this book are Frank Christianson, Ed Cutler, Rick Duerden, Jill Rudy, Leslee Thorne-Murphy, Paul Westover, and Matt Wickman. Colleagues at other universities whose input has pushed this book in productive new directions include Jennifer Ashton, Walter Benn-Michaels, Andrew Elfenbein, Andrew Franta, Anthony Jarrells, Paul Keen, Simon Kovesi, Devoney Looser, Peter Manning, Tom Mole, Mark Parker, and, above all, John Strachan, my co-laborer in the field of advertising history and a fountain of knowledge on seemingly every niche of Romantic-era popular culture. Most recently, the L.E.L. chapter improved considerably thanks to feedback from Angela Esterhammer, Patrick Vincent, Sara Nyffenegger, and the other participants in the British Romanticism research group at the University of Zurich. Finally, Matt McAdam, Melissa Solarz, Anne Whitmore, and others at the Johns Hopkins University Press have been highly supportive, insightful, and professional through the final stages of bringing this book to life.

Several sections of this book would not have been possible without the collections and staff at the New York Public Library, the Metropolitan Museum of Art, the Huntington Library, the British Library, the British Library Newspaper Reading Room, the British Museum, the Bodleian Library, the National Library of Scotland, the Stony Brook University Libraries, and the Harold B. Lee Library at BYU. I also profited immensely from having ready access to such game-changing digital databases as Google Book, ECCO, and LION.

The College of Humanities and Department of English at BYU have been unfailingly supportive of this project, both intellectually and financially. Research for this book has also been funded in part by a number of timely and generous fellowships and grants, including a Carl H. Pforzheimer, Jr., Research Grant from the Keats-Shelley Association of America, a Bibliographical Society of America Fellowship, a Fletcher Jones Foundation Fellowship from the Huntington Library, and a Ray and Ida Lee Beckham Lectureship from BYU's Department of Communications.

Thanks are also in order for the various presses who have allowed me to include material previously published elsewhere. An earlier version of the section on the consumer revolution found in Chapter 1 appeared in "Consumer Culture: Getting and Spending in Romantic Britain" (*A Concise Companion to Romanticism*, edited by Jon Klancher [Oxford: Blackwell, 2009], 189–211; used with permission). Portions of Chapters 2 and 5 were published in "'The Quack has become God': Puffery, Print, and the 'Death' of Literature in Romantic-Era Britain" (*Nineteenth-Century Literature* 60 [2005]: 1–31; used with permission). A previous version of Chapter 4 appeared as "Building Brand Byron: Early-Nineteenth-Century Advertising and the Marketing of *Childe Harold's Pilgrimage*" (*Modern Language Quarterly* 63 [2002]: 411–41; used with permission).

Finally, a note of personal thanks to the family members whose love, companionship, and good will makes every day a pleasure—specifically, my brothers (Matt, Patrick, and Christian Mason), parents (Mike and LeAnn Mason), in-laws (Leonard and Katheryn Gunderson), children (Sam, Anna, Michael, and Ellen Mason), and, above all, my wife, Stacie. Not even the most audacious puffs in the pages below can do justice to just how unprecedented, unrivaled, and eminently fashionable you all are.

Literary Advertising and the Shaping of British Romanticism

INTRODUCTION

Entangled Histories

In the summer of 1817 the up-and-coming Edinburgh publisher and bookseller William Blackwood pulled aside John Wilson and John Gibson Lockhart, two free-spirited, Oxford-trained attorneys who frequented his shop, and made them a proposal. The magazine he had launched in April of that year, the *Edinburgh Monthly*, was floundering, and he hoped they would help him make it fresher, bolder, and smarter. More than anything, he wanted his periodical, which would be rechristened *Blackwood's Edinburgh Magazine*, to break the stranglehold giant publishing houses had on British literature. While *Blackwood's* would be openly partisan on political matters, as per the custom of the age, it would offer a sharp break from the two dominant literary periodicals (Archibald Constable's *Edinburgh Review* and John Murray's *Quarterly Review*) in its critical impartiality and its dedication to publishing the best original poetry and short fiction of the day.[1]

The rebranded magazine Blackwood, Lockhart, and Wilson introduced to an astonished public in October 1817 was, in today's vernacular, quintessentially "indie." The first issue of "Maga," as the magazine came to be known, featured open mockery of Leigh Hunt's "Cockney School of Poetry," a withering critique of Coleridge's *Biographia Literaria*, and the "Chaldee Manuscript," an outrageous, biblical-styled parody of Edinburgh's Whig literary and political establishment. Simply put, this was an all-out declaration of war on the literary status quo, a thorough repudiation of the backroom, back-scratching world of mainstream publishing. And from the start, a central fixation was upon reforming literary criticism, which, in the eyes of many, had devolved into yet another branch of the nation's hydra-headed advertising system. "If one looks around among our periodicals," Lockhart lamented in the March 1823 number of *Blackwood's*,

> there is scarcely one of them that is not labouring away to hoist up some heavy bottom. The Quarterly and the British Critic tell us that [Henry] Milman is a mighty poet. The New Monthly Magazine, and five or six inferior books, keep up a perpetual blast about Barry Cornwall—Waugh [the publisher of the *Edinburgh Monthly Review*] winds his sultry horn for the glory of Mrs. [Felicia] Hemans—Taylor and Hessey [owners of the *London Magazine*] pound the public with [Bernard] Barton and Allan Cunningham. ("Noctes Ambrosianae, No. VII," 376)

If, as this indictment alleges, deeply politicized criticism and advertisements masquerading as book reviews were the norm at other magazines, *Blackwood's* intended to aim for the opposite extreme. William Blackwood informed a prospective contributor to his magazine in 1820, "I would rather see any publication of mine, or of any of my friends, cut to pieces in the Magazine than that there should be the slightest appearance of favour or partiality—for this is perfect destruction to 'Maga' and would render her no better than a petty bookselling job" (qtd. in Oliphant, 1:377).

Yet, despite these founding ideals, even before Lockhart's pontification, *Blackwood's* was slipping into the mire of literary puffery. The power to influence which books their readers might purchase proved too great a temptation for a publisher with new titles to promote and a team of magazine insiders anxious about the fates of their own books and those of their friends. A rather telling case in point comes from the spring of 1822, when John Wilson learned that Blackwood had commissioned Henry Mackenzie, the senior statesman of Scottish letters, to review Wilson's new book, *The Lights and Shadows of Scottish Life*. After seeing a draft of Mackenzie's lukewarm review, Wilson fired off a letter to Blackwood, calling the piece "loathsome" and "sickening" and demanding that he be allowed to find his own reviewer for the volume. When Blackwood conceded, Wilson contemplated reviewing the book himself before deciding to enlist his close friend Lockhart in the cause. Predictably, Lockhart's review, which ran in the June 1822 issue of the magazine, dealt in superlatives. *Lights and Shadows*, we are told, was "most indubitably full of exquisite poetry" (670), and "every page overflows with images of the most pure and beautiful tenderness" (677).[2]

Two years later, while preparing for the release of his own new book, *The History of Matthew Wald*, Lockhart had no compunctions about urging Wilson to return the favor, asking, "Pray write a first-rate but *brief* puff of *Matthew* for [the] next number [of] Blackwood['s], or if not, say so, that I may do it myself" (qtd. in Strout, 120). When Wilson apparently proved too busy to come through, Lockhart, as promised, took the task upon himself—a fact verified by Blackwood's account book, which shows Lockhart being paid the standard contributor's fee to review his own novel (Murray, 150). Again, not surprisingly, the review was glowing.

Flash forward 180 years and turn 4,500 miles due west and we find another group of booklovers in another northern cultural outpost dreaming up ways to take on the literary establishment through a new medium. This time, though, it is not a group of twenty-something Tories launching literary raids from north of the Tweed but a confederacy of bookworms and computer geeks huddled together in the Seattle office of a new company, visualizing how the Internet might allow anyone anywhere to buy any book in print. In creating "the world's largest bookstore," they imagined themselves wresting contemporary literature away from international conglomerates and corporate superstores and putting it back in the hands of writers and readers. As James Marcus, one of the company's earliest employees, recalls, their principal mission was, quite simply, "to preach the gospel of literature from the Internet pulpit" (22).

After naming their company after the world's largest river, the group took their website, amazon.com, live in 1995 and quickly began attracting a core of loyal customers. While they were more than happy to sell you an automobile repair manual or the latest Danielle Steele novel, the company's carefully crafted ethos was as a haven for former English majors and other assorted bibliophiles. One day Amazon's home page might recommend Richard Holmes's new biography of Coleridge; the next it might feature an interview with Toni Morrison or Salman Rushdie. And, rather astonishingly, despite stiff competition from Barnes and Noble, Borders, and a host of imitators, Amazon's formula actually paid off. By 1999 it had become the darling of the dot.com boom, with both its sales and its stock price skyrocketing. Even its editorial team—the twenty-five or so bookworms and bohemians charged with writing heady reviews and author profiles—cashed in on the moment. In the words of one Amazon reviewer, their company stock options made them "the best paid editorial staff since the invention of moveable type" (J. Marcus, 77).

Yet, even as the stock price soared and the company's founder, Jeff Bezos, was crowned *Time* magazine's "Person of the Year" for 1999, Amazon's image as the savior of literature was beginning to crack. Behind the scenes, the company had hired a team of corporate veterans who immediately proposed merging the editorial and marketing divisions. (The new division, one high-ranking executive boasted, would be dubbed "Marketorial" [J. Marcus, 107].) Soon the company that at one time had promised to level the playing field occupied by both giant multinational publishers and struggling basement presses began reverting to the old rules of brick-and-mortar retail, where prominent display space comes with a price. The precise moment of Amazon's fall from public grace can be dated to February 8, 1999, when, adjacent to accounts of the Clinton impeachment debates and the death of Jordan's King Hussein, the *New York Times* ran a page-one exposé entitled "For Sale: On-Line Bookstore's Recommendations." As detailed in that story, Amazon had recently begun offering a $10,000-per-book package to advertisers that included the top position on its home page, an author profile, and "complete Amazon.com editorial review treatment." In the first few months of this campaign, several $10,000 books had made their way onto Amazon's supposedly objective lists of books deemed "New and Notable," "What We're Reading," and "Destined for Greatness," and nowhere on the website was any distinction made between unsolicited and paid reviews (Carvajal).

Amazon's eventual solution for this public relations disaster was sacking its editorial staff and replacing them with an army of volunteer reviewers. While most consumer reviews on the site are ostensibly disinterested, this system, too, rapidly morphed into an engine for puffery, as evidenced in 2004, when a glitch in Amazon's Canadian site temporarily unmasked thousands of hitherto anonymous reviewers. Self-reviewing, it seems, was a pastime not only for the likes of Kent Braithwaite, a California high school teacher who promoted his debut novel, *The Wonderland Murders*, via a series of glowing reviews he had posted under a range of aliases; as it turns out, it was also an occasional hobby of award-winning, highbrow writers like Dave Eggers, John Rechy, and Jonathan Franzen, all of whom were caught pseudonymously dishing out five-star reviews for either their own works or those of close friends (Giles, 14; Harmon).[3]

What, then, to make of the parallel morality tales of *Blackwood's Magazine* and amazon.com? For some, such narratives only reinforce the notion that literature is locked with commerce in a long-term battle for its very soul. While many writers and publishers enter the fray with the best of intentions, the commercial logic of late capitalist societies, it would seem, has a way of reducing even the most profound, beautiful, and sacred texts into mere commodities. As Theodor Adorno rather dolefully puts it, "Entertainment sells the neutralized dregs of serious art." The art world, he continues, "has become vulgar ever since the mechanism of exchange has sunk its fangs into artistic production, turning art into a commodity" (434). Rather than surrendering to the commercial impulse, however, many contend that art can still be shielded from what Allen Ginsberg dubbed "the nitroglycerine shrieks of the fairies of advertising" ("Howl," line 56). At the very least, they insist, art should be treated as what the legal theorist Margaret Jane Radin has called a "contested commodity." In Radin's ethical system, some goods and services—ranging from adopted babies to donor kidneys to pollution permits—defy the basic laws of commodity pricing and market exchange (xi–xiv, 1–15). Literature, too, many would have it, warrants such protection from the dehumanizing forces of modern markets.

Yet, as persuasive as these arguments might be, three flights up in the marketing division or across the quad in the School of Business, thoroughly reasonable and learned people find such pleas for literary exceptionalism more than a little quixotic. The reality, they tell us, is that a wide range of studies suggest that consumers use the same cognitive processes in selecting books as in choosing among brands of coffee, breakfast cereal, or cigarettes (Holbrook, 96–97). In their world, it makes perfect sense that Amazon would lure a top manager away from the snack food giant Frito-Lay and that Borders would find its new CEO at the supermarket chain American Stores. And, like Len Riggio, the head of Barnes and Noble, they have little patience for "the elitists who say we can't sell books like we sell toothpaste" (qtd. in Miller, 97; see also Stephen Brown, "Preface," xiii). When book sales are essentially flat—as they have been in the United States for some time now—the industry has no other recourse, in their estimation, than to borrow marketing methods that have long proven successful in peddling everything from bacon to body wash (Green, 80).

While I have no fantasies about definitively resolving such debates with this book, one of my major aims is to provide fresh historical perspectives on the 250-year-old clash between literary idealism and market realism. Specifically, this book is an endeavor to show that, far from being inherently antagonistic institutions, modern literature and advertising actually share a common genealogy and in very real ways can be said to have co-produced each other, having both arisen out of the historically unprecedented cultural and economic upheavals of late-eighteenth- and early-nineteenth-century Britain. As the chapters that follow will suggest, such basic components of modern literature as periodical criticism and the author function were born out of the advertising logic that permeated Britain during what has come to be called the "Romantic Century" (1750–1850).[4] At the same time, many of the core methodologies and philosophies of modern advertising trace their origins to the British literary book trade of this era. And, in perhaps the oddest historical twist of all, the very literary idealism that inspired the founders of both *Blackwood's* and amazon.com can be seen as a distinctive outgrowth of Romantic-era advertising culture.

Although this is the first extended attempt to trace the shared "rise" narratives of advertising and modern literature, it draws heavily upon two generations of theoretical and historical scholarship on advertising's methods and cultural impact. In the 1970s and '80s, thinkers as diverse as Roland Barthes, Raymond Williams, and Dick Hebdige reflected at length on how advertising shapes our relation to the world and, by extension, our interactions with written and electronic texts.[5] Following Barthes's lead, structuralist and poststructuralist theorists proved particularly adept at teaching us to read advertisements more discerningly, and in several instances—most notably Gérard Genette's *Paratexts* and Sara Thornton's recent study *Advertising, Subjectivity, and the Nineteenth-Century Novel*—they have helped us better understand the structural links between advertising and literature. Genette's book meshes particularly well with the project at hand, as he devotes an entire section to tracing how our interpretive experience is often shaped by such extratextual (or "epitextual") materials as book advertisements, prearranged reviews, and authorial commentaries. The "public epitext," as Genette suggests and this book reaffirms, can play as great a role in determining our experience with a text as the actual story or poem itself.

This book is equally indebted to a wide variety of literary critics and historians who over the past two decades have begun filling the sizeable gaps in our understanding of advertising's modern development. Until relatively recently, two commonly accepted myths thwarted the in-depth study of advertising history. The first of these held that, as *Time* magazine proclaimed in its 12 October 1962 cover story, advertising is "a uniquely American contribution to economic life" ("The Mammoth Mirror," 85). According to this school of thought, modern advertising began, for all intents and purposes, with P. T. Barnum and the mass-circulation American magazines of the late nineteenth century. Beholden to this view, conventional American histories of advertising have often completely bypassed British precedents. A case in point is Stephen Fox's widely read *The Mirror Makers* (1984)—hailed by the *New York Review of Books* as "arguably the best general history of advertising" (Draper, 14)—which asserts that advertising as we know it originated in the post–Civil War United States. All prior modes of marketing, he alleges, belong to advertising's "prehistory" and are thus of little consequence (Fox, 13). In addition to perpetuating the fallacy that advertising is fundamentally American, Fox's study upholds the second myth of advertising history: that advertising did not begin to assume its modern forms until the late nineteenth century. This latter belief appears to have taken root sometime around the turn of the twentieth century, as evidenced in Earnest Elmo Calkins and Ralph Holden's *The Art of Modern Advertising* (1905), which maintains that the entire history of advertising, "from the first spoken announcement down to within the last fifty years, or even later, would be of no value to the advertising man of to-day. Advertising, as we understand it, is a development of the past half century" (13).[6] Three-quarters of a century later, in his otherwise penetrating essay "Advertising: The Magic System" (1980), Raymond Williams repeats this storyline, arguing that "in the last hundred years, . . . advertising has developed from the simple announcements of shopkeepers and the persuasive arts of a few marginal dealers into a major part of capitalist business organization" (184). Elsewhere in his essay, Williams pushes modern advertising's birth date even farther forward, claiming that, "if we look at advertising before, say, 1914, its comparative crudeness is immediately evident" (179). More than thirty years after Williams's essay, this basic chronology remains widely unquestioned, especially in advertising circles. For evidence of this, one need look no farther than the title of a recent trade history by the French advertising conglomerate Publicis: *Born in 1842: A History of Advertising* (Pincas and Loiseau).

Not surprisingly, as scholarly interest in the historical structures and mechanisms of consumer culture surged in the late 1980s and early 1990s, a wide range of scholars began challenging both the place of birth and date of birth of modern advertising. In eighteenth-century studies, Neil McKendrick, John Brewer, and J. H. Plumb's groundbreaking collaboration, *The Birth of a Consumer Society* (1982), sparked widespread interest in how the rise of advertising contributed to the so-called "consumer revolution" Britain experienced in the latter half of the eighteenth century. The result has been a range of publications—most notably those by Hoh-Cheung Mui and Lorna H. Mui, Peter M. Briggs, James Raven, Jill Campbell, and Cynthia Wall[7]—detailing, in Briggs's words, "how extremely various and vital eighteenth-century advertising actually was" ("'News from the little World,'" 30). The impulse to reassess advertising history has been equally strong in Victorian studies. As one might expect, given their disciplinary prejudices, Victorianists have often too-readily accepted the traditional "advertising as late-nineteenth-century invention" narrative. Thomas Richards, for instance, insists in *The Commodity Culture of Victorian Britain* (1990) that, prior to the Great Exhibition of 1851, advertising remained in a "primitive state," controlled by a small band of hucksters who "had a few old tricks, a fixed repertoire at least several hundred years old, and nothing more" (6). And Lori Anne Loeb's *Consuming Angels: Advertising and Victorian Women* (1994) leans heavily upon the assumption that pre-Victorian advertisements were "almost always simple announcements that relied on repetition, bold headlines, and small logos," promoting "a small range of products by a few well-publicized producers" (7).

These historical biases aside, however, scholars of Victorian advertising have brilliantly countered the Americentric tendencies of advertising history and have done more than scholars of any other period to begin contemplating the historical and structural ties between advertising and literature. Perhaps the best such study is still Jennifer Wicke's groundbreaking *Advertising Fictions: Literature, Advertisement, and Social Reading* (1988), which argues that advertising, as "a preeminent discourse of modern culture," is "a language and literature in its own right" and that the late-nineteenth- and early-twentieth-century novel "relies on the conditions of advertising to permit it to become the major literary form" (1). In very real ways, the book you are reading functions as something of a revision and extension of Wicke's thesis, sharing her interest in the dialectical engagement of advertising and literature but locating their historical relationship a century earlier.

In contrast to the widespread interest in advertising history among eighteenth-century scholars and Victorianists, Romanticists have engaged relatively infrequently with the subject. Advertising usually receives passing notice in studies of Romantic-era book history and print culture,[8] but rarely has it been treated as a major mode of late-eighteenth- and early-nineteenth-century commercial or literary discourse. The two laudable exceptions to this are Marcus Wood's *Radical Satire and Print Culture, 1790–1822* (1994) and John Strachan's *Advertising and Satirical Culture in the Romantic Period* (2007), both of which, as their titles suggest, focus particularly on advertising's enormous impact on the satirical literature of the age.[9] For its part, Wood's book offers a wealth of evidence related to advertising's central place in late-eighteenth- and early-nineteenth-century popular culture, showing particularly how heavily influenced radical satirists such as William Hone and George Cruikshank were by the marketing forms and techniques of well-known manufacturers. Strachan picks up where Wood leaves off, setting out first to examine "the cultural practices evident in contemporary advertising literature in the context of the wider aesthetic landscape of the [Romantic] period" and then to treat "advertising as a cultural form that is sociohistorically revealing" (13). In chapters covering everything from shoe-blacking verses to lottery jingles to "the poetry of hair-cutting," Strachan compellingly catalogues an enormous array of Romantic-era advertisements and the satirical texts that engage them.

While this book joins Wood and Strachan in calling for broader recognition of the profound effect the fledgling advertising system had on Romantic-era Britain, my subject matter is more traditionally literary than either of theirs. Wood's principal focus is radical publishing and Strachan's is popular culture in all its modes, while mine is specifically literary culture. Essentially, this book asks two interrelated questions, neither of which has been extensively explored. First, what role did British writers and publishers of the eighteenth and early nineteenth centuries play in the development of the modern advertising system? And, second, how did the new forms, methods, and philosophies of advertising influence the production, distribution, and reception of Romantic-era literature?

My first chapter provides a historical overview of the systemic changes advertising and literature underwent in Britain between 1750 and 1850, showing how a series of economic, social, and legal milestones dramatically transformed these fields. The chapters that follow offer a loosely chronological survey of literature's and advertising's shared histories. Chapter 2 focuses on the mid-to-late eighteenth century, chronicling the rise of "puffery," the various methods merchants and manufacturers developed to pass off paid advertisements as news stories, public service announcements, or objective book reviews. In particular, I describe how the two great literary genres to emerge from eighteenth-century Britain, the novel and the book review, originated largely in booksellers' needs to creatively promote their works in an increasingly crowded marketplace. Chapter 3 examines another major innovation in late-eighteenth-century marketing, the birth of the brand-name product. After chronicling the arrival of household brands, I show how the marketing campaign behind cantos 1 and 2 of *Childe Harold's Pilgrimage* appropriated both the logic and the techniques of branding to transform Lord Byron into the world's most successful literary brand.

Chapter 4 turns to the poet many hailed as "the female Byron," Letitia Elizabeth Landon. Moving beyond traditional studies of Landon's engagement with the marketplace, which focus primarily on her strategic employment of the initials "L.E.L.," I argue that the commercial genius of Landon and her publisher, William Jerdan, was actually best displayed in their pioneering experiments at bandwagon and visual marketing. Chapter 5 returns to the subject of puffery, recounting how the techniques developed in the eighteenth century became normalized in the early nineteenth century. So rampant did puffery become during the later Romantic period that, when the book market floundered following the banking crash of 1826, a chorus of renowned cultural commentators, including Carlyle, Macaulay, and *Blackwood's* "Christopher North," hastened to charge puffing booksellers, critics, and authors with having "killed" literature. Paradoxically, though, at this very moment, other writers began contemplating the idea that, far from the death of literature, advertising might actually revitalize the literary arts. This is the story told in my conclusion, which documents how advertising became so naturalized and so conjoined with literature and commerce that from the 1820s forward the British commentariat increasingly spoke of the "art of advertising" and imagined the ad-man as a close cousin to the inspired, solitary genius of Romantic poetry.

I hope that by book's end readers will have come to think of literature and advertising differently, appreciating both their common history and the commercial and aesthetic pioneers who brought them together.

CHAPTER 1

Advertising in the Romantic Century

Of the preeminent transitional years in British literary history, none is more appropriately situated than 1850. Not only did this year witness the symbolic culmination of Romanticism in the death of Wordsworth and the posthumous publication of his great Romantic epic, the fourteen-book *Prelude*, but it also saw the enshrinement of High Victorian poetics in the appointment of Tennyson as Wordsworth's successor to the poet laureateship and the publication of his *In Memoriam*. It wasn't just in regards to literature, though, that midcentury Britons had occasion to contemplate the mediality of their moment. In the build-up to the Great Exhibition of 1851, many famously hailed the event as the birth of a new age. Less enthusiastically, in 1852 a spiritually bereft Matthew Arnold mused that his society was "wandering between two worlds, one dead, / The other powerless to be born" ("Stanzas from the Grande Chartreuse," lines 85–86).

Among the most insightful contemporary reflections on the Janus-like nature of 1850 was George Henry Francis's six-part *Fraser's Magazine* series, "The Age of Veneer," the first installment of which fittingly preceded in the September 1850 issue the magazine's review of *In Memoriam*.[1] This once-heralded but now little-known essay series functions as a valuable retrospective, using the century's midpoint as an opportunity to reflect on the advances and disappointments of the previous half-century and to chart a better course for the half-century to come.

In Francis's estimation, one of the most lamentable developments of the century's first fifty years was the rise of a culture of deception, or "veneering." And at the heart of this new hucksterism was advertising. So insidious was advertising, in Francis's mind, that he opted to devote the entire final installment of his series to it. Appearing in January 1852, this concluding essay, titled "The Science of Puffing," offers both an astute analysis of midcentury marketing norms and, perhaps more importantly, one of the earliest histories of British advertising. What makes Francis's essay particularly relevant here, though, is how closely its claims anticipate my own. To begin with, both this book and "The Science of Puffing" argue that the modern advertising system was in Britain by the early nineteenth century. While conceding that "charlatans have existed in every age and in every country," Francis insisted that there was something distinctive about the modern age of "manufactured opinion." In recent generations, his account suggests, advances in transportation and the availability of printed materials had given birth to a commercial environment in which "the tradesman, who had hitherto been content with the profits of private custom, found it to his account to seek a more extended patronage" through advertising. Consequently, advertising "became regularly reduced to a *system*" and was "*scientifically employed*" throughout Britain (87, my emphasis).

In and of itself, this suggestion that advertising had come to function as both a system and a science by the late Georgian age is remarkable enough, offering as it does a counternarrative to twentieth-century theories of the Victorian invention of advertising (see Introduction). But Francis's arguments even more directly anticipate my own when he proceeds to speculate that nineteenth-century advertising's fundamental modernity was inextricable from its literariness. "Advertising," he asserted, "may be said first to have attained the dignity of an art when it employed its own Laureate, and court poetry sought inspiration in the neighbourhood of Aldgate" (87). While this observation requires some unpacking for the modern reader, the point is crucial. In essence, Francis implied that the first clear sign of advertising's sophistication and fundamental modernity came early in the century, when several famous poets were rumored to have descended from Parnassus into Grub Street (or, in this case, working-class Aldgate), where they were reportedly paid lavish sums to pen puffs and jingles for such household products as Packwood's razor strops and Warren's boot blacking.[2]

Unfortunately, after briefly entertaining this notion, the essay immediately veers off into a stylistic analysis of recent puffs, never to return to the historicity or literariness of advertising. Perhaps Francis lacked the chronological distance or archival resources to flesh out his narrative, or perhaps he simply took the propinquity of advertising and literature as self-evident, requiring no elaboration. Regardless, what Francis began to hypothesize at the midpoint of the nineteenth century can be substantially proven a century and a half later. As the remainder of this chapter will demonstrate, Francis was fundamentally correct in suggesting that by the dawn of the nineteenth century not only had advertising emerged as a system and a science but "the art employed by modern advertisers far transcend[ed]" (88) anything previously imagined.

PRECONDITIONS FOR MODERN ADVERTISING

As almost every historian of advertising has pointed out, there is nothing distinctively modern about the act of publicizing one's wares.[3] Several ancient records portray street criers making the rounds in Athens, muralists publicizing coming gladiator bouts on the walls of Pompeii, and Roman shopkeepers posting fliers on the pillars of the Forum. As might be expected, prior to the era of mass literacy most merchants relied primarily on oral advertising. In early modern Europe, this often meant employing street criers or doorway barkers to drum up business. Thus, on a typical trip to the high street, a fifteenth- or sixteenth-century shopper was likely to be greeted at several doors by barkers demanding, "What do you lack, mistress?" (Presbrey, 14). Another strategy shopkeepers used to attract the attention of illiterate passersby was hanging ornate signs outside their premises. Over time, a language of symbols and colors developed on these signs: three golden balls came to stand for the pawnbroker, a figure of a black boy became the trademark of tobacco shops, and an ivy bush represented the tavern (Gloag, 19–21). In response to this growing practice, Shakespeare quipped in the epilogue to *As You Like It* that "Good wine needs no bush."

With the coming of the printing press in the fifteenth century and the gradual emergence of print culture and the bourgeois public sphere in the seventeenth and eighteenth centuries, advertising was thoroughly transformed. Significantly, each new milestone in the spread of print was accompanied by a corresponding breakthrough in advertising. For instance, William Caxton published the first English advertising handbill only a year after bringing the first press to Britain in 1476. An interval of less than five years passed between publication of the first English newspaper (1621) and appearance of the earliest English newspaper advertisement (1625). And the introduction of printing presses to the provinces was quickly followed by the posting of broadsides, handbills, and campaign posters on town walls and rural park palings.

It wasn't until the early eighteenth century, however, that print advertising came into its own as a major market force in Britain. Three fundamental social and technological shifts paved the way for advertising's explosion in the eighteenth century. First, literacy rates climbed to the point where printed advertisements could reach a large percentage of the populace. Of course, given the paucity of reliable evidence and shifting definitions of what exactly makes a person literate, computing historical literacy rates is notoriously difficult. According to John Brewer's admittedly rough figures, in 1500 approximately 10 percent of English males and 1 percent of English females were literate. Over the next two centuries, as the commercial world increasingly relied on reading and writing and many Britons embraced a Protestant emphasis on personal Bible study, the number of readers and writers surged. By 1714 the literacy rate had reached roughly 45 percent for men and 25 percent for women, and by 1750 it had climbed to 60 percent for men and 40 percent for women (Brewer, 167; see also D. Vincent).

Closely related to the rise of literacy—and the second development paving the way for the advertising boom of the eighteenth century—was the gradual harnessing of print's capacities. As has been well documented elsewhere, however much Gutenberg's contemporaries marveled over the printing press, it wasn't until two centuries later that European society began to realize the full potential of print (see Kernan, *Samuel Johnson*, esp. 48–90; McLuhan; Ong; Plumb; and Sher, esp. 2–6). Print's greatest institution, the periodical press, did not emerge in England until the 1620s, and another century passed before newspapers became widely popular (Harris, 82; Feather, *The Provincial Book Trade*, 44; and Plumb, 268–69). The number of London dailies rose from one in 1702 to six in 1730, nine in 1770, and sixteen in 1793 (Raven, *Business of Books*, 258). Over the course of the same period the number of printing presses in the metropolis rose by some 400 percent, and much of what they produced either functioned as direct advertising (e.g., trade cards, handbills, posters) or as a medium for advertising (e.g., newspapers and magazines) (St. Clair, *The Reading Nation*, 87–88). The combination, then, of a government generally willing to allow the spread of print, a citizenry increasingly capable of reading advertisements, and a network of printers with the capacity to flood the marketplace with promotional materials left eighteenth-century Britain ideally suited to witness history's first advertising boom (R. Williams, "Advertising," 171; Ferdinand, 393).

The third, and perhaps most significant, cultural development facilitating the growth of British advertising during the eighteenth century was the dramatic transformation of the nation's productive capacities and consumer attitudes. While capitalism's European roots stretch back to the sixteenth century, most economic historians see eighteenth-century Britain, with its expanding stock market, burgeoning networks for global trade, and growing fascination with political economy, as the first fully capitalist society (E. Wood; Fulcher, 19–22). In terms of its domestic retail economy, Britain had a significant advantage in its push toward full-fledged capitalism in having a geographically concentrated market (largely in the south of England) and an extensive system of roads and canals (Corley, 158). As a result, by the latter half of the eighteenth century, two interrelated economic "revolutions" were under way in Britain: the industrial and the consumer. Little need be said about the former, as the basics of the nation's shift from a rural-agricultural to an urban-industrial economy have long been widely understood. This early initiation of the "consumer revolution," however, has until relatively recently been widely ignored or underappreciated.

As noted earlier, the collection that has had the greatest impact in encouraging scholars across several disciplines to study eighteenth-century British consumerism is McKendrick, Brewer, and Plumb's *The Birth of a Consumer Society*. McKendrick's chapters in that volume have proven particularly influential, as at the heart of his argument is the claim that, in the eighteenth century,

> more men and women than ever before in human history enjoyed the experience of acquiring material possessions. Objects which for centuries had been the privileged possessions of the rich came, within the space of a few generations, to be within the reach of a larger part of society than ever before, and, for the first time, to be within the legitimate aspirations of almost all of it. Objects which were once acquired as the result of inheritance at best, came to be the legitimate pursuit of a whole new class of consumers. (Introduction, 1)

Drawing heavily upon Veblen's theories of conspicuous consumption, McKendrick suggests that most of the energy behind Britain's consumer revolution came from its newly affluent middle classes, whose growing preoccupation with social status and respectability led to obsessive efforts to emulate aristocratic fashions and tastes. Manufacturers in textiles, china, shaving products, and the like were quick to recognize and exploit this shift in consumer attitudes, aggressively advertising their products as the "must-have" items of the season. Under the spell of marketing geniuses like the china manufacturer Josiah Wedgwood—the tradesman who, above all others, emerges as the hero of McKendrick's tale—Britain's grocers, bank clerks, and attorneys, not to mention their spouses, developed insatiable desires for the newest "Queensware" table settings or Chippendale chairs.

Among literary scholars in general and Romanticists in particular, perhaps the most intriguing offshoot of McKendrick's consumer revolution thesis is Colin Campbell's *The Romantic Ethic and the Spirit of Modern Consumerism* (1987). As his title suggests—with its overt allusion to Max Weber's landmark study, *The Protestant Ethic and the Spirit of Capitalism* (1905)—Campbell seeks to update the Weberian theory that European society's transition from feudalism to capitalism was facilitated by the rise of Protestantism and the accompanying social emphasis upon personal accountability and the gospel of work. Equally central to Campbell's project is revising McKendrick's claims that middle-class emulation of the aristocracy fueled Britain's late-eighteenth-century consumer revolution. Using Weber and McKendrick as his starting points, then, Campbell sought to develop a better understanding of the sociological shifts that prompted so many late-eighteenth-century Britons to display consumer instincts so dramatically different from their forebears'.

His answer came via a detailed survey of how the asceticism of early Protestantism gradually gave way to its mirror image, what he calls the hedonism of Romanticism. At the heart of the Romantic project, Campbell explains, are two interconnected impulses: to seek pleasure and to imagine future pleasures. Not surprisingly, then, when Romanticism gained cultural preeminence in the late eighteenth and early nineteenth centuries, heeding these impulses became increasingly socially acceptable, nowhere more so than in the marketplace. What resulted was "a distinctively modern form of pleasure-seeking," a sort of "autonomous, self-illusory hedonism." In contrast to traditional hedonism, which turns to material goods to alleviate life's discomforts, modern Romantic hedonism produces an endless series of imagined desires, none of which once attained offers more than fleeting pleasure. Hence, the modern consumer-cum-hedonist "is continually withdrawing from reality as fast as he encounters it, ever-casting his day-dreams forward in time, attaching them to objects of desire, and then subsequently 'unhooking' them from these objects as and when they are attained and experienced" (86–87). Viewed from this perspective, it was not through—as McKendrick would have it—the instinctual desire to emulate one's social betters or the individual's helplessness in the face of the modern advertising machine that eighteenth- and nineteenth-century consumerism came to be; rather it was through the ascendance of a Romantic ideology that trapped consumers in a cycle of constantly imagining that their next purchase would finally be the one that delivered the long-anticipated gratification.

As influential as McKendrick's and Campbell's theses have been, they have their detractors. Within the humanities the liveliest set of debates in their wake has focused on whether the eighteenth century (rather than the seventeenth, the nineteenth, or even the twentieth) was indeed the moment when a consumer society was "born" and whether this "birth" actually first occurred in Britain or elsewhere (see Richards; de Vries; and Benson and Ugolini). Among economists the most pointed critiques of the eighteenth-century consumer revolution thesis charge that McKendrick and his followers have developed an oversimplified narrative of consumer behavior around a dataset composed almost wholly of exceptional retailers and products. Were we to concentrate less on fringe products like Wedgwood china and high-end clothing, they argue, and more on staples like grain and coal, the narrative would look quite different. As Ben Fine has remarked, "It would be far-fetched to view the rise in coal consumption as originating out of the emulative behaviour of the lower classes (with fashion emanating from London as the major domestic market)" (164). Instead, a coal-centered narrative leads us back to the more traditional industrial revolution model, in which shifts in productive capacities rather than consumer demands serve as the principal catalysts for socioeconomic change.

THE ADVERTISING BOOM OF GEORGIAN BRITAIN

Yet, even if McKendrick, Campbell, and others have oversold the historical particularity of the eighteenth century or how widely experienced the new consumer mindset may have been, it is impossible to deny that widespread changes occurred in the demand side of the British economy between 1700 and 1800. Perhaps nothing better demonstrates these changes than the growth of advertising. A wealth of evidence, both statistical and anecdotal, illustrates how, over the course of the Georgian era, advertising moved from the periphery to the center of the British retail economy. In 1713, the year after the first advertising duty took effect, 18,220 advertisements were taxed in Britain. This number rose to nearly 125,000 per year in 1750 and 500,000 per year in 1800—marking a twenty-five-fold increase in less than a century (Bruttini, 21; Nevett, *Advertising in Britain*, 26–27). By Adriano Bruttini's counts, "during the period 1700–1720 London newspapers carried an average of 15 advertisements per edition, and the provincial ones carried five; in 1720–1745, the figures rose to 35 and 12 respectively and finally, during the period 1750–1800, London newspapers and those from 'industrial areas,' which took the lion's share, had an average around 45" (21).[4] So great did the demand for periodical advertisements become in the late eighteenth and early nineteenth centuries that newspapers were for the first time able to wean themselves from the government subsidies they had traditionally received (Asquith, "The Structure," 111). In some cases, in fact, newspaper proprietors not only got by on advertising income but became fabulously wealthy. James Perry, the owner of the *Morning Chronicle*, for instance, died in 1821 with a net worth between £130,000 and £190,000, almost all of which was attributable to his paper's popularity with advertisers (Asquith, "Advertising and the Press," 721).

As one might expect from these figures, anecdotal and circumstantial evidence of advertising's growing cultural presence in Georgian Britain appears at every turn. In the realm of semantics, the rise of advertising brought a range of new usages, such as the commercial sense of the verb "advertise" (as in "I will advertise my books") in 1750 and the participial form "advertising" (as in "the advertising merchants of London") in 1779.[5] In the age's leading periodicals, such luminaries as Addison, Fielding, and Johnson offered detailed analyses of the new advertising system and its potential impact on the national character (see Chapter 2). Also taking up the pen to comment on the proliferation of newspaper advertisements were London's coffeehouse owners, who made up a sizable percentage of the average newspaper's subscriber base. In 1728 several of them banded together to publish *The Case of the Coffee-Men of London and Westminster*, in which they protested:

> [We] stipulate for *News*; not for *Advertisements*: Yet the Papers are ordinarily more than half full of them. The *Daily Post*, for Example, is often equipped with Thirty; which yield *Three Pounds Fifteen Shillings* that Day to the Proprietors, for the least: And sometimes that Paper has more. Well may they divide Twelve Hundred Pounds a Year and upwards: They are paid on both Hands; paid by the *Advertisers* for taking in *Advertisements*; and paid by the Coffee-Men for delivering them out. (A Coffee-Man, 16)

So ubiquitous, it seems, was advertising by century's end that even the consecrated ground of a country church had become fair game. Since the early nineteenth century, visitors to the parish church in Goldalming, Surrey, have been greeted by a tablet in the south chapel which reads:

SACRED
To the Memory of
NATHANIEL GODBOLD Esq.[r]
Inventor and Proprietor
of that excellent Medicine
The Vegetable Balsam,
For the Cure of Consumptions & Asthmas.
He departed this Life
The 17th day of Dec. 1799
Aged 69 years.
Hic Cineres, ubique Fama.[6]

Nearly a half-century later, a *Notes and Queries* entry on this epitaph quipped, "I submit that the inscription is so clearly a posthumous advertisement, that if the

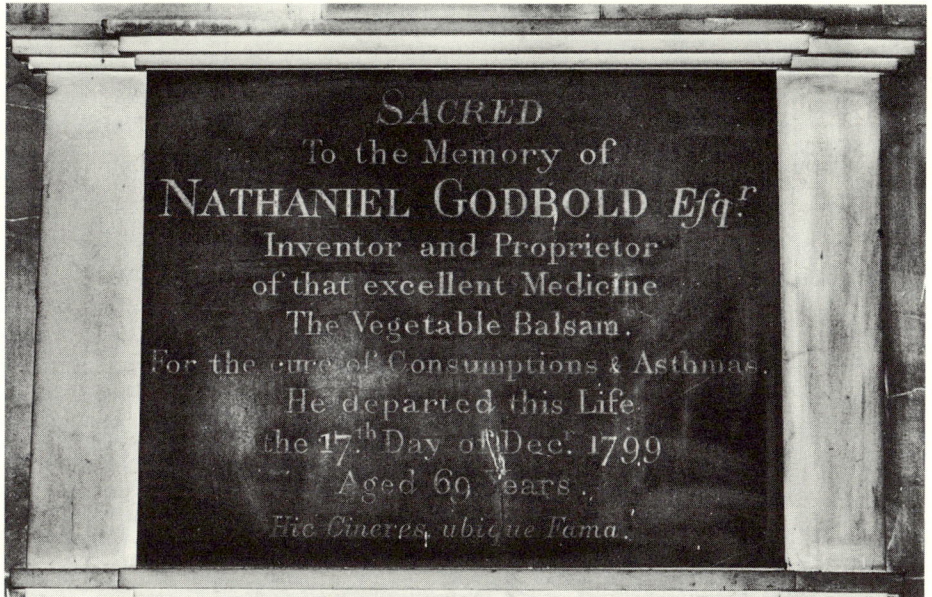

Figure 1.1. Memorial tablet to Nathaniel Godbold in the Parish Church of St Peter and St Paul, Godalming, Surrey. (Photo by author, courtesy of the Parish Church of St Peter and St Paul, Godalming.)

Chancellor of the Exchequer were to charge an annual duty in respect of it, no one could blame him" ("Monumental Advertisements," 33).

The tax referred to here, of course, is the national advertising duty, which, along with the stamp tax, was first levied in the early eighteenth century as a means of slowing the spread of potentially seditious periodicals. Not even these duties, however, could halt advertising's proliferation. When the advertising and stamp duties became law in 1712, initial rates were set at one shilling for each printed advertisement and one penny for each stamped sheet of newsprint. Over the next century, the stamp tax quadrupled to four pennies per sheet and the advertising duty grew nearly as quickly, peaking at three shillings and six pence in 1815 (Presbrey, 74–75; E. S. Turner, 24–48; Nevett, *Advertising in Britain*, 25–27).[7] Yet, by this time advertising had become so essential in many industries that the taxes seem to have had little effect. If anything, the rising expense of newspaper advertising fueled creativity. One response to the advertising duty was to experiment with tax-exempt modes of marketing. As is detailed at length in Chapters 2 and 5, several merchants outwitted both the taxman and the ad-resistant reader by bribing editors to insert "puffs," or paid advertisements masquerading as news stories, heralding the arrival of a new line of exotic hats at the local haberdashery or the discovery of a miracle cure by the town pharmacologist. Less cunningly, other merchants distributed trade cards in their shops or on street corners. Not only were these cards tax-exempt, but they also allowed much greater freedom than the traditional newspaper advertisement in such design elements as typography and illustration (Nevett, *Advertising in Britain*, 22; McKendrick, "The Commercialization of Fashion," 83–84).

What the trade card was to the high-end shop, the poster was to the common advertiser. Traditionally, bill-sticking has been considered a Victorian phenomenon, largely because of the descriptions by Dickens and other mid-nineteenth-century writers of a London pasted over with posters. In reality, the professional bill-sticker was well established a century before Dickens's time, having emerged in the wake of the advertisement duty (Nevett, *Advertising in Britain*, 21–22). In the 1805 *Prelude*, for instance, Wordsworth portrays a late-eighteenth-century London in which "files of ballads dangle from dead walls; / Advertisements, of giant-size, from high / Press forward, in all colours, on the sight" (Book 7, lines 209–11). Less grand forms of advertising that arose or reached new levels of popularity in the era of the advertising tax include the handbill, the horse-drawn billboard, and the sandwich-board carrier. The lengths to which some tradesmen resorted to attract tax-exempt publicity is seen in such stunts as the barber who exhibited a live bear in his shop to promote his bear's grease and the quack medicine dealer who painted his pony a garish purple to attract the gaze of all as he rode through London's streets (Strachan, *Advertising and Satirical Culture*, ch. 5; McKendrick, "The Commercialization of Fashion," 93).

In contrast to such outlandish tactics, newspaper advertisements remained relatively conservative through the end of the Romantic period, largely because of industrywide column-width and typeface restrictions. That said, the rhetorical flair of newspaper advertisements noticeably intensified between the reigns of George I and George IV. The greatest impetus for this change was the proliferation of the number of advertisements in the average day's paper. In 1710, for instance, when most newspapers printed only a small number of advertisements, each notice had a high probability of being read; but in the latter half of the century, when the number of advertisements per issue rose to fifty or more, advertisers had to resort to gimmickry and puffery to stand out from the crowd. By the first half of the nineteenth century, several advertisers employed jingles, slogans, and clever word play to attract the attention of newspaper readers. Typical of the times was the fad of pulling in readers with bold headlines ("*The Duke of Wellington*

Shot...") before introducing them to the product in smaller print ("... a glance of admiration at our hats") (E. S. Turner, 60).

The more familiar one becomes with the advertising norms of this period, the more apparent it is that slick and sophisticated marketing campaigns are by no means original to the electronic age. As James Raven puts it, in the eighteenth century "advances were made in customer psychology which would cheer any twenty-first-century marketing consultancy" (*The Business of Books*, 269). One medicine dealer's trade card from this era pledges, "NO CURE, NO PAY." Another trade card carries a chimney sweep's promise to refund his customers' money if they aren't fully satisfied with his services (McKendrick, "The Commercialization of Fashion," 83–84). Not to be outdone, the potter Josiah Wedgwood offered free delivery to any customer able to pay ready cash, and several grocers experimented with "loss leaders," advertising products at or below cost in hopes that bargain hunters would buy additional items with a higher markup (McKendrick, "The Commercialization of Fashion," 94). Even product placement traces its roots to this era, with Wedgwood and Matthew Boulton bestowing complimentary dinnerware and buttons on fashionable families.

By the early Romantic age, advertising in Britain was also rapidly professionalizing (detailed in Chapter 3). For the first time, a wide range of merchants and manufacturers abandoned traditional practices of generic and local retailing and began marketing their goods as national brands. Entrepreneurs in numerous product lines developed elaborate marketing strategies to generate nationwide demand for their mass-produced pottery, shoe blacking, and razor strops. With the emergence of the first advertising agents in the 1790s and early 1800s, Georgian Britain was well on its way to creating a prototype for Madison Avenue culture. As T. R. Nevett and others have shown, the old myth that the advertising agent was a Victorian invention is belied by the careers of William Tayler, James White, Charles Barker, and other early-nineteenth-century professionals who specialized in managing the advertising campaigns of clients. While their primary role was to coordinate the placement of advertisements in hundreds of newspapers across the country, they also had a hand in the creative side of advertising, helping clients design the most effective advertisements for their target audience (Nevett, "London's Early Advertising Agents"; Dunbar; and St. Clair, *The Reading Nation*, 186). Robert Southey attests to the existence of these early advertising agents in his *Letters from England* (1807), where he relates how a successful author friend of his had recently been besieged by ad-men promising to boost his sales dramatically and ensure his works were properly circulating among "people of fashion" (343–44). The Romantic-era ad-man also makes a conspicuous appearance in

W. T. Moncrieff's 1819 play *Wanted a Wife*, which opens in the advertising office of the conniving Irishman Barney McShift.

All told, then, while there's no question that advertising continued to expand and professionalize rapidly over the course of the Victorian period, it is time to definitively lay to rest the old notion that advertising remained mired in a sort of prehistory prior to the Great Exhibition of 1851. As a host of economists, philosophers, and cultural critics have theorized over the past half-century, advertising is at the heart of modern consumerism, buoying up the demand side of capitalist economies through the perpetual creation of new wants and desires. Extending the logic of these claims back a few centuries, it becomes clear that, without advertising, the new consumerism of the late eighteenth century would merely have been a passing fad, not, as it has turned out, the dominant mode of economic consciousness of the modern industrialized world.

As for the other large-scale historical premise of this book—that, like advertising, literature as we know it is fundamentally a creation of the late eighteenth and early nineteenth centuries—four decades of scholarship have essentially left this a settled point. In fact, it has become somewhat axiomatic among British literary historians to speak of the "Romantic invention of literature."[8] The basic argument holds that, as a byproduct of the print revolution and the Enlightenment-era reclassification of knowledge, the category of "literature" narrowed from including all worthwhile books to just the best writing in imaginative genres (i.e., fiction, poetry, and drama). Undergirding these categorical shifts were the concomitant emergence and naturalization of such core institutions of modern literature as periodical criticism, copyright legislation, national literary canons, and the author function.[9] On the heels of multiple generations of historicist scholarship on the "invention" of literature, the general narrative is now largely understood. What has yet to be fully appreciated, though, is what the chapters that follow aim to prove—namely, that a remarkable number of these core developments in the literary field were deeply dependent on simultaneous developments in advertising. Writers and booksellers had a curious tendency to be on the scene at crucial moments in advertising history; but, by the same token, without the landmark advancements in advertising that took place over the course of the Romantic Century, we might all be steeped in tales of the "Victorian invention of literature."

CHAPTER 2

The Progress of Puffery

While, for all intents and purposes, the story of the twin rises of modern advertising and literature begins in eighteenth-century Britain, the prologue is actually set several centuries earlier in the workshop of William Caxton. Just one year after Caxton made history by introducing the printing press to England, he earned a second claim to fame by recognizing that his press had the capacity not only to mass-produce books but also to publicize those same books widely and inexpensively. Beginning in 1477, Caxton effectively became England's first mass advertiser when he printed and circulated a handbill for *The Pyes of Salisbury*, a book he had published and sold in his shop. The significance of this early conjunction of England's literary and advertising systems has not been lost on scholars. The marketing researcher Stephen Brown, for instance, has dubbed Caxton "one of the first modern marketing men" and suggested that the "marketing orientation" of England's earliest bookmakers "predates the emergence of the modern marketing concept" ("Rattles," 9–10; see also Eisenstein, 60). Similarly, the book historian John Feather has noted that "printed books were the first products to be manufactured in large quantities for sale. The makers and sellers of printed books were therefore the first producers to be confronted with modern problems of marketing and advertising" (*English Book Prospectuses*, 22). And the linguist Michael Baird Saenger has posited that early modern book announcements like Caxton's "constitute something like the birth of modern advertising" (197).

For the first century and a half after Caxton, English book advertisements tended to come in two forms: title pages posted in public places and catalogs shipped to booksellers and collectors.[1] The arrival of the first English newspapers in the early seventeenth century offered a third method of marketing new titles, and, not surprisingly, printers and booksellers were again quick to recognize the promotional potential of this new medium. In fact, the first wave of English newspaper advertisements (ca. 1621–25) was devoted almost exclusively to books and other printed goods (Clarke, 140).

Long before 1700, then, bookmaking and advertising had forged a special relationship in Britain. Over the course of the eighteenth century, these two modern systems became only more tightly intertwined, with each experiencing exponential growth and undergoing major structural shifts as the direct result of their kinship. As nearly every major cultural commentator of the time noted, eighteenth-century Britain was deluged with print in general and printed advertisements in particular. Perhaps most famously, Samuel Johnson lamented in 1759, "Advertisements are now so numerous that they are very negligently perused, and it is therefore become necessary to gain attention by magnificence of promises, and by eloquence sometimes sublime and sometimes pathetic" (*The Idler*, 125).

This pressure to discover ever more original ways of capturing consumers' attention was felt most acutely in two trades, quack medicine and bookselling, both hyper-competitive industries selling nonessential goods, often on a national scale. To grasp the remarkable originality and moxie of seventeenth- and eighteenth-century quack medicine ads, one can turn to the work of Roy Porter and a train of scholars who have followed in his wake.[2] My particular focus in this chapter, however, is eighteenth-century British booksellers and authors, a group that may have enjoyed greater occupational prestige than contemporaneous dealers of nostrums, fever powders, and healing balms but was no less cunning in its harnessing and expansion of emergent advertising practices. In fact, several core promotional strategies that still form the backbone of modern advertising were first developed in the publishing houses of eighteenth-century Britain. No less significantly, the advertising logic that took hold during the so-called "consumer revolution" had a revolutionary impact on eighteenth-century British literature, playing a crucial role in such landmark developments as the rise of the novel and the professionalization of literary criticism.

ADVERTISING PIONEERS IN THE EIGHTEENTH-CENTURY BOOK TRADE

Unlike seventeenth-century journalism, which went through cycles of boom (e.g., the Civil War–era wars of words) and bust (e.g., the crackdown on the press during the Restoration), newspaper advertising developed slowly but unabatedly between its introduction in the 1620s and the century's end. By the mid-seventeenth century a number of newspapers were branching beyond generic descriptions of items for sale to include personal ads for runaway servants, public notices for lost or stolen goods, and miscellaneous queries of the public. That this new mode of personal advertising carried with it not only few stigmas but, in fact, a certain cachet is evidenced by how many of the English elite were quick to place personal ads, especially when they happened to misplace a cherished possession. Even the royal family, as C. John Sommerville quips, was "always losing things" (70). In 1660, for example, the household of Charles II ran a series of notices in the *Mercurius Publicus* imploring the public to help the king recover a favorite dog that had been stolen from Whitehall (Elliott, 47). Even more remarkably, following the coronation of James II in 1685, the royal jeweler placed a lost-and-found ad for "the Button off His Majesties Scepter, set about with 24 small Diamonds, three rubies and three Emeralds: a Pendant Pearl from His Majesties Crown, about 9 Carats or 30 Common Grains, and about 16 Great Links of a Gold Chain" (qtd. in F. G. Price, 166). The latter half of the seventeenth century also saw the first English weekly given over wholly to advertisements (the *Publick Adviser*, est. 1657), the first English periodical dedicated to reviewing new books (the *Works of the Learned*, est. 1691), and the first wave of complaints about advertisements crowding news out of newspapers (Sommerville, 55, 100–113; Presbrey, 42). Even the word "advertisement" traces its earliest commercial usages to this period, first appearing, rather tellingly, in a bookseller's list of recently published titles (Presbrey, 46; Elliott, 50–51).

Yet, despite these advances, it would not be until the mid-eighteenth century, when the realization of print culture and the rise of the new consumerism radically transformed British society, that advertising would enter its modern era. In regards to the book trade, it bears remembering that at the turn of the eighteenth century Britain still had no daily newspapers, no literary magazines, no circulating libraries, and few coffeehouses. Authors were generally either independently wealthy or beholden to patrons, and their works rarely circulated beyond a small coterie of fellow writers and well-educated readers. While during the seventeenth century the nation's economy had clearly entered an early capitalist stage, most retailing remained highly localized and a Puritan ethic restrained middle-class spending on luxury goods. With markets essentially fixed, merchants and manufacturers tended to see little need to advertise either extensively or creatively. As C. Y. Ferdinand has suggested, the relatively small-scale and forthright nature of seventeenth-century advertising reflected the "limitations of a pre-consumer-society market: wages were lower than they would be in the eighteenth century;

demand was relatively inflexible; luxury commodities went to a small, well-defined group; and other forms of advertising—handbills, word-of-mouth, town criers, shop signs—were evidently adequate to promote local goods and services" (394).

At the dawn of the eighteenth century, then, print advertisements remained relatively straightforward and unobtrusive. Most newspaper advertisements were as matter-of-fact as one from the 2 January 1705 issue of the *Daily Courant* that informed readers, "Coffee, Tea, and Chocolate, by Wholesale or Retail at the King's Arms next the King's Arms Tavern on Ludgate-hill near the Bridge." Book advertisements during the century's early decades tended to be similarly unadorned. In the advertising pages of the *Spectator* for 15 May 1711, readers saw this notice for Alexander Pope's new book:

> This Day is publish'd
> An Essay on Criticism. Printed for
> W. Lewis in Russel[l] Street, Covent Garden; and Sold by W. Taylor, at
> the Ship in Pater Noster Row; T. Osborn, in Grays-Inn near the Walks;
> J. Graves, in St. James's-Street; and J. Morphew, near Stationers-Hall.
> Price 1s.

In sampling early-eighteenth-century advertisements such as these, it is difficult not to sense that the advertisers themselves were often sheepish about joining the likes of quack medicine dealers in hawking goods in so public a forum. In fact, one of the major professional, and to some extent ethical, dilemmas for retailers throughout the eighteenth century and into the early nineteenth would be how to heed the mounting commercial imperative to advertise aggressively without violating personal or professional decorum. This was particularly the case among physicians, high-end shopkeepers, professional writers, and booksellers, all of whom yearned for respectability but faced widespread prejudices, especially among the genteel ranks, about the nature of their education, breeding, and connections to "trade."

As might be expected, the most thorough archive of this vacillation between self-promotion and professional restraint was left behind by writers themselves. Daniel Defoe, for instance, was at once one of the first great literary self-promoters and a pointed critic of the deceitful "shop-rhetorick" he saw suffusing London. In *The Complete English Tradesman* (1725), Defoe blasts the humbuggery of much early-eighteenth-century salesmanship, declaring that far too much of the age's marketing was "composed of a mass of rattling flattery to the buyer, and that fill'd with hypocrisy, compliment, self-praises, falshood, and in short, a complication of wickedness" (304).³ Even more interesting is Alexander Pope's elaborate negotiation of the new rituals of advertising. On the one hand, Pope frequently grouped advertising with other modes of printed media that were, in his mind, dulling the public's intellect and vitiating its tastes. As early as 1712, in a letter he contributed to *Spectator* No. 452, the twenty-four-year-old Pope lamented that so debased had newspaper readers' powers of discrimination become that they "read the Advertisements with the same Curiosity as the Articles of Publick News" and were "as pleased to hear of a Pye-bald Horse that is stray'd out of a field near *Islington*, as of a whole Troop that has been engaged in any Foreign Adventure" (2; see also M. Wood, 28–33). Later in his career, Pope would famously skewer the banality of modern publicity campaigns in the *Dunciad* (1728–43), which includes a slew of mock prefaces and puffs celebrating dullness.

Yet, for all his complaining about advertising, Pope was quite possibly the most widely advertised writer of his era. From early in his career, each of his major publications was accompanied by an unusually intense marketing blitz. Consider his 1715 translation of the *Iliad*, the proceeds from which made Pope independently wealthy. Pope's *Iliad* was heralded by a flurry of advertisements in the *Evening Post* and the *Post-Man* and several supposed "news" stories in the *Weekly Journal* marveling at his unsurpassed understanding of the Greek bard (Barnard, 116–17). Pope's career retrospective in the "Epistle to Dr. Arbuthnot" (1735) intimates that he had nothing to do with the advertising campaigns behind his books:

> What tho' my Name stood rubric on the walls?
> Or plaister'd posts, with Claps [posters] in capitals?
> Or smoking forth, a hundred Hawkers load,
> On Wings of Winds came flying all abroad?
> I sought no homage from the Race that write;
> I kept, like *Asian* monarchs, from their sight[.]
> (lines 210–15)

Pope's private correspondence, however, tells a different story, as on multiple occasions we see him directing his publisher to place advertisements he himself has written. On one particularly telling occasion, Pope began a letter to the publisher Samuel Buckley with detailed instructions on how to promote his forthcoming translation of the *Odyssey*. Mid-letter, though, he abruptly changed course and insisted that any advertising in his behalf be conducted with an eye to propriety. "What I particularly recommend to your care," he wrote, "is to cause it [his advertisement] to be distinguished with proper dignity, & the title in Capitals, as here drawn. Also to stand at the head of the more vulgar advertisements at least rankd before Eloped wives, if not before Lost Spaniels & Strayd Geldings" (*Correspondence*, 2:285; see also 3:473).

For all of Pope's skillful negotiations of the commercial world, however, his self-publicizing efforts paled beside those practiced by the generation of writers and booksellers that came in his wake. Like many sectors of Britain's retail economy, bookselling underwent enormous changes during the latter two-thirds of the eighteenth century. On the positive side, consumer spending was skyrocketing and the spread of print culture had more people doing more reading than ever before in human history. Naturally enough, this led to a dramatic expansion of the book industry. Over the course of a single generation, a trade that had long catered to a relatively small and fixed customer base was forced to adapt its business practices to an increasingly middle-class, and in some cases working-class, clientele. Whereas at the dawn of the eighteenth century Britain's publishing industry was confined to a few blocks in London, by its latter half publishers had set up shops not only throughout the greater London area but in several provincial centers as well (Brewer, *Pleasures*, 138–39). Soon nearly every market town in the kingdom had its own printer, providing Britons with their initial exposure to such basic printed items as handbills, labels, tickets, advertising posters, and local newspapers (Belanger, 6; Harris, 83–84).

Along with this transformation of the book industry, however, came heightened levels of competition and risk. For every Robert Dodsley, John Newbery, or James Lackington who amassed an immense fortune through the book trade, dozens of publishers were forced into poverty or bankruptcy because they lacked the requisite capital, ambition, or good fortune to compete in the changing marketplace (Raven, *Judging New Wealth*, 47–50). To publish a typical edition often required expending hundreds of pounds up front in author's fees, printing costs, and incidental expenses, which meant that a publisher needed sufficient capital on hand to continue with other projects until books on the market began to produce revenue. If a book were to sell slowly or flop altogether, the financial loss would fall wholly on the bookseller's shoulders (Raven, *Judging New Wealth*, 39; Kernan, *Samuel Johnson*, 67–68).

It was out of this newly reconfigured publishing landscape that literature as we know it emerged, with its narrowed focus on imaginative genres and its institutions of copyright and authorial genius. Crucially, these very circumstances also drove authors and booksellers to move beyond the conventionally straightforward marketing practices that many trades were just then discovering and to begin experimenting with a range of groundbreaking methods for stoking demand for their new titles. At some level, consumers clearly benefited from the new market conditions, as publishers were forced to offer a wider range of books, often in higher-quality editions and at more competitive prices. Some booksellers also wooed customers with early forms of the "special, limited time offer." In the early 1780s, for instance, John Bell offered purchasers of his 109-volume *Poets* series a specially designed and ostensibly discounted set of bookshelves to house their new collection. Other publishers pioneered "free gift" marketing campaigns, which promised loyal buyers bonus materials such as limited-edition sheet music, art prints, and embroidery patterns (Raven, *Business of Books*, 281–82).

Yet, whatever warm glow may have surrounded such consumer-friendly promotions as these, many of the most innovative book marketing practices of this era were purposely designed to con the public. Some booksellers capitalized on the craze for novelty by slapping new title pages on decade-old works and promoting them as hot off the press.[4] Others either egregiously postdated their title pages or advertised books as "just published" several months — and, in some cases, several years — after their original release (Raven, *Judging New Wealth*, 63; Tierney, 114).[5] Another common trick was to print unusually small or intentionally misnumbered editions so as to rapidly reach a fourth or fifth edition and thereby give the illusion of runaway sales. Contemplating this practice, John Trusler complained, in his 1785 novel *Modern Times, or The Adventures of Gabriel Outcast*, "by way of deception, though they print but five hundred copies, the title-page shall be altered five times in such an edition, the second hundred having the words *second edition* in the title, of the third hundred the *third edition*, and so on: so that the third edition of a book shall be advertised and selling, before a sufficient number are sold to pay even paper or print" (3:103).

Another favorite marketing ploy was leading readers to mistake the work of a hack for that of a literary legend. Sometimes this took the form of publishing the "lost" works of a Shakespeare or a Jonson; more conventionally it involved coaxing would-be readers to believe an anonymously published volume had been penned by a literary lion or a notorious aristocrat. In the *Champion* for 1 March 1740, Henry Fielding blasted such practices:

> One Bookseller is reported to have maintained certain Writers in his Garret, because they had the same Names with some of their eminent Cotemporaries. Others have contented themselves with concealing the Name of the Author in the Title-Page, and only spreading Whispers through the Coffee-Houses, that he is a very considerable Person, my Lord, or Mr. Such-a-one, which the Whisperer hath discovered by his Stile, or been credibly informed of by some who have seen the Manuscript. But the most usual Way is to throw out certain Hints

in the Advertisements, such as by a Lady of Quality. By a celebrated Physician. By D----r S----t. By a certain Dean, &c. (1:323–24)[6]

If any one figure embodies the innovation, ambition, and penchant for hucksterism of eighteenth-century publishers, it is John Newbery. Newbery, of course, is well remembered today through the prestigious children's book medal that bears his name, but he deserves to be at least as well remembered as one of the pioneers of modern advertising. List virtually any major eighteenth-century marketing innovation, and it is likely Newbery was among its earliest practitioners. He was among the first, for instance, to make use of the "bonus gift" promotion, offering purchasers of *A Little Pretty Pocket Book* (1744) — on the front page of the *Daily Gazetteer* for 19 May 1744—a "Ball and Pincusheon [sic], the Use of which will infallibly make *Tommy* a good Boy, and *Polly* a good Girl" ("Some Publishers' Puffs," 491). He also experimented with a "free book" campaign, informing readers of the *Public Advertiser* for 18 December 1753 that *Nurse Truelove's Christmas Box* would be "given gratis to all little good Boys and Girls . . . , they paying for the Binding, which is only *One Penny* each book."[7] At the same time, Newbery was also experimenting with promoting books as part of a series rather than as stand-alone products. A full 250 years before the launch of today's "For Idiots" and "For Dummies" brands, Newbery established his "Circle of the Sciences" series, which featured such titles as *The Art of Rhetorick Laid Down in an Easy and Entertaining Manner* (1746), *Grammar Made Familiar and Easy for Young Gentle-Ladies and Foreigners* (1748), and *Arithmetic Made Familiar and Easy to Young Gentlemen and Ladies* (1748).

Perhaps Newbery's greatest contribution to modern advertising, however, came in his groundbreaking use of product placement, or the insinuation of advertisements into the plots of novels and other entertainments. Many a Newbery book contains multiple passages in which characters delightedly pore over other Newbery titles. The protagonists of *The Twelfth Day Gift* (1767), for instance, routinely liven up a dull day by pulling out such Newbery titles as *The New Year's Gift*, the *Lilliputian Magazine*, *Newtonian Philosophy of Tops and Balls*, and *A Valentine's Gift* (Welsh, 107). Product placement was also a staple in Newbery's nonfiction titles, such as *The Art of Poetry on a New Plan* (1762), which takes a disproportionate percentage of its samples of model poetry from the publisher's back catalogue of verse (Buck, 203).

What's more, Newbery used his literary titles as occasions to promote his other major product line, patent medicines. Like several other booksellers (see Figure 2.1), from the early 1740s Newbery was at least part owner of a range of drugs, including the enormously profitable Dr. James's Fever Powders. Far from distancing his literary and pharmaceutical endeavors, Newbery enthusiastically took every opportunity to market them in tandem. Above the door of his St. Paul's Churchyard bookstore, he proclaimed in large golden letters that the shop also doubled as a "Medicinal Warehouse" ("On the Learning," 1:53–54). He published several books heralding the miraculous powers of Dr. James's Powders, including *A Dissertation on Fevers and Inflammatory Distempers* (written in 1748 by Dr. Robert James himself)[8] and Christopher Smart's *Hymn to the Supreme Being, on Recovery from a Dangerous Fit of Illness* (1756), the dedication to which prophesies that "millions yet unborn will celebrate the man, who wrote the *Medicinal Dictionary*, and invented the *Fever Powder*" (ii). Even Newbery's children's fiction got in on the act; the opening lines of *Goody Two-Shoes* (1766) read: "Care and Discontent shortened the Days of Little *Margery*'s Father.—He was forced from his Family, and seized with a violent Fever in a Place where Dr. *James*'s Powder was not to be had, and where he died miserably" (*History of Goody Two-Shoes*, 13).[9]

RICHARDSON, FIELDING, AND THE BIRTH OF THE PUFF

What most clearly separates Newbery and his peers in the book trade from previous generations of retailers, however, is one profound and thoroughly modern insight: namely that virtually any space and any mode of discourse can be appropriated for promotional purposes. As we have seen, prior to the 1730s and 1740s, advertisements almost invariably were clearly demarcated as such, appearing in such established and unambiguous forms as handbills, posters, shop signs, and newspaper advertisements.[10] The print explosion of the early eighteenth century severely challenged the efficacy of such traditional genres, since there were more ads than ever competing for the gaze of consumers, and a sizeable percentage of shoppers had grown so weary of advertising that they consciously tuned out advertisements altogether. Add to this the fact that the stamp and advertisement duties, which were introduced in 1712 and were raised several times by century's end, made advertising increasingly expensive, and there was ample incentive to bend the rules of traditional marketing.

That booksellers by the early 1730s were coming to be associated with unconventional and ethically suspect advertising is evidenced by the entrance of a new term into the marketing lexicon: the puff. Today "puff" and "puffery" are often used as synonyms for advertising in general and hyperbolic marketing in particular. The original, eighteenth-century usage of the word "puff," however, was much narrower. In yet another sign of just how closely associated the fledgling

a

CHARLES PUNCHARD,
Bookseller, Binder, Stationer, and Printer,
At his CIRCULATING LIBRARY,
In the BUTTER MARKET, IPSWICH:
Let out to Read, Novels, Plays, &c. &c. At *four Shillings* per Quarter — *twelve Shillings*, per Year.—Or, *one Penny* per Evening for each Volume or Play.
☞ New Books and Plays purchased as soon as Published.—Catalogues may be had GRATIS at his SHOP.
ALSO *may be had, the following* USEFUL FAMILY MEDICINES, *viz.*

Betton's British Oil.	Leyden Pill.	Speediman's Pills.
Dr. James's Fever Powders.	Maredant's Drops.	Smith's Specific Drops.
Glass's Magnesia.	Mayerne's Drops.	Turlington's Balsam.
Leake's Pills & Drops.	Ridley's Asthmatic Pills.	Walker's Jesuit Drops.

With many others, as mentioned in his SHOP-BILL.
He begs leave to inform his Friends, and the Public in General, that of him may be had (on the Shortest Notice) *every Book or Medicine advertis'd in Mr.* SHAVE's *Ipswich Journal, though his Name be not inserted.*—*All Orders will be thankfully received, and gratefully acknowledged.*
BOOKBINDING *in all its Branches*—PRINTING NEATLY *and* CORRECTLY *Perform'd.*
COPPER-PLATE PRINTING BY COMMISSION.

b

Robert Peck
PRINTER,
Proprietor & Publisher of the
HULL PACKET,
No 31, Scale Lane, Hull,
Warehouse for Writing Paper; &
Genuine Patent Medicines
Retail, Wholesale, and for Exportation.

c

JOSEPH HEATH,
BOOKSELLER and STATIONER,
Near the *Trees* in the *Market-Place*,
NOTTINGHAM.

SELLS all forts of Bibles, Common-Prayer-Books, School-Books Modern Books, &c. as *Cheap as in* LONDON.

Alfo all Sorts of *Stationary-Wares Wholefale* and *Retail.* Great variety of Paper-Hangings for Rooms, of the Newest Patterns, at 2d. Farthing a Yard, & upward.

Subfcriptions taken in for all Sorts of MAGAZINES, and all other Periodical Works.

Binds all forts of BOOKS in all variety of Bindings in the neatest Manner. Leidgers, &c. Rul'd & Bound to particular directions

PRINTS Advertifements, Tradefmen's Bills, Blank Receipts, Certificates, &c.

SELLS Dr. *Daffy's* Original Elixir, *the fame which was Sold by the late.* Mrs. Ann Peach in *Nottingham*. Dr. *Benj. Godfrey's* Cordial, HILL's *Ormfkirk* Medicine, for the Bite, of a *Mad-Dog*. with all other publick MEDICINES, &c. &c. Wholefale & Retail.

Figure 2.1. Eighteenth-century trade cards illustrating the kinship between the book and patent medicine trades: (a) Charles Punchard, Ipswich (John Johnson Collection, Bodleian Library, Oxford); (b) Robert Peck, Hull (Huntington Library, San Marino, California); (c) Joseph Heath, Nottingham (Huntington Library, San Marino, California)

advertising system was with the book trade, the commercial sense of the word "puff" originated specifically to describe publishers' attempts to promote their books outside traditional forms of advertising. The earliest known usage of "puff" in this sense comes in the *Weekly Register* of 27 May 1732, which reports, "Puff is become a cant Word to signify the Applause that Writers or Booksellers give to what they write or publish, in Order to increase its Reputation and Sale."[11] In 1735, again in his "Epistle to Dr. Arbuthnot," Pope caricatured the self-important literary patron as "full-blown *Bufo*, puff'd by ev'ry quill" (line 227). That same year the *Grub-Street Journal* ran a two-part "Short Dissertation upon Puffs," satirizing booksellers' new proclivity for deception. Indulging the age's scatological tastes, the essay of 12 June 1735 muses that perhaps the recent coinage of the term "puff" derived from the similarity between self-hype and flatulence. Puffs, the satirist points out, "are frequently exploded from the *posteriors* or back-side of a News-paper; and in that they give the book-seller some ease under the pains occasioned by flatulent compositions, which are very apt to afflict him with the spleen, or a hypochondriacal and windy melancholy" (1).[12]

As defined in all these instances, a puff has two distinguishing features. First, it is thoroughly hyperbolic, regularly taking the form of an exuberant endorsement of a lackluster product. Second, and more important, a puff is an advertisement in disguise, sometimes masquerading as a news story or opinion piece, sometimes as a bit of eager praise strategically shared at a literary gathering on the eve of a book's publication. By 1739 such forms of stealth advertising had become so rampant in the book trade that the *Scots Magazine* grumbled, "The art of puffing increases beyond belief" (Toupee, 181).

A year later, Henry Fielding began what would be a multiyear battle against literary puffery. First, in the *Champion* of 16 February 1740, he adopted the satirical persona of the puffer extraordinaire "Gustavus Puffendorff," announcing that "*Puffs* . . . of all Degrees and Magnitudes, for all Arts, Mysteries and Professions are to be had of me, if *properly bespoke*, at my House, the Sign of the *Powder-Puff*, in *Blow-Bladder-Street*, and no where else in the Three Kingdoms" (*The Champion*, 1:281). Two weeks later in the same journal, he devoted an entire essay to the subject, this time attempting a serious analysis of this new phenomenon in literary marketing. Here he concludes that the rising generation's impatience for fame "hath given Rise to several Inventions among Authors, to get themselves and their Works a Name. And has introduc'd that famous Art call'd Puffing, which . . . [has been] brought to great Perfection in this Age" (1:322–23).

Fielding's most notable attacks on puffery, however, came a year later, when his mock-novel *Shamela* took direct aim at the promotional campaign behind

Samuel Richardson's *Pamela*. At the time, Richardson's novel was experiencing unprecedented popularity, having sparked what William B. Warner has aptly termed a "media event" not just in Britain but across much of the Western world. At the same moment that entrepreneurs were displaying *Pamela*-inspired wax figures off Fleet Street and sportsmen were naming race horses after characters in the novel (Keymer and Sabor, *Pamela in the Marketplace*, 2–3), Fielding and others were taking to press to lambaste what they saw as the novel's ill-gotten acclaim. What many suspected then has recently been given further credence in Thomas Keymer and Peter Sabor's *Pamela in the Marketplace*, which argues that "*Pamela*'s success lay as much in commercial strategy as in literary achievement." Quite simply, Keymer and Sabor reveal, Richardson "targeted his market" and "manipulated it with a virtuoso publicity campaign" (22). Having spent over three decades in the book trade prior to turning novelist, Richardson had had a front-row seat at some of the most inventive advertising campaigns thus far staged; so when it came time to release his own book, he was equipped with a remarkable understanding of the principles of modern publicity.

Somewhat surprisingly, the direct advertising campaign behind *Pamela* was unexceptional, consisting primarily of a few standard newspaper notices circulated on the eve of its publication. Richardson expended considerably more energy in compiling the promotional materials he would include as prefaces to the novel. The first edition features a preface by the anonymous "editor" extolling the deep-seated piety of Pamela's letters and commendations from two friends of Richardson predicting the morally salubrious effects the book would have on readers. However presumptuous these prefaces might seem to modern readers, such paratextual self-praise wasn't out of the ordinary at the time. Where Richardson truly crossed the line, though, was in the second and subsequent editions, which supplemented the first edition's prefatory encomia with several additional commendatory letters, an elaborate self-congratulating introduction, and a set of "Verses, sent to the Bookseller, for the Unknown Author of the beautiful new Piece call'd PAMELA."[13]

More than anything, it was the audacity of these prefaces that goaded Fielding into writing his parody. *Shamela* appeared a mere six weeks after the second edition of *Pamela*. It opens with a gleefully erotic dedication and a set of biting "Letters to the Editor." The first of these letters, "The EDITOR to *Himself*," insinuates that Richardson himself had authored the commendatory letters in *Pamela*. The second, titled "JOHN PUFF, *Esq; to the* EDITOR," pants, "Who is he, what is he that could write so excellent a Book? he must be doubtless most agreeable to the Age, and to *his Honour* himself; for he is able to draw every thing to Perfection but Virtue" (*An Apology*, xiv). Fielding caps off this introductory section with a notice that "several other COMMENDATORY LETTERS and COPIES OF VERSES will be prepared against the NEXT EDITION" (xv).

Equally obnoxious as these paratextual puffs, in the eyes of Fielding and others, were Richardson's epitextual efforts to ensure a buzz surrounding *Pamela*'s release. In October 1740, for instance, Richardson evidently leaned on William Webster, a business associate whom he had recently released from a £90 debt, to publish a lead article in the *Weekly Miscellany* hyping *Pamela*. Richardson also appears to have prodded his long-time acquaintance Alexander Pope into publicly declaring that *Pamela* would "do more good than a great many of the new Sermons." Perhaps most notoriously, Richardson enlisted Dr. Benjamin Slocock, chaplain of St. Saviour's Chapel in Southwark and the original for *Shamela*'s Parson Thomas Tickletext, to devote his inaugural sermon of 1741 to recommending *Pamela* as an unrivaled piece of devotional literature (Keymer and Sabor, *Pamela in the Marketplace*, 23–26; see also Warner, 203–12, and Eaves and Kimpel, 119–27).

That Richardson would see the benefit of having his tale on the subject of "virtue rewarded" endorsed from the pulpit is easily understood. What is more remarkable is how, at the same time as he was hyping the righteousness of his tale, Richardson was also seemingly laboring behind the scenes to guarantee that his novel's lightly veiled eroticism was not lost upon less pious readers. As Keymer and Sabor detail in one of the most intriguing sections of *Pamela in the Marketplace*, abundant circumstantial evidence links Richardson to *Pamela Censured*, the highly controversial 1741 pamphlet that goes to great pains to locate all the most potentially titillating passages from *Pamela*, ostensibly in the name of denouncing the book as little more than an extended exercise in literary pornography. Despite the pamphlet's avowed moral squeamishness, many from the start suspected its real purpose was to cultivate a secondary market of libertine readers. As the eminent critic Aaron Hill reported to Richardson in May of 1741, there was considerable speculation afoot that *Pamela Censured* was little more than "a Bookseller's Contrivance for recommending ye Purchase of *Pamela* to such Light and Loose Readers, as the names of Religion and Virtue might well have scar'd from any Purpose to look into it" (qtd. in Keymer and Sabor, *Pamela in the Marketplace*, 34–35). Further suspicion regarding Richardson's rumored involvement in *Pamela Censured* is raised by the fact that it was published by James Robert, a long-term business associate of Richardson who depended on the author of *Pamela* for much of his printing work (35). In light of all this, Keymer and Sabor seem justified in suggesting that *Pamela Censured* might very well be "the most ingenious marketing ploy surrounding the novel" (36).

Yet, even if Richardson had nothing to do with *Pamela Censured*, the promotional campaign he engineered for *Pamela* still warrants recognition as a milestone in British advertising. With 20,000 authorized copies and nearly as many pirated copies in circulation within a year of the book's release, the novel's commercial success definitively showed what an innovative and tireless advertising campaign could accomplish. It also demonstrated that the new age of product marketing would see advertisements freed from the confines of the newspaper or handbill, appearing just as frequently in such diverse media as Sunday sermons, celebrity endorsements, newspaper puffs, and staged denunciations. All told, then, *Pamela* warrants recognition not just as one of the first great English novels but, perhaps as importantly, one of the first modern products.

Advertising, in turn, can be credited as the force that made possible the *Pamela* media event. Pushing the case even further, Jill Campbell has contended that a deep, formal relationship exists between early advertising and novels (251–54). Given how frequently eighteenth-century novelists were in fact moonlighting journal editors, it is hardly surprising, she notes, that similar modes of particularized description appear in both the ad copy and the tales of adventure these writers produced. Furthermore, Campbell argues, the forms and logic of eighteenth-century advertising play a pivotal role in such foundational early novels as Richardson's *Clarissa*, Burney's *Cecilia*, and Edgeworth's *Belinda*. In short, "the novel and advertising grew up together" (251), and it is quite likely that we are only beginning to grasp the depth of the contextual, structural, and epistemological links between the two.

PUFFERY AND THE RISE OF THE BOOK REVIEW

However significant an impact the nascent culture of advertising had on the early novel, it had even greater bearing on another monumental development in mid-eighteenth-century British letters, the emergence of modern literary criticism. Properly speaking, of course, criticism is nearly as old as art itself, dating back to the instance when someone first uttered an opinion on a drawing, story, or song. But through the end of the seventeenth century, literary and cultural criticism in Britain was primarily the pursuit of gentlemanly amateurs, often finding its fullest expression in polite conversation rather than published essays. In the early eighteenth century, however, this courtly tradition began to fade, giving way, as

H. B. Nisbet and Claude Rawson have put it, to "the beginnings of what might be called critical careers, of whole lifetimes devoted to extensive consideration both of literary principles and of the practice of authors" (xvi).[14] At least initially, the evolving role of the critic had little impact on the tone, style, and subject matter of most criticism. Like the gentleman critic of the seventeenth century, the professional writing for such early-eighteenth-century periodicals as the *Tatler*, the *Spectator*, and the *Gentleman's Magazine* had two basic aims: to exhibit his (or, in some cases, her) own refined taste and to impart that cultivation to others (Patey, "The Institution of Criticism," 11–16). Only rarely did the critic working in this mode transition beyond general musings on aesthetics, judgment, and taste and into the careful analysis of discrete literary works. In fact, much of what we tend to think of as the "literary" criticism of the early eighteenth century is better considered "cultural" criticism. As Terry Eagleton has pointed out, for the *Tatler*, the *Spectator*, and their various imitators, "the examination of literary texts is one relatively marginal moment of a broader enterprise which explores attitudes to servants and the rules of gallantry, the status of women and familial affections, the purity of the English language, the character of conjugal love, the psychology of the sentiments and the laws of the toilet" (*The Function*, 18).

To find the effective point of origin for modern literary criticism, then, we need to look beyond the age of Addison and Steele to the century's middle decades, when book reviewing as we know it began taking shape. For it was during the 1740s and 1750s that the literary review—a genre that remains largely unchanged in twenty-first-century periodicals like the *Times Literary Supplement* and the *New York Review of Books*—took root in Britain. Prior to this time, a number of British publishers had attempted to imitate the *Journal des Scavans*, the Parisian journal founded in 1665 with the explicit aim of surveying new scientific and scholarly books. In one such attempt, in the 1690s, the exiled French Huguenots Jean de la Crose and Peter Anthony Motteaux launched a series of short-lived, London-based monthlies dedicated to reviewing new scholarly books; and in the 1730s, another wave of publishers either founded scholarly reviews (most notably Jacob Robinson's *History of the Works of the Learned*) or began including lists of new scientific publications in their journals (such as the catalogue found in the *Gentleman's Magazine*) (Sommerville, 110–13; Feather, *A History*, 102–5). All of these efforts, however, had one significant blind-spot: they failed to realize that readers craved not only concise recaps of theological, astronomical, and mathematical treatises but also critical reviews of the best new titles from the world of belles lettres.

The bookseller generally credited with first seriously addressing this gap in the market is Ralph Griffiths, the founder and long-time editor of the *Monthly Review*. It was presumably while working for Robinson, one of Britain's most innovative publishers of scholarly journals, that Griffiths first conceived of a monthly periodical that would treat novels, plays, and books of verse alongside discourses on anatomy, theology, and physics. And, thus, a few months shy of his thirtieth birthday and only a few years after setting up on his own as a publisher, Griffiths launched the *Monthly Review*.[15] The inaugural issue, that of May 1749, clearly signaled the *Monthly*'s eclectic and belletristic intentions. Of the six publications reviewed in this first number, two were collections of verse, one a new play, and the other three treatises on patriotism, moral philosophy, and the physical senses. As if this disruption of the traditionally limited scope of review periodicals weren't enough, Griffiths took an even bolder step two months later, announcing in the July 1749 issue that the *Monthly* would thenceforward attempt to touch upon *all* new titles, "without exception to any, on account of their lowness of rank, or price" ("Monthly Catalogue," 238). This new journal, Griffiths insisted, would offer an invaluable public service, relieving the anxiety increasingly experienced by learned and general readers alike over being unable to keep up with the flood of new books appearing each month. Not only would the *Monthly* provide objective and expert reviews by some of the best scholars of the day, but it would save its readers considerable time and money by steering them away from inferior titles. In short, Griffiths's journal would be, as James Basker puts it, a "consumer's guide for what was, after all, the first mass-production industry in history" ("Criticism," 328).[16]

It was not just the newly expanded world of print, however, that Griffiths promised to help readers navigate; just as important, the *Monthly* would protect readers against the worst exploits of the nation's burgeoning advertising system. Two sentences into the précis announcing the establishment of the *Monthly*, Griffiths justifies the need for such a publication via an indictment of advertising in general and of book trade puffery in particular. "The abuse of title-pages," he laments, "is obviously come to such a pass, that few readers care to take in a book, any more than a servant, without a recommendation." Accordingly, he pledges that the *Monthly Review* will strive to inoculate readers against lying title pages and other advertising cons, by exercising high standards and strict critical independence. In short, its reputation will be built on "candour, and justness of distinction" (i).

Just how impermeable the barriers turned out to be between the burgeoning advertising system and Griffiths's *Monthly* has long been subject to debate. In fact, almost immediately after the *Monthly*'s founding, allegations began swirling throughout literary London that the review's so-called critical independence was yet another booksellers' ruse. The 26 June 1753 number of the *Universal Advertiser*, for instance, suggests that it had already become common practice for authors hoping to receive an extended review in the *Monthly* to make an under-the-table payment to the "Guardians of the *Temple of Fame*." "I know a Writer," the anonymous essayist reports, "who has paid dearly for telling the Author of the *Monthly Review*, that he would no more buy a Puff from him, than he would a Wind from a *Lapland Witch*" ("*Universal Advertiser*, No. 50," 57). Such charges are expanded upon in the 7 September 1754 issue of *Gray's-Inn Journal*, which stages a mock trial in which Griffiths and his team of "Hirelings" (Murphy, 2:269) are indicted for, first, being "obscure, hackney Scriblers, who deal out Malice and Invective by the Sheet" (2:272); second, "recommend[ing] their own native Dulness, or indeed, the Dulness of any other Person, provided he or his Bookseller condescend to make Interest with them" (2:268); and, third, denouncing "all Works that have the least Ray of Genius, according as they happen to dislike the Author's Face, or that of the Bookseller, who may have purchased the Copy" (2:268). By the mid-1750s it had become something of a point of doctrine among the *Monthly*'s detractors that Griffiths employed a team of garreted hacks who labored under strict orders to reserve praise exclusively for associates of the publisher and those who had paid the requisite bribe.[17] Feeding off these sentiments, in the final weeks of 1755 Tobias Smollett promoted the launch of the *Critical Review* by repeatedly announcing that, unlike the *Monthly*, his journal would be staffed by true men of genius and taste, not "obscure Hackney Writers, accidentally enlisted in the Service of an undistinguishing Bookseller," and that the *Critical* would be steadfastly independent from booksellers or other corrupting interests.[18]

Over the course of the nineteenth century, this image of Griffiths as a rascally, self-serving huckster took even deeper hold through a series of biographies of Smollett and Oliver Goldsmith, two increasingly revered writers who had squabbled with Griffiths. The twentieth century, in contrast, was considerably kinder to the legacy of Griffiths and his review. The first major revaluation of the publisher's reputation came in Benjamin Christie Nangle's 1934 study *The Monthly Review, First Series, 1749–1789*. Nangle begins by arguing that Griffiths staffed his journal not with "Hackney Writers" but with "the most eminent scholars in the kingdom" (viii). He insists that "Griffiths made a strenuous effort to maintain a high standard of honesty himself, and to ensure impartiality in the reviews. . . . He rejected emphatically any proposal which endeavoured to secure by undue influence the insertion of a favourable review" (ix–x). In

Nangle's wake, a number of scholars—most prominently Derek Roper, James Basker, and Frank Donoghue—have come to similar conclusions. Summarizing the late-twentieth-century scholarly consensus, Basker states, "In assessing Griffiths's *Monthly*, no modern scholar has so far found anything terribly corrupt or unusually self-serving about his editorial practices" (*Tobias Smollett*, 36–37; Roper, 30–36; Donoghue, 19–27).

Applied to Griffiths's entire fifty-four-year tenure as head editor at the *Monthly* (he continued to run the review until his death in 1803), such a claim generally holds true, as most extant evidence suggests he became increasingly intent over the years on promoting strict critical disinterestedness. Yet, if we focus particularly on the *Monthly*'s first five years, it is difficult to deny that the journal was at least in part conceived of as an advertising organ for Griffiths's fledgling bookselling operations. To begin with, the early numbers of the *Monthly* frequently featured either oblique or direct advertisements for Griffiths's new titles—this despite the fact that the *Monthly* ostensibly ran no advertisements. The second review in the journal's opening issue, for instance, concerns a recent French edition of Claude Nicolas LeCat's *Physical Essay on the Senses*. As much as the reviewer—whom we learn from the publisher's marked copy of the *Monthly* was Griffiths himself—may admire LeCat's scholarship, what soon becomes clear is that the immediate occasion for this review was not the publication of the French original but the English translation of LeCat that was then being prepared for publication in Griffiths's shop. In other words, the second essay in the inaugural issue of the first modern reviewing periodical was essentially an advertisement. This becomes even clearer in the "review's" opening paragraphs, when Griffiths informs his readers: "A translation into *English* of Mr. *Le Cat*'s book is now in the press, and advertising to be speedily published, with all the original plates, in one volume 8vo. To raise the curiosity of the public . . . for this excellent work, I need only say that it is mentioned with approbation in the *Philosophical Transactions*, No. 466, by Dr. *Persons*, F.R.S." (Review of *Physical Essay*, 28–29). Ten months later, upon the actual publication of Griffiths's English edition of LeCat, the *Monthly* ran an entirely new review of the book, and subsequent essays on Griffiths's English edition would appear in the September, October, and November 1750 numbers.

Griffiths also devoted considerable space in the *Monthly*'s early issues to reviewing two other periodicals he was then launching, *Le Nouveau Magasin Francois* and *Magazine de Londres*. Every issue between June and October 1749 contained a lightly disguised advertisement for the *Magazine de Londres*. In the June issue, the advertisement is formatted like a review but reads like straightforward advertising copy. It also comes at the issue's end, where one typically would find formal advertisements in other periodicals. In August, however, the review/advertisement appears in the heart of the issue, flanked on either side by ostensibly objective reviews of non-Griffiths publications. Three years later Griffiths returned to this advertisement-cum-review format in a February 1752 notice of his new publication *The Pillars of Priestcraft and Orthodoxy Shaken*. That nearly three years after establishing his journal Griffiths was still navigating the gray area between a review and an advertisement—and possibly trying to dodge the advertising duty—is evidenced in the headline to this notice: "Article XX. *The Pillars of Priestcraft* . . . " (Figure 2.2). While this headline follows the format of all other formal reviews in this number, its placement at issue's end—several pages after all the other full reviews—clearly sets it off as a direct advertisement. The cumulative impression in reviewing cases like these is that Griffiths was at war with himself, at once intent on using his journal to promote his other publishing interests and conscience-stricken over his ethical obligation to be straightforward with readers. His fall-back, then, was crafting odd hybrids such as these that blurred the lines between the direct advertisement, the formal review, and the bookseller's puff.

In fairness, not everything in the *Monthly*'s early numbers that might initially look like a puff necessarily was one. When you set out to review *every* new book proceeding from British presses, there is nothing particularly unprincipled about noticing your own publications. Moreover, one can certainly find instances from the *Monthly*'s early years of the journal voicing mixed opinions on a Griffiths title. In the December 1750 number, for example, Griffiths offered a rather lukewarm assessment of John Cleland's *Oeconomy of a Winter's Day*, despite the fact that Cleland was a friend and frequent contributor to the *Monthly*. That said, one would be hard-pressed to find an unequivocally negative review of a Griffiths title in the *Monthly*'s first ten volumes. It wouldn't be until 1755—perhaps not coincidentally in the midst of the growing outcry by Smollett and others against the supposed corruption at the *Monthly*—that the journal began negatively critiquing Griffiths titles with any regularity.[19]

Meanwhile, the early numbers of the *Monthly* featured several clear-cut puffs for Griffiths titles. On a number of occasions Griffiths himself penned celebratory reviews of his firm's books.[20] The most notorious of these instances—and the one Griffiths's twentieth-century apologists found hardest to justify—was his March 1750 notice of a new, somewhat sanitized edition of Cleland's erotic novel, *Fanny Hill*. Griffiths had been involved from the beginning in the commissioning and publication of this book, apparently agreeing to secure Cleland's release from debtors' prison in exchange for the novel's copyrights. According to some to the standard necessary to maturation; which is promoted by hot and stimulating medicines. Besides these he observes, that some different medicines sometimes conduce to this end, by exciting an intestine motion in the humours already stagnant in, or just effusing into the cavity; or by occasioning such a slight incipient putrefaction, as sometimes disposes to suppuration. He concludes the operation of digestives, which are applied to the humid part itself that is to be formed into *Pus*, to be pretty similar.

The third chapter of the classes of suppurating medicines, enumerates many of the officinal medicines and some others, which correspond to the different intentions above mentioned.

The fourth chapter of the use of suppurating medicines in external diseases, contains many practical directions, applicable to a general variety of cases, and directs several other topical compositions. It seems indeed, a therapeutic and judicious extension of the former. But, as this valuable tract is of a small bulk and purchase, and can entertain only our chirurgical readers, we chuse to refer them to the work itself, which we conceive they will approve, as methodical and satisfactory. The translator, Mr. *Dargent*'s language is very clear and intelligible; though we imagin'd a gallicism or two in it, which might possibly be only typographical errors. *H*

(*End of the Catalogue.*)

ART. XX. *The Pillars of Priestcraft and Orthodoxy shaken. In two vols.* 12mo. 6s. *bound.* Griffiths.

THESE two volumes are intended as a supplement to those published the last year, in three volumes, entitled *a Cordial for Low Spirits*. The tracts are of the same kind, and the design of the editor the same in both. Mr. *Barron* tells us in his preface, that he is greatly mistaken, if this collection be not as well received as the former. It consists, says he, of very curious and entertaining pieces, some of them so scarce, that they are not to be purchased for any money; and he assures us, that they are faithfully printed, according to their respective originals, or best editions.

The pieces contained in these volumes, are,

1. A discourse on *Isaiah* lxvi. 7, 8. preached on the 10th. of *June*; being the birth-day of the *Pretender*.

2.

Figure 2.2. Griffiths's quasi-review of his publishing house's *The Pillars of Priestcraft*. (*Monthly Review* 6 [February 1752]: 159.)

(likely exaggerated) reports, Griffiths earned upwards of £10,000 from the combined sales of *Memoirs of a Woman of Pleasure* (the original 1749 title) and *Memoirs of Fanny Hill* (the edited 1750 version).[21] And yet, in his review of *Fanny Hill* for the *Monthly*, Griffiths feigned both ignorance concerning the book's authorship and surprise over the public outcry surrounding its alleged lewdness:

> Though this book is said to be taken from a very loose work, printed about two years ago, in two volumes, and on that account a strong prejudice has arisen against it, yet it does not appear to us that this performance, whatever the two volumes might be, (for we have not seen them) has any thing in it more offensive to decency, or delicacy of sentiment and expression, than our novels and books of entertainment in general have. . . . The author of *Fanny Hill* does not seem to have expressed any thing with a view to countenance the practice of any immoralities, but meerly to exhibit truth and nature to the world, and to lay open those mysteries of iniquity that, in our opinion, need only to be exposed to view, in order to their being abhorred and shunned by those who might otherwise unwarily fall into them. The stile has a peculiar neatness, and the characters are naturally drawn. (431–32)

While this comically disingenuous review has gone down as the most notorious puff from the *Monthly*'s early years, its audacity was matched by several self-reviewals that appeared in the journal's early issues. The November 1749 number, for instance, praises the anonymous author of *The Case of the Unfortunate Bosavern Penlez*—since revealed as John Cleland—for possessing an unusual "regard for candour" and "knowledge of facts" and a real flair for "just description." The reviewer in this instance, as recorded in Griffiths's marked copy of the journal, was none other than Cleland himself. Griffiths also allowed Smollett—with whom he still had a collegial relationship in the *Monthly*'s early years—to puff an edition of William Smellie's *Theory and Practice of Midwifery*, which Smollett himself had edited and prefaced (Basker, *Tobias Smollett*, 37). And in 1750 John Hill, the apothecary-turned-actor, who was a major contributor to the *Monthly* from its founding, was permitted to review two of his own books, *The Adventures of Mr. Loveill* and *The Actor: A Treatise on the Art of Playing*. The review of *Mr. Loveill* begins by referencing (or possibly inventing) rumors that this "fashionable" novel was written by "an author of considerable rank" and moves on to praising the story for possessing "a spirit and fire thro' the whole that few performances of this kind have had to boast of" (58). Hill's much longer review of *The Actor* is even more laudatory. In a remarkable series of superlatives, the review asserts that the author "argues very sensibly," "very rationally pleads," "concludes very justly," "very pleasantly cautions," and "very justly observes" (189–97). In short, it declares, "This work must be allow'd to deserve the character it generally has obtained, of the most sensible performance ever published on the subject" (196).

What becomes increasingly clear in surveying such examples is that, even in a periodical ostensibly dedicated to neutralizing the reach and sophistication of modern advertising, the siren-call of puffery was always within earshot. Whatever his principal motives may have been in founding the *Monthly*, Griffiths—like Richardson before him—had unmistakably absorbed the commercial ethic of the age and was thus prepared to use every medium at his disposal to boost the sales of his and his close associates' titles. Far from an antidote to the age of puffery, then, Griffiths's *Monthly* can be said to have further accelerated the incursion of advertising logic into the production and dissemination of literature.

THE BRAVE NEW WORLD OF *THE CRITIC*

In the decades to follow, as the success of the *Monthly* inspired dozens of imitators, the debate over whether the fledgling institutions of literary criticism principally served the needs of booksellers or those of the reading public only intensified. One point on which virtually everyone involved in the world of letters agreed was that review criticism had a sizeable impact on sales and an even greater impact on authors' reputations. In the postscript to his 1767 book *Lexiphanes*, Archibald Campbell reflected a widely shared view when he lamented, "The greatest number now a-days, will not so much as cast their eyes on a new production, unless, it may be, a Romance or a Novel manufactured for a circulating library, till they have consulted their monthly Oracles, a Magazine, a Museum, or a Review" (165). While Campbell likely oversimplified the buying habits of the average reader, his general point holds true if one considers, first, that a large percentage of late-eighteenth-century readers got their books from circulating libraries and book clubs and, second, that these libraries and clubs often based their purchasing decisions largely on the recommendation of the reviews. As the *Antijacobin Review* remarked in a 1798 essay on book clubs, "Few publications are purchased [by book clubs] until the lords paramount of literature, the Reviewers, have fixed on them the seal of their approbation" ("Book Clubs," 475). "Had the reviewer not existed," William Christie rightly suggests, "print culture would have had to invent him" (18).[22]

Not surprisingly, as the influence of reviews expanded, the temptation to exploit the commercial possibilities of criticism became harder to resist. A letter from the Scottish writer James Beattie to his friend Thomas Blacklock suggests that by 1770 critical puffing had become naturalized in at least some circles. At the time, Beattie was preparing his *Essay on the Nature and Immutability of Truth* for publication, and he justified urging his friend to review it by saying, "Puffing is so constantly used on these occasions that the omission of it would seem to bespeak either total unconcern about public approbation or that the production is altogether unsupported or friendless" (qtd. in Forbes, 46). In 1787 the *Busy Body* reported much the same, claiming, "the art of puffing is now become so common, no publication whatever can be sold without it" (Oulton, 1:19). And years later, the *Dublin University Magazine* recorded how, upon hearing Edmund Kean's complaints about critics' lack of appreciation for his acting, David Garrick's widow replied: "You should write your own criticisms. David always did so" ("On Criticism," 730).[23]

While, as Antonia Forster points out, few extant records detail quid-pro-quo puffs or bribes, "there is plenty of evidence in private correspondence, most of it as yet unpublished, that there were then, as there are now, other kinds of corruption in reviewing and that such apparently admirable factors as friendship, compassion, and kindliness could do as much as bribery to pervert the supposedly high-minded business of criticism" ("Avarice or Interest," 169). With this in mind, one could reasonably argue that much of the puffery that took place during this age wasn't as unequivocally unprincipled as we might imagine. Yet, from the perspective of novice or otherwise unconnected authors, there was nothing respectable at all about the situational ethics of the age's book reviewing, even when a puff was rooted in benevolent motives. Thomas Chatterton spoke for a good portion of the age's disenfranchised authors when, in 1770 at the age of seventeen, he dashed off a thirty-eight-line satire titled "The Art of Puffing." Adopting an arch pose from the start, he implores the great publishers and reviewers of the age to "Teach the young Author how to please the Town, / And make the heavy drug of Rhime go down" (lines 3-4). Looking upon literary London from the outside, he can only marvel at how, on the one hand, "they puff the heavy Goldsmith's Line, / And hail his Sentiment tho' trite, divine" (lines 19-20), while, on the other, they either curtly dismiss or completely ignore unknown writers with genuine merit. The lesson, as Chatterton sees it, is simple: a book, in the eyes of many late-eighteenth-century reviewers, is only as good as its publisher's imprint, as "Merit's no more, / Than a good Frontispiece to grace the door" (lines 33-34).

Dozens of other poems, essays, and squibs express similar frustration over the perceived degradation of the age's critical practices.[24] Far and away the most famous indictment of the depths to which institutionalized criticism had sunk in the three decades since the *Monthly*'s founding is Richard Brinsley Sheridan's 1779 play *The Critic*. While scholars have traditionally focused on the second and third acts of this play, which lampoon the culture of the English stage, Sheridan himself was proudest of Act I, maintaining into his later years that it was the best thing he had ever written (Crane, xiv). Whereas Acts II and III take place at the rehearsal of a new play, Act I is set in the home of the self-important drama critic Dangle. Through a series of visits to Dangle by favor-seeking friends, playwrights, and musicians, Sheridan captures just how multifaceted the publicity machine behind the English theater had become by the 1770s. Rather than being the narrow pursuit of a select few, theatrical puffery is presented as the common cause of critics, playwrights, theater managers, and an emerging guild of professional ad-men.

Although there has been some debate over which character is the "critic" of the play's title, the most likely candidate is Dangle, a regular of the theater scene who is more renowned for his enthusiasm than his discrimination. Dangle's lack of prestige among the elite of the theater world is disclosed in the play's first scene, when his exasperated wife asks: "Why should you affect the character of a critic? I have no patience with you! Haven't you made yourself the jest of all your acquaintance by your interference in matters where you have no business? Are not you called a theatrical quidnunc, and a mock Maecenas to secondhand authors?" (Sheridan, I.i.33–37). Reviled as Dangle may be in fashionable circles, however, the connections he has acquired through his zeal have made him seem, at least in the eyes of the "lackeys of literature" (I.i.55), a person with considerable influence in the dramatic community. If Act I—which is presented as a typical morning in Dangle's life—is any indication, each day he admits to his home a steady stream of visitors seeking his imprimatur upon their works.

Why authors and actors should be so desperate to secure recommendations from a second-rate critic is perhaps most succinctly explained by Dangle's colleague Sneer. Reflecting upon one thin-skinned writer's habit of pestering critics to weigh in on his work, Sneer opines that he is "so covetous of popularity, that he had rather be abused than not mentioned at all" (I.i.179–80). Sneer goes on to expound upon the elaborate system that had emerged in the theater world to create hype for new plays and to induce critics to pen favorable reviews. For instance, when asked if he plans to attend the opening of a new play at Drury Lane, Sneer responds, "I suppose one shan't be able to get in, for on the first night of a new piece they always fill the house with orders to support it" (I.i.102–4). "Orders"—free tickets distributed to friends of the actor, playwright, or theater owner—would ensure boisterous applause for even the most disastrous productions and might thereby persuade fickle critics into rethinking or tempering their critiques of the performance (Hogan, 36).[25]

If there is a central theme of Sheridan's first act, it is how puffery had infested English culture. Less than ten lines into the play's first scene, Dangle reads aloud a puff he has just encountered in the "Theatrical Intelligence Extraordinary" column of the *Morning Chronicle*: "We hear there is a new tragedy in rehearsal at Drury Lane Theatre, called *The Spanish Armada*, said to be written by Mr. Puff, a gentleman well known in the theatrical world. If we may allow ourselves to give credit to the report of the performers, who, truth to say, are in general but indifferent judges, this piece abounds with the most striking and received beauties of modern composition" (I.i.10–15). The Mr. Puff spoken of here is the character who later in Act I professes to be the foremost living expert in the art of puffing. Nine of ten puffs in London's newspapers, by his account, come from his pen, and entire professions, most recently the auctioneers, have turned to him for training in the art of composing "panegyrical superlatives" and "variegated chips of exotic metaphor" (I.ii.84–87). So skilled at producing puffs is Mr. Puff that he claims to have lived handsomely for two years off a series of sham newspaper appeals for charity.

That this self-proclaimed "professor of the art of puffing" has begun to theorize his craft is evidenced in the most famous passage of Sheridan's first act, Mr. Puff's taxonomy of puffery.[26] After long, scientific reflection, Mr. Puff determines that most puffs can be grouped into one of five categories (I.ii.151–258):

1. *The puff direct*, or a glowing newspaper review paid for and often written by the theater manager prior to the opening of a production;
2. *The puff preliminary*, such as a scheme whereby a young rake attracts the attention of a lady he has admired from afar by placing a personal advertisement warning her that he is a dangerous character who should be avoided;
3. *The puff collateral*, or a sham news story that is in reality a vehicle for praising a certain product or shop;
4. *The puff collusive*, such as a review that drums up interest in a book by casting aspersions on its decency and the morality of its author; and
5. *The puff oblique, or puff by implication*, or attempts to further the good name of a person or political cause by subtly leaking news of honorable deeds in the press.

However whimsical Puff's taxonomy may be, it marks a significant milestone in advertising history insofar as it bears witness to the diversity and sophistication puffs had attained by the late eighteenth century. For over a century after the initial performance of Sheridan's play, writers would continue to reference Sheridan's categories, and observers of puffery would offer up revised and expanded versions of Mr. Puff's taxonomy.[27]

From a historical perspective, the genius of Sheridan's play lies in its pitch-perfect satires on the runaway advertising culture of the late eighteenth century. In the world satirized in *The Critic*, advertising was not only proliferating but was also rapidly becoming professionalized, systematized, and naturalized. In the space of a few generations, advertising had evolved from being a minor component of retailing practices into a major, if often inconspicuous, part of the everyday lives of millions of Britons. Not only was advertising omnipresent, but it also completely complicated the reader's relationship to print. If, as Sheridan suggests, the veiled wizard behind the institutions of print was likely either a Mr. Puff or one of his protégés, it had become impossible to hold to the long-cherished assumption that if it was printed, it must be true. In a very real sense, then, less than a century into the era of print culture, the aura and efficacy of the printed word were deeply in jeopardy. And, in one of the great ironic subplots of literary history, the culprits were not uncultured philistines or bibliophobes but authors, critics, and booksellers.

CHAPTER 3

Building Brand Byron

Four months to the day after Samuel Johnson's death drew a curtain on the "Age of Johnson," the *Public Advertiser* heralded the beginning of a new epoch in English cultural history. The 13 April 1785 issue of the London daily announced, "This is the *Age of Advertising*." "Look at the London papers," it insisted, "what is the sum total? — Ladies' heads — masquerade dresses — giants — pigs — and patent snuffers. When we consider the language and artful manner of these advertisements, the lures they throw out, and the success they have, we may say, *Lead us not into temptation*" ("The Advertising Age"). This wasn't the first such claim. From early in the eighteenth century, in a continuous stream, cultural commentators have identified theirs as the great era of advertising. Still, the *Public Advertiser* seems to have intuited something, as there was clearly a widely shared sentiment in late-eighteenth-century Britain that a new stage in advertising history was under way.

As we have seen, Sheridan sensed this and satirized it broadly in *The Critic* (1779). Two years later, Thomas Sternhold offered an equally forceful testament to how thoroughly advertising logic had suffused English culture in his book-length satirical poem *The Daily Advertiser, In Metre* (1781). Dispensing from the outset with outmoded distinctions between high- and low-brow forms, Sternhold quipped that the time had come when poetry and advertising had to be seen as wholly compatible. To model this, he transposed an entire issue of a London daily newspaper into verse. Amid a stream of intentionally pedestrian passages are a number of remarkable riffs on the generally haphazard, often carnivalesque organization of the average London daily. Near the beginning, we read:

Figure 3.1. Robert Seymour, "Cheap Advertisements." (*McLean's Monthly Sheet of Caricatures, or, The Looking Glass.* No. 15 [March 1831]: 1.)

>Yesterday died *John Doze*, the Special Pleader—
>The fattest Ox e'er seen—*Cruttenden*, Feeder—
>Last Monday died, suppos'd of suffocation—
>'Tis by a simple outward application—
>Perish'd thro' Want, a most ingenious Writer—
>*Warren*'s fam'd Paste makes dirty hands look whiter.— (13)

The vertiginous heterogeneity of this and similar passages suggests a print world gone mad and the onset of a new, attention-deprived mode of consciousness brought on by a barrage of unsolicited and thoroughly randomized texts (see Figure 3.1). The effect here is not unlike the one Sara Thornton identifies as the new commercial subjectivity experienced by the nineteenth-century Londoner, who each day was barraged by hundreds of messages on billboards, sandwich-boards, advertising vans, and handbills. In such a world, Thornton suggests, "text was no longer something which had to be sought out and paid for dearly; it now sought out the subject, moved into the line of his or her gaze, and asked to be read" (32).

By the dawn of the nineteenth century, Britain had its first advertising agents, its earliest nationwide ad campaigns, and packages and handbills that showcased remarkable advances in graphic technology (Nevett, "London's Earliest Advertising Agents," 15–17; Strachan, *Advertising*, 3–4, 14–23). Just how thoroughly ad-saturated the nation had become is amply illustrated, as Marcus Wood and John Strachan have shown, in the era's satire, which routinely drew upon well-known advertisements as points of parodic departure.

Perhaps the most productive vein for advertising-related satire during the period was a widely circulated story involving a captain of industry who secretly employed one of the age's great poets to write his advertising jingles. Originating soon after the turn of the century, when the first wave of brand-name products was filling the advertising columns of the nation's newspapers, this rumor took various forms, with the names of several different manufacturers and poets being inserted in the basic narrative. One of the earliest published versions of the anecdote appears in Maria Edgeworth's *Ennui* (1809), where the narrator recounts: "A gentleman of my acquaintance lately went to buy some razors at Packwood's. Mrs. Packwood alone was visible. Upon the gentleman's complimenting her on the infinite variety of her husband's ingenious and poetical advertisements, she replied, 'La! sir, and do you think husband has time to write them there things his-self? Why, sir, we keeps a poet to do all that there work'" (187).

Other versions locate the action not at Packwood's but at 30 Strand, the legendary home of Warren's Blacking (i.e., shoe polish). In one of the most widely circulated accounts, Lord Byron is Warren's poet of choice. As late as 1843 the *Edinburgh Review* linked Byron with Warren's, explaining,

> The most attractive vehicle [for advertising in the early nineteenth century] was verse, and the praises of blacking were sung in strains which would have done no discredit to "Childe Harold" himself, even in his own opinion—for when accused of receiving six hundred a-year for his services as Poet-Laureat to Mrs. Warren,—of being, in short, the actual personage alluded to in her famous boast, "We keeps a poet"—he showed no anxiety to repudiate the charge. (Hayward, 3)

Another strain of the legend relates how Byron earned five hundred pounds by fulfilling the offices of "Poet-Laureat" for Warren's chief competitor, Day and Martin's.

Not surprisingly, Byron's rival satirists pounced on these rumors. In the fourth installment of *Blackwood's* "Noctes Ambrosianae" (July 1822), the fictional Morgan Odoherty, who has himself taken credit for Day and Martin's jingles in a previous episode, composes lines on the blacking verses attributed to Byron:

> Is Byron surprised that his enemies say
> He makes puffing verses for Martin and Day?
> Why, what other task could his Lordship take part in
> More fit than the service of Day, and of Martin?
> So shining, so dark—all his writing displays
> A type of this liquid of Martin and Day's—
> Gouvernantes—Kings—laurel-crown'd Poets attacking—
> Oh! he's master complete of the science of Blacking!
> (Maginn, 110)[1]

Two years later, Horace Smith advised the aspiring poets of Oxbridge to "Renounce Aristotle, and take to the bottle / That wears 'Patent Blacking' inscribed on its throttle" (lines 13–14). Also in 1824, William Frederick Deacon published *Warreniana*, an entire volume of parodies based on the premise that Warren commissioned the age's leading poets to write his advertisements. Among the more amusing poems in this volume is "The Childe's Pilgrimage," in which one Childe Higgins embarks on a holy quest to find 30 Strand.[2]

Byron's only recorded response to the blacking rumors appears in the appendix to *The Two Foscari* (1821), where he deems "laughable" the accusation that he "received five hundred pounds for writing advertisements for Day and Martin's patent blacking." Affecting unconcern, he quips, "This is the highest compliment to my literary powers which I ever received" (*Complete Poetical Works* [CPW], 6:222). Complimentary or not, the rumors linking Byron to the blacking industry colorfully capture the kinship between the poet and the major household brands of the early nineteenth century. Not only did his unmatched celebrity make Byron the natural candidate to be named in those rumors, but as the great poetic brand of the 1810s and 1820s he had become the literary world's equivalent of Day and Martin's Blacking.

Reading Byron's rise to fame against the backdrop of the early-nineteenth-century explosion of product branding in Britain shows how the phenomenon that came to be known as "Byromania" followed branding's core principles and techniques. As this chapter's first section details, during Byron's lifetime (1788–1824) Britain was in the midst of what we might call an "onomastic revolution." The most significant commercial manifestation of this shift from generic to specific modes of identification was the proliferation of brand-name products, and by the first decade of the nineteenth century, when Byron set out to make his name as a poet, branding logic was ascendant in a range of retail sectors, including bookselling. While one could certainly devote an entire chapter, if not a book, to chronicling the maintenance and expansion of the Byron brand over the last decade of the poet's life, my focus here is on how the events leading up to the 1812 publication of cantos 1 and 2 of *Childe Harold's Pilgrimage* helped establish the Byron brand. This recasting of the mythical tale of Byron's rise to fame as a crucial chapter in the histories of both British advertising and the commodification of the aesthetic reveals that, more than the "Wellington of literature" or the "first rock star," Byron embodied the moment when Britain's nascent system of product branding most visibly spread to the book trade.

THE ONOMASTIC REVOLUTION AND THE BIRTH OF BRANDING

Of all the cultural conditions underlying the rise of branding, perhaps the most basic was society's general shift towards more precise modes of identification. A hankering for taxonomy was at the heart of the Enlightenment project, and the eighteenth century witnessed a systematic "disciplining" of knowledge that required ever more exact labels for previously generalized fields of study. In this respect, the quintessential eighteenth-century European was Carl Linnaeus, the Swedish botanist whose *Systema Naturae* (1735) issued a clarion call for scientists everywhere to be more precise in their naming practices. The Linnaean system meshed perfectly with the spirit of the age, and by century's end binominal nomenclature was well on its way to becoming the universal standard in the life sciences.[3]

While the basic story of the Linnaean revolution remains common knowledge, the simultaneous upheavals in child naming practices have gone all but unnoticed, even by scholars of the eighteenth and nineteenth centuries. Briefly, at the same moment when Linnaeus's followers were attempting to more precisely label virtually every living thing, Britain was undergoing its first major change in infant-naming norms in five hundred years. With uncanny consistency, between the fourteenth and the late eighteenth centuries English names followed what might be called the 20-50-80 rule: roughly 20 percent of newborns received the most common name for their sex (in most eras, John for boys, Mary for girls), 50 percent received one of the three most common names, and 80 percent received one of the top ten names. Consequently, if a sixteenth- or seventeenth-century Londoner couldn't remember an acquaintance's given (or Christian) name, he or she could confidently narrow it down to John, William, or Thomas for males or Mary, Elizabeth, or Anne for females. While this pattern was largely owing to traditions of naming daughters after mothers and sons after fathers, it also reflected a general sense that, outside of preserving family customs, given names were of little consequence and had minimal bearing on one's identity (Galbi; Smith-Banister, 150).

For compelling evidence that at the beginning of the Romantic Century these practices were beginning to fade, one need only turn to the first volume of Sterne's *Tristram Shandy* (1759). Here we are treated to a chapter-long discourse on the disastrous results of "careless" and "indifferent" naming (1:122). If there is anything in life that Walter Shandy held true, we are told, it was "that there was a strange kind of magick bias, which good or bad names, as he called them, irresistibly impress'd upon our characters and conduct." "How many CAESARS and POMPEYS," he asks, "by mere inspiration of the names, have been render'd worthy of them? And how many . . . are there who might have done exceeding well in the world, had not their characters and spirits been totally depress'd and NICODEMUS'D into nothing?" (1:115–16).

Apparently, Shandy wasn't alone in worrying about the importance of Christian names, as his generation and those that followed displayed dramatically new approaches in christening newborns. While the old naming practices began to wane in the late eighteenth century, the most momentous changes came during the nineteenth century. Between 1800 and 1900, the frequency with which the most popular name was given to a child plummeted from 24 percent for girls and 22 percent for boys to 7 percent and 9 percent respectively. Over the same period, the frequency of the top ten names dropped from 82 percent to 39 percent for girls and 85 percent to 51 percent for boys (Galbi) (see Figure 3.2).

In response to these shifts, publishers began selling lists of common names (e.g., James Buchanan's *A New Pocket-Book* [1757]), guides to help immigrants pronounce fashionable English names (e.g., Thomas Nugent's *A New Pocket Dictionary* [1767]), and the first full-length baby-name books (e.g., Charlotte Yonge's *History of Christian Names* [1863]). Authors too were forced to adapt; they, like parents, faced increased pressure to give their offspring distinctive names. An 1825 essay on "Euonomy: or, The Art of Novel Writing" from *La Belle Assemblée* magazine warned, "Jones, Brown, Smith, Tomkins, Jenkins, Perkins, &c., are perfectly unsentimental" and should thus be avoided when naming characters; likewise, "John manifestly belongs to a footman or coachman," and "Plain William is a confidential secretary—a modest youth of strict integrity," but certainly no hero ("Euonomy," 97).

Considering these momentous changes in the naming of species and new-

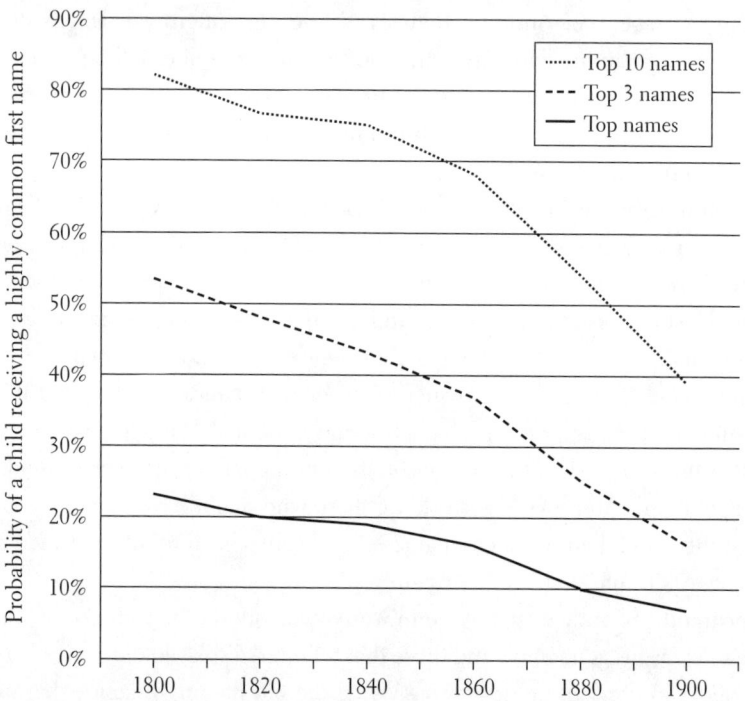

Figure 3.2. Changes in naming of children, as indicated by frequency of most common given names in England, 1800–1900. (Data from Galbi, "Long-Term Trends"; "A Chapter on Names"; Whitaker, "Name Choosing"; "Christian Names.")

borns, it is little surprise that a similar and simultaneous shift occurred in the world of goods. Prior to the late eighteenth century, most British retailing consisted of neighborhood merchants selling locally produced goods. Consumers tended to have few purchasing options, and manufacturers therefore felt little need to distinguish their products from those of their rivals. Even if producers had been inclined to develop distinctive brands, the high cost of paper and other packaging materials, combined with the lack of technology for mass-producing unique containers, would have limited their ability to do so. Only with the late-eighteenth- and early-nineteenth-century inventions of transfer printing, the lithograph, and the papermaking machine was the large-scale production of distinctively labeled products possible (Davis, 26, 38–39).[4] Thus, shopping prior to the late eighteenth century typically meant asking a store clerk for a particular commodity, expecting there to be little variety in the store's stock, and receiving a generically packaged, locally produced product.

The one significant exception to this tradition of generic retailing came in the patent medicine trade. More than a century before branding came into vogue with other commodities, Britain's dealers in healing balms and fever powders were taking to the newspapers to convince the public of their various products' uniqueness. Daniel Defoe's *A Journal of the Plague Year* suggests that the Plague of 1665 gave rise to unprecedented numbers and types of medicine advertisements:

> It is incredible, and scarce to be imagin'd, how the Posts of Houses, and Corners of Streets were plaster'd over with Doctors Bills, and Papers of ignorant Fellows; quacking and tampering in Physick, and inviting the People to come to them for Remedies; which was generally set off, with such flourishes as these, (*viz.*) INFALLIBLE preventive Pills against the Plague. NEVER-FAILING Preservatives against the Infection. . . . The ONLY-TRUE Plague-Water. The ROYAL ANTIDOTE against all Kinds of Infection; and such a Number more that I cannot reckon up; and if I could, would fill a Book of themselves to set them down. (36-37)

By late 1665 those who could afford up to three pounds an ounce for medicines might purchase such cure-alls as the "Quintessence Animae Mundi," the "Oil of the Heathen Gods," and "Lady Kent's Powder." "Constantine Rhodocanace's Grecian," boasted its proprietor, was the very potion "wherewith Hippocrates, the Prince of all Physicians, preserved the whole land of Greece" (Leasor, 30). In the following decades, branding became increasingly common in the medicine trade; advertisements for such products as "Dr. Clark's Opthalmic Secret," "Warham's Apoplectic Balsam and Snuff," and "Dr. James's Fever Powders" dominated the columns of early-eighteenth-century dailies.

That so disreputable a group as the "quacks" pioneered the art of branding explains much about its slow spread to other trades. Throughout much of the eighteenth century, medicine advertisements routinely emphasized a brand name, while notices for foodstuffs and other household goods did little more than announce the sale of a generic product and tell where it might be purchased. In the 1760s, however, this began to change. Encouraged by the population boom in London's suburbs and improvements in transportation, several manufacturers established regional, national, or even international distribution networks for their products. Shedding its stigma, branding proved an ideal method of expanding distribution, since, as Susan Strasser explains, it allowed producers to establish "reputations and relationships with consumers as surely as the corner grocer did through personal contact and personality" (28; see also Ohmann, chs. 5 and 6). Early brand-name advertising, like advertising today, aimed to convince the consumer that a certain product was worth asking for by name. If a merchant either did not carry it or tried instead to push a substitute, shoppers were to insist that no alternative would suffice.

More than any other manufacturer, the famed potter Josiah Wedgwood helped counter the stigma attached to branding. Wedgwood had first made a name for his pottery with innovative designs and textures, which allowed him to charge much higher prices than his rivals. Even at the peak of his early success, however, he feared his competitors would eventually match his quality and force him to lower his prices. To prevent a decline in his prestige, he lit upon a scheme to present the royal family and influential aristocrats with specially designed china sets. Their use of his products, he correctly reasoned, would make Wedgwood the brand of choice in fashion-conscious homes across the kingdom (Reilly, 1:49, 200–201; McKendrick, "Josiah Wedgwood," 105–8). By the late 1760s Wedgwood was promoting himself as "The Queen's Potter" and manufacturing the highly successful "Queensware" line of china. In a letter dated 12 March 1767, he exults:

> The demand for this said *Creamcolour*, Alias, *Queen's Ware*, Alias, *Ivory*, still increases. It is really amazing how rapidly the use of it has spread allmost [sic] over the whole Globe, & how universally it is liked.—How much of this general use, & estimation, is owing to the mode of its introduction—& how much to its real utility & beauty? are questions in which we may be a good deal interested, for the government of our future Conduct. (*Correspondence*, 1:127)

In the decades to come, Wedgwood continued to make brand building central to his business operations. His long-term prosperity—by his death in 1795, he had amassed a fortune of half a million pounds (McKendrick, "Josiah Wedgwood," 103)—provided clear proof that branding could be profitable outside the patent medicine trade.

Despite Wedgwood's success in the 1760s, advertisements for brand-name household commodities did not appear with regularity for another decade.[5] In 1776 William Bayley began what would be a decade-long advertising campaign for "Bayley's Blacking Cakes." Bayley's inventiveness is manifest in a lightly disguised advertisement that ran repeatedly in several London newspapers between October 1775 and August 1776. Here we find a confession from one John Desoer, a rival businessman who supposedly so admired Bayley's Blacking that he had stolen the recipe (see Figure 3.3). One of the first notices for a brand-name food product came in the 4–6 April 1776 issue of the *St. James Chronicle*, which advertised "Bon Gout, or Cherokee Sauce," a condiment that promised to lend "the most pleasing Flavour to all Sorts of Made Dishes." Over the next two decades, these advertisements were joined by notices for a growing number of branded goods, including Sharp's Elastic Hair Cushions, Andrews's Powder for Cleaning Woollen Cloth, Dr. Oliver's Bath Biscuit, and Hillyer's Maldon Salt.[6]

By far the most legendary advertiser of the 1790s was George Packwood, who in 1794 began one of the most expensive, sustained, and original advertising campaigns England had thus far witnessed. Nearly every week, Packwood contrived some new gimmick to keep his brand visible (see Figure 3.4). One of his favorite advertising genres was the dialogue, in which characters would contrast the hazards of shaving with non-Packwood products to the remarkably smooth shaves that his razor strops ensured. Much of the supposed humor in these dialogues drew upon ethnic and racial stereotypes, such as in "A Dialogue between a Jew and a Christian," which takes as its premise the inability of Frolick (the titular Christian) to comprehend the heavily inflected English of Levi (the Jew). After a series of misunderstandings, they finally discover one subject where there is no confusion: shaving products. As Levi insists and Frolick agrees, the buyer of shaving supplies must "shee dat Packwood's name ish on de Strop, and on de bills round de Box of Paste, and a seal on with the impression of a bird, and the world FIDELLE, ash imposishions are libale (from de beginning of de vorld unto dish day) to be practised by humble immitations on all such valuable articles" (Packwood, *Packwood's Whim*, 27). Another Packwood advertisement, "A Dialogue between a Merchant and his Black Servant," builds on a similar premise, as the clownish slave Scipio receives a handsome reward from his "massa" for using Packwood's shaving products (Packwood, "A Dialogue").[7]

Basking in his newfound prominence, the razor maker in 1796 published *Packwood's Whim*, a forty-eight-page compendium of his advertisements.[8] By the turn of the century Packwood had become a legend of British popular culture. In Edgeworth's 1801 novel *Belinda*, the title character's aunt tries so fanatically to marry her off that one gentleman observes: "You heard of nothing, wherever you went, but of Belinda Portman, and Belinda Portman's accomplishments. Belinda Portman, and her accomplishments, I'll swear, were as well advertised, as Packwood's razor strops" (25). Six years later Eaton Stannard Barrett quipped: "Many say that *radical reform* (quasi radix et forma) signifies digging up an old tree, and making snuffboxes out of its roots; and adduce Shakspeare's mulberry-tree as an instance. Others again derive it from *rado*, to shave, and *formico*, to

To the PUBLIC.

WHEREAS I, JOHN DESOER, of Kirkby-street, Hatton-garden, have, for some Time past, made and sold a certain Composition, in Imitation of the *Patent Cakes* for making *Shining Liquid Blacking*, and have thereby infringed the Patent, and otherwise injured the Patentee in the Sale and Character of his Cakes, for which an *Action* has been justly commenced against me; but the Patentee having obligingly condescended to stop all farther Proceedings, on Condition of my paying Costs of Suit, and thus publicly acknowledging the Offence, I do hereby confess myself under every Obligation for his Lenity on the Occasion, and do promise, that I will not, at any Time hereafter, directly or indirectly, make or sell any Composition whatsoever in Imitation of the Patent Cakes, or otherwise infringe the Patent in any Manner howsoever. Witness my Hand, the 16th Day of October, 1775. JOHN DESOER.

The genuine Cakes, which have a Label pasted on each, with these Words, *By the King's Patent, Cakes for Shining Liquid Blacking*, are greatly superior to any other Thing whatever, for making a most curious and beautiful glossy Blacking for Shoes, Boots, &c. which will always preserve the Leather from cracking, and keep it soft and pliable to the very last. It is also perfectly free from any Smell, and the Shoes that are blacked with it will neither soil the Fingers in putting on, nor the Stockings in wearing. Price 6d. each Cake, which makes a full Pint of Liquid Blacking, by the Addition of Water only.

Sold Wholesale and Retail only by the Patentee, W. Bayley, Perfumer, in Cockspur-street, London. Sold also Retail by J. Price, Perfumer, No. 150, Leadenhall-street; F. Newbery, Bookseller, the Corner of St. Paul's Church-yard; J. Grosvenor, Perfumer, near Turnstile, Holborn; and A. Rotnwell, Perfumer, in New Bond-street.

Figure 3.3. Advertisement for Bayley's Blacking. This alleged confession from a patent-infringing rival was reprinted at least eighty times, in Lloyd's Evening Post, the St. James Chronicle, the London Chronicle, and the Morning Post between October 1775 and August 1776. (Lloyd's Evening Post, 18–20 October 1775: 379.)

> Many a good Razor has been cast aside as useless and good for nothing, till
> # PRO BONO PUBLICO,
> ### A FACT; or, PROOF POSITIVE.
> #### STEP'D FORWARD,
> To give ease to the Cheek, comfort to the upper Lip, a pleasant familiarity to the Chin and an uncommon agreeable
> ## SURPRIZE
> To the bearded Physiognomy which takes place by a RAZOR being strop'd or sharpen'd on
> ### PACKWOOD's NEW INVENTED RAZOR STROP:
> It acts with such Power, as to take Notches out of a Razor, Penknife, or Surgeon's Instrument; and afterwards to leave so smooth an edge, as to Shave yourself with that comfort and ease before describ'd—☞ The Strop acts by Virtue of a Paste, and may be spread on one side of your old Razor Strap very thin with a knife, as you would a plaister, &c. Let it stay two days before you use it, and if your strop is dry it will make it Supple, and the effect will
> ## ASTONISH
> you past belief—If any Emery or Dirt is on, be careful it is first scraped off.—The Paste will hang to the back of the Razor at first using, but you must keep working it on the Strop and it will stick fast enough afterwards.—It is necessary to renew the Strop with fresh Paste when by use it will not give an edge.—☞ Be particular to read the red Directions on the Case of the Strop before you use it.—The Proprietor himself has strop'd a Notch out of his own common Sixpenny Knife, and shav'd himself dry (though a hard Beard without a Lather.) much cleaner and smoother than he has done for many years back.
> This is a material acquisition for the use of Counting-Houses, Infirmaries, and Barbers Shops, &c.—To pass a proper Encomium on this strop would swell this Advertisment beyond a common hand-bill.—To give you a faint idea, permit the Proprietor to observe, that a diamond or flint will cut glass, and this strap will have as powerful an effect on steel by way of polishing, and give a fine tho' not a wiry-edge to any small Instrument not larger than a common case-knife, one particular remark is necessary, when you shave lay the razor flat on your Face, and bear very light for the composition has the power to make the edge of the Razor too sharp, is a reason that the other side of the strop is to counter-act and bring the Razor to suit your own Beard, whether hard or soft, the Strops are sold for 3s. 6d. 5s. and 10s. 6d each.—The Composition that will keep the Strop in good order for Years, per box as. 6d. and G. Packwood will also engage to make an old Razor Strop as good as new with this Paste for only 2s. & 6d.
> The Proprietor wishes to divest Gentlemen of that Prejudice which generally takes place with advertisements like this, as a proof G. Packwood offers to return the Money within one week after the purchase if not found to answer Agreeable to the Advertisement.
> ☞ G. Packwood can answer for no Strop or box of Paste except it is seal'd with the Impression of a *Bird* and the word *Fidelle*. *** Letters post paid duly attended to.
>
> Sold by the Proprietor, G. PACKWOOD, 16, Gracechurch-street London, *(turn over)*

Figure 3.4. Inventive advertisement for Packwood's razor strops (ca. 1795). (British Library, General Reference Collection Cup.21.g.42/46.)

rise in pimples; and say that it refers to *Packwood's razor-strops*, not Shakspeare's mulberry-tree" (32–33).

Among the commercial icons of the 1790s and early 1800s, perhaps only Robert Warren outshone Packwood. Today, Warren is primarily remembered as an answer to a Dickens trivia question, since the young Charles Dickens worked long, dreary hours as a label paster at a counterfeit Warren's Blacking operation.[9] During Robert Warren's lifetime, however, his notoriety throughout England was for his creative and seemingly omnipresent advertisements. In the first quarter of the nineteenth century, he engaged in a fierce competition with Day and Martin for supremacy in the highly lucrative shoe polish trade.[10] In the process, Warren developed a variety of strategies to make his advertisements distinctive. His most famous ads recount in both image and verse how animals marveled when they saw their reflections in boots shined with Warren's Blacking.[11] In his widely reprinted "The Cat and the Boot; or, An Improvement upon Mirrors"—the illustration for which was drawn by George Cruikshank—a confused cat attempts to attack a pair of Warren's-shined boots (see Figure 3.5).

Such advertisements were only one phase of Warren's sophisticated brand building. When Day and Martin began covering city walls with pasted bills advertising their blacking, Warren did them one better, painting his ads directly on the walls themselves. Thomas Hood related how Warren "had his name whitewashed in letters twice as long as [a] Magazine upon the walls of the metropolis and the Park-palings of the country" ("The Art of Advertizing," 247). Others reported seeing "Buy Warren's Blacking!" scrawled across such world heritage sites as the Acropolis, the Temple of Sunium, and Pompey's Pillar ("Advertisement" [*New American*], 144; Review of *Letters*, 190; Wynter, 111).[12] Years later, P. T. Barnum approvingly recounted how,

> when the great blacking-maker of London dispatched his agent to Egypt to write on the pyramids of Ghiza, in huge letters, "Buy Warren's Blacking, 30 Strand, London," he was not "cheating" travelers upon the Nile. His blacking was really a superior article, and well worth the price charged for it, but he was "humbugging" the public by this queer way of arresting attention. (21)

Perhaps the best testament to Warren's fame is Deacon's *Warreniana*, the volume dedicated to spoofing the blacking manufacturer's poetical advertisements. Here, alongside the mock panegyrics to Warren by such literary luminaries as "Sir W. S.," "Lord B," and "S. T. C," is W.W.'s "Old Cumberland Pedler," which recounts how the wandering author "beheld / Graven on the tawny rock these magic words, / 'BUY WARREN'S BLACKING.'"[13] Overcome by so poignant a juxtaposition of nature and Warren, the enraptured poet exclaims, "My stars, how we improve!" (28).

BECOMING BYRON

While it was into this marketplace of Packwoods, Warrens, Days, and Martins that Byron emerged in the early nineteenth century, scholars and general readers

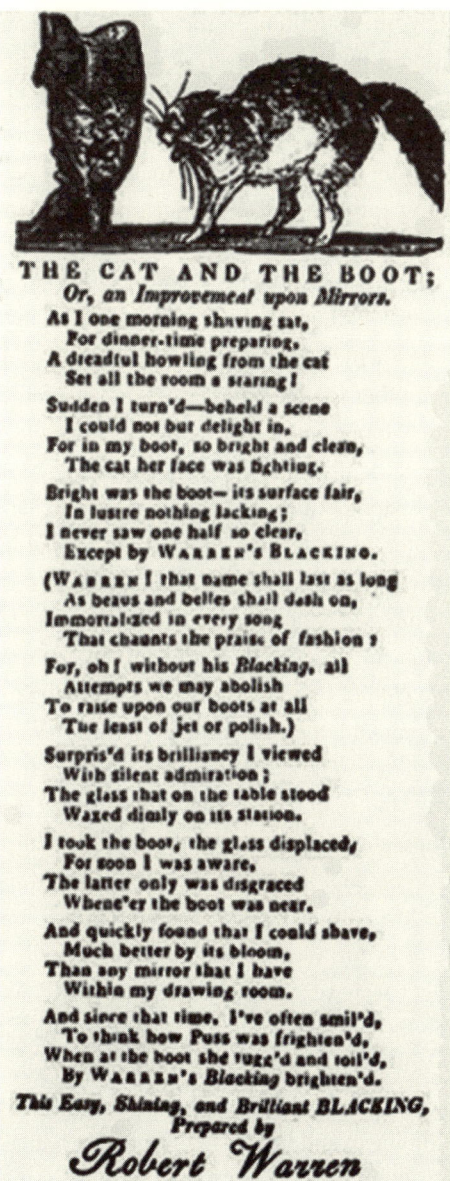

Figure 3.5. Warren's famous "The Cat and the Boot" advertisement. The poem first began appearing ca. 1817; the George Cruikshank image was added in 1822. Warren continued reprinting this advertisement into the 1830s. (*The Lancaster Gazette and General Advertiser*, 23 November 1822: 4.)

have paid surprisingly little attention to the commercial contexts for "Byromania." From the beginning, most attempts to explain why the first edition of *Childe Harold* I and II (the initial two cantos, published together in 1812) sold out in three days have looked primarily at the poem's internal features, emphasizing the distinctiveness of its style, tone, and subject matter. Two years after the poem's publication, for instance, Byron's close friend John Cam Hobhouse speculated in his diary, "the great success of 'Childe Harold' is due chiefly to Byron's having dared to give utterance to certain feelings which every one must have encouraged in the melancholy and therefore morbid hours of his existence, and also by the intimate knowledge which he has shown of the turns taken by the passion of women" (1:100). Another friend, Thomas Moore, generally concurred, attributing much of Byron's initial fame to his original style and refreshing honesty when contemplating difficult social and religious issues (*Letters*, 1:432–36). In 1833 Edward Bulwer-Lytton perhaps best captured how the late-Romantic literary establishment had come to understand the *Childe Harold* phenomenon when he recounted how the first two cantos "touched the most sensitive chord in the public heart—they expressed what every one felt" (*England*, 2:71).

Throughout most of the nineteenth and twentieth centuries, this notion that the success of *Childe Harold* I and II was essentially owing to the poem's ability to speak to its age remained largely unquestioned.[14] In recent decades, however, critics have become increasingly skeptical of the idea that the text sold itself and have begun exploring the material factors that helped it become a bestseller. Peter J. Manning, for instance, has argued that the innovative marketing strategies of John Murray, the book's publisher, were chiefly responsible for the remarkable run on the first edition, and Jerome Christensen has detailed how the cultural commodity of Byron was the "collaborative invention of a gifted poet, a canny publisher, eager reviewers, and rapt readers" (xx).[15] While neither Manning nor Christensen focuses on branding's place in this narrative, their work has helped more fully contextualize Byron's ascent to fame.

Even in the wake of such studies, however, there is still a strong tendency in recent classroom anthologies and literary encyclopedias to treat Byron's legendary boast "I awoke one morning and found myself famous" as a one-sentence summary of his early life. Thomas Moore, in whose *Letters and Journals of Lord Byron* this remark first appeared, used it to support his argument that the immediacy and scope of his late friend's fame was unprecedented in British literary history:

> Never did there exist before, and, it is most probable, never will exist again, a combination of such vast mental power and surpassing genius, with so many

other of those advantages and attractions, by which the world is, in general, dazzled and captivated. The effect was, accordingly, electric;—his fame had not to wait for any of the ordinary gradations, but seemed to spring up, like the palace of a fairy tale, in a night. As he himself briefly described it in his Memoranda,—'I awoke one morning and found myself famous.'" (1:346–47)

The regular invocation of this claim in explaining the runaway success of *Childe Harold* is to some degree understandable, as overnight fame *seems* right for a figure whose entire legend is built on hyperbole. Yet, not only does Byron's quip diminish the fame he had enjoyed prior to *Childe Harold*, but it leads to a mystification of the processes involved in producing and marketing a bestseller. The notion of becoming famous overnight carries with it the sense that a book sells itself, independent of the promotional efforts of the author, publisher, and retailer. In essence, the literary text seems to transcend the mundane processes that mark the exchange of other commodities. While the author sleeps, the text magically labors to circulate his name.

In reality, it would have been virtually impossible for *Childe Harold* I and II to sell out in three days solely because of the poem's intrinsic merits, since content-based sales are usually built by word of mouth, which travels relatively slowly. The few readers who stumbled on the volume on the morning of its release would have to have taken it home immediately, read it at once, and persuaded all their friends that the relatively slim quarto was worth the then-exorbitant sum of thirty shillings unbound or fifty shillings bound.[16] Later editions, released after word had had time to spread, very likely did sell well because of the poem's merits; but to account for the phenomenal success of the first edition, we need to look beyond the poem itself. The real story of *Childe Harold* I and II, I would argue, is not so much one of a text speaking to its age as one of a marketing-savvy publisher, an ambitious agent, and a poet with a penchant for self-promotion converging at an ideal moment in literary and advertising history.

Byron's flair for attracting publicity, of course, has been well chronicled. In the poet's day, the Irish barrister John Philpot Curran complained, "my Lord weeps for the press, and wipes his eyes with the public" (qtd. in Kilgour, 25). Thackeray alleged, more harshly, that Byron "*never* wrote from his heart. He got up rapture and enthusiasm with an eye to the public" (*Notes*, 76). At least in his teenage years and early adulthood, however, the real Byron was much less cocksure and self-aggrandizing than the popular image would suggest. Byron's letters from this period reveal that, however remarkable he was in several respects, he experienced typical adolescent fluctuations between supreme self-confidence and debilitating self-doubt. In one of his earliest surviving letters, written to his mother from boarding school, the sixteen-year-old Byron proclaims: "[T]he way to *riches* to *Greatness* lies before me, I can, I will cut myself a path through the world or perish in the attempt. others [sic] have begun life with nothing and ended Greatly. And shall I who have a competent if not a large fortune, remain idle, No, I will carve myself the passage to Grandeur, but never with Dishonour" (*Byron's Letters and Journals*, ed. Marchand [*BLJ*], 1:49). Between such buoyant moments as this, however, Byron was often plagued by insecurity over his lingering Scottish accent, lackluster early education, propensity for weight gain, and, most particularly, club foot (Eisler, 33, 49, 52, 118, 121). As a result, the young lord became, by Moore's account, "naturally shy, *very* shy, which people who did not know him mistook for pride" (*Letters*, 1:78).

This pattern of there being two Byrons—one self-assured, the other self-abasing—carried over into his early attempts at establishing a literary career. In 1806, when he was all of 18 years old, he had the confidence to self-publish thirty-eight of his poems—many of them deeply personal and frankly erotic—under the title *Fugitive Pieces*. But when some of the volume's initial readers expressed discomfort over its sexual content, Byron immediately recalled and burned as many copies as he could. Just a few weeks later, however, this bout of self-doubt gave way to renewed ambition, resulting in another self-published volume, this time titled *Poems on Various Occasions*. While most copies went to friends and relatives, Byron summoned the courage to send copies to Alexander Fraser Tytler and Henry Mackenzie, two of Scotland's leading men of letters (*BLJ*, 1:110–12). In the months that followed the printing of *Poems*, he meticulously noted readers' responses, at times congratulating himself on "the applause of all the County Lords & Squires" and at others retreating into the defensive posture that any praise owed more to his youth than his talent (*BLJ*, 1:109). True to form, in March 1807 he told one friend, "[P]oetic fame is by no means the '*acme*' of my Wishes," yet in April he told another, "Let me but 'hear my fame on the winds' and the song of the Bards in my Norman house, I ask no more" (*BLJ*, 1:112, 114).

This emotional roller-coaster ride only accelerated in the months ahead, when Byron released his first publicly circulating volume, *Hours of Idleness*. In the preface to this collection the poet insists that he will be content with "a posthumous page in 'The Catalogue of Royal and Noble Authors'" (*CPW*, 1:34). Privately, however, he was not so demure, telling his confidante Elizabeth Bridget Pigot that he was "a *Man* whose works are praised by *Reviewers*, admired by *Duchesses* & sold by every Bookseller of the Metropolis." He goes on to confess, "[I]n every

Bookseller's I see my *own name*, & *say nothing*, but enjoy my *fame in secret*" (*BLJ*, 1:130–31; see also 1:139). When the largely positive—and generally prearranged—initial reviews of *Hours of Idleness* gave way to much harsher critiques, including a withering attack in the *Edinburgh Review*, Byron challenged at least two critics to duels but privately lamented that the reviewers had "completely demolished my little fabric of fame" (*BLJ*, 1:159; see also 1:150 and 167).

Far, then, from the image he would cultivate in later years as the gloomy outsider who had "not loved the world, nor the world me" (line 1049, *CPW*, 2:118), the pre-*Childe Harold* Byron was obsessed with tracking the ebbs and flows of his fame. And, of particular import for the present argument, he paid special attention to what the "Byron" name signified in the world at large. On the one hand, it was an ancient and noble surname, linked to the family estate at Newstead Abbey since the reign of Henry VIII. More recently, however, the name had been sullied by spendthrifts and scoundrels, not the least of whom was the poet's father, "Mad Jack." As the young lord complained to his half sister, Augusta, his mother took every opportunity to remind him just how degraded their family name had become. Seemingly every mother-son argument, he reported, ended the same way: "[She] rakes up the ashes of my *father*, abuses him, says I shall be a true Byronne, which is the worst epithet she can invent" (*BLJ*, 1:56).

Not altogether surprisingly, his mother's abuse seems to have driven the teenaged Byron to take even greater pride in his paternal lineage. One of his earliest poems, "On Leaving Newstead Abbey," celebrates the long and glorious service his paternal forebears had rendered to king and country, and pledges to uphold the family name:

> Shades of heroes, farewell! your descendent, departing
> From the seat of his ancestors, bids you, adieu!
> Abroad, or at home, your remembrance imparting
> New courage, he'll think upon glory, and you.
> (lines 21–24, *CPW*, 1:35–36)[17]

When, four years after drafting this poem, the nineteen-year-old Byron became the subject of Nottinghamshire gossip, he angrily confronted those besmirching his name, declaring, "[A]s a young man very lately entered into the world, I feel compelled to state, that I can permit no suspicion to be attached to my name with impunity" (*BLJ*, 1:105).

This early obsession with name and reputation factored significantly into the composition and publication of Byron's first major poem, *English Bards and*

Scotch Reviewers. Read as a product of the age of Wedgwood, Packwood, and Warren, Byron's satirical send-up of his critics and rival poets is a particularly effective early case of what today we would call "rebranding." As Byron himself fully realized, whatever celebrity he enjoyed prior to the March 1809 publication of *English Bards* was almost entirely owing to his rank and the precocity of publishing *Hours of Idleness* while still in his teens (*BLJ*, 1:118–19). The *Hours* poems themselves, as the *Edinburgh Review* was quick to point out, were generally characterized by tired conceits, plodding rhymes, and school-boy philosophizing (Brougham, 285–89). For *English Bards*, Byron would consciously take on an entirely new persona. Gone were the persistent apologies for his youth and earnest encomia to his literary and political idols, replaced by belligerent pledges to be entirely his own man in poetry and "not to be terrified by abuse, or bullied by reviewers" (*CPW*, 1:228). Whereas the teenaged Byron published anonymously (in *Hours*) or in privately circulating editions (*Fugitive Pieces* and *Poems*), the adult Byron openly defied friends who encouraged him not to publish *English Bards* and, just as significantly, made this the first public edition to bear his name.[18] More than just Byron's coming-out as a serious, adult poet, however, *English Bards* went a step further, in systematically undercutting all competing poetic brands. Here Walter Scott is an overexposed sell-out (lines 171–84), Robert Southey a "Ballad-monger" (line 202), and William Wordsworth a prosaic idiot (lines 235–54); all other "rival rhymesters" are guilty of either outright imbecility or "mental prostitution" ("Preface," lines 34–35).

While Byron would later regret *English Bards* and work actively (if unsuccessfully) to prevent his publisher, James Cawthorn, from releasing post–*Childe Harold* editions of the poem, it clearly played a significant, albeit now underappreciated, role in establishing the Byron brand. Three years before *Childe Harold* allegedly transformed him from an unknown into a superstar, *English Bards* made Byron a literary sensation. In an age when the vast majority of verse collections failed to get past a first edition, *English Bards* went through four editions in two years and would have gone into at least a fifth had Byron not suppressed it.[19] By May 1810 the poet's mother could report to her son, then traveling on the Continent, "Your 'E. Bards' is in the *third edition*, and I hear the universal opinion is that since the days of Pope nothing has equalled it" (qtd. in D. Moore, 122). Byron himself would long afterward attest to the poem's impact, reportedly telling Thomas Medwin that *English Bards* had "made a prodigious impression, more perhaps than any of my works, except 'The Corsair'" (Medwin, 144).

"THE BEST ADVERTISEMENT FOR CHILDE HAROLD'S PILGRIMAGE"

Prior to the summer of 1809, when he set off on the two-year Mediterranean voyage that would inspire *Childe Harold's Pilgrimage*, Byron was already well on his way to making a name for himself. Whether his name yet fully functioned as a poetic brand, however, is doubtful. If, by definition, a brand is a fixed identity that grows up around a product based on its distinctive and largely unchanging qualities, it would be a stretch to say that Byron had achieved anything like this before *Childe Harold*. Readers encountering his name on a book's spine or title page in 1810 or 1811 would likely have had few preconceptions about the style, tone, or contents of the poems within. Of course, the young Byron was hardly alone in this respect, as few writers at this point in consumer history had enjoyed anything like brand-name status. One could certainly make the case that Pope's poetic essays, Richardson's epistolary novels, and Blair's homiletic sermons all functioned to one degree or another as eighteenth-century versions of the literary brand; and, as Judith Pascoe, Claire Brock, and Eric Eisner have shown, Mary Robinson clearly traded upon her "Perdita" persona to achieve a sort of branded identity in the century's waning decades (Pascoe, 172; Brock, ch. 3; Eisner, 21–23). Yet, all of these writers came on the scene well before the logic of branding had become normalized in British society. Accordingly, we need to turn to the likes of Byron and Walter Scott for the earliest instances in which British authors from the age of branding produced the sort of cultlike devotion associated with modern "power brands."

As we have seen, from the time of his initial experiments in publication, Byron was well aware of the importance of an author's name, and he frequently obsessed, in his late teens and early twenties, over what his name was coming to signify. One advantage he clearly had over most rival poets was his title; in a post-courtly era, when few peers published works of any kind, the very idea of a publicly circulating volume of poems—and a largely autobiographical one at that—by a lord was newsworthy. That Byron was fully cognizant of this is evidenced in his preface to *Hours of Idleness*, which concludes by quoting Dr. Johnson's assertion that "when a man of rank appeared in the character of an author, his merit should be handsomely acknowledged" (*CPW*, 1:34).[20] At the same time, Byron realized that novelty's dividends are limited, and he consequently involved himself fully in the marketing of his poems. As early as 1807, as *Hours* was being prepared for press, he asked Cawthorn, "[H]ave you done as I directed about the extracts for the advertisements?" (*BLJ*, 1:152). Meanwhile, he was also sitting for the first of many portraits he would commission over the course of his adult life. As Christine Kenyon Jones has written, from the 1807 George Sanders portrait (see Figure 3.6) forward, "Byron played a major part in creating images of himself that accord with and enhance the representation of the 'Byron' displayed in the verse, prophesying with uncanny accuracy the kinds of images subsequent generations would require of the poet." In fact, even before commissioning his first portrait, the poet "created his own 'look' or image for the public—or for his own gratification—by direct means, such as dieting and weight control, clothes, hairstyles, and the disguise of his lameness" (19).[21]

Byron's anxieties over his name and public image only intensified in the months preceding the publication of *Childe Harold*. In his more confident moments, he worked actively behind the scenes to ensure the best possible reception for his poem. For example, less than two weeks after returning from his tour, he began lobbying William Miller, a London publisher with a much stronger literary reputation than Cawthorn, to take him on as an author (*BLJ*, 2:63). After Miller balked because of concerns over *Childe Harold*'s political and religious unorthodoxy, Byron strategized with his distant relation and unofficial agent, Robert Charles Dallas, to place the poem with another eminent member of "the trade," John Murray. When Dallas's pitch to Murray succeeded, Byron turned his energies—even during a harrowing three-month stretch that saw the death of his mother and several close friends—to preparing the poem for publication. Working closely with both Dallas and Murray, he thoroughly revised the poem, usually with an eye toward its reception. When Murray balked at one particularly heretical passage, the poet presciently responded, "As for the '*Orthodox*,' let us hope they will buy, on purpose to abuse—you will forgive the one if they will do the other" (*BLJ*, 2:91). At the same time, he urged Cawthorn to delay publication of his new satirical poem, *Hints from Horace*. Writing to Dallas on 23 September 1811, he insisted that *Hints* "must not precede the 'Romaunt' [*Childe Harold*]." Even if Cawthorn turned "savage," Dallas must "keep *them* back, & *him* in *good humour* if we can, but do not let him publish" (*BLJ*, 2:104).

If Byron's more optimistic moments saw him maneuvering to rehabilitate his brand and avoid overexposure, in his darker hours he lamented that he would forever be known for the callowness of *Hours* and the petulance of *English Bards*. On more than one occasion in the build-up to *Childe Harold*, he contemplated giving up poetry altogether. In a 2 September 1811 letter to Augusta, for instance, he mopes, "Nothing so fretful, so despicable as a Scribbler, see what *I* am, & what a parcel of Scoundrels I have brought about my ears, & what language I

Figure 3.6. "Lord Byron at the Age of 19." Engraving by William Finden based on George Sanders's portrait *Byron and Robert Rushton* (1807–8). (Thomas Moore, ed., *Letters and Journals of Lord Byron: With Notices of his Life*, 3rd ed., vol. 3 of 3, London: John Murray, 1833, between pp. 598 and 599.)

have been obliged to treat them with to deal with them in their own way;—all this comes of Authorship, but now I am in for it" (*BLJ*, 2:88). For a short while, he even convinced himself that *Childe Harold* must appear anonymously. "I don't think my name will answer the purpose," he told Dallas in late August, "& you must be aware that my plaguy Satire will bring the North & South Grubstreets down on the 'Pilgrimage'" (*BLJ*, 2:75).[22]

Realizing that, tarnished or not, Byron's name still had the potential to sell thousands of copies, Dallas and Murray dug in on the point of authorship. The poet eventually relented, pledging to "man" himself and do what he could to bolster his reputation prior to *Childe Harold*'s release (*BLJ*, 2:151). As a first step, he set out to repair relations with several writers he had targeted in *English Bards*. In early November he arranged an armistice dinner with three of the age's leading poets, Samuel Rogers, Thomas Campbell, and Thomas Moore, the last of whom had been so incensed with the young lord at one point that he contemplated challenging him to a duel. At the dinner, Byron was apparently all charm and contrition. By 16 November, Byron could report to Hobhouse, "Moore & I are on the best of terms" (*BLJ*, 2:127–29).[23] Despite his habitual reserve and tendency to confine himself to a small circle of friends, Byron also took pains to develop connections in society at large. This paid off when he was among the 6 of 354 candidates selected for initiation into the prestigious Alfred Club (*BLJ*, 2:128, 141).

While cutting a figure in literary and social circles certainly improved Byron's reputation, his forays into national politics brought him and his forthcoming volume of poetry still greater attention. In January 1812 he returned to the House of Lords for the first time in nearly three years, and on 27 February he delivered his maiden political speech, opposing Tory efforts to make Luddite frame-breaking a capital offense. In hindsight, what is most interesting about Byron's address is not what he said but that he spoke at all. By the time he took the floor, the debates over Nottinghamshire Luddism had all but ended and it was generally assumed that the frame-breaking bill had enough votes to pass. For an inexperienced member of the House to have any influence on the vote at this point was virtually impossible. Yet Byron proceeded, delivering a speech filled with blunt accusations and invective.

The Tories apparently regarded the speech as inconsequential, for they voiced no official rebuttal. It was left to Lord Holland, leader of Byron's Whig Party, to break the awkward silence. The *Sun* reported the following day that Holland "rose, and expressed his surprise, that after what had fallen from his Noble Friend the Bill should be suffered to go to question, without another word being offered in its defence. After the speech of his Noble Friend, which was fraught with an eloquence not very usual in first speeches, he felt at a loss to offer additional objections to the measure." In the parlors and drawing rooms of London, however, the young lord and his bravado quickly became favorite topics of gossip. The Tory authors of the bill mocked the impudence and fervor of the upstart. On the Whig side, several members came forward to offer Byron congratulatory handshakes, but privately they lamented that he had shown his youthful inexperience in going to such lengths on behalf of a dangerous, largely unsupported, cause (Marchand, *Byron*, 1:321–22). Byron paid little attention to his critics, focusing instead on the encouraging words of radicals such as Sir Francis Burdett, who reportedly called the oration "the best speech by a *Lord* since the 'Lord knows when'" (*BLJ*, 2:167). While the speech itself and his subsequent poem "Ode to the Framers of the Frame Bill" attest to his sincere interest in the Luddite cause (Mole, "Byron's 'Ode'"), Byron seems to have been well aware that, even if the speech ultimately did little for the poor of Nottinghamshire, it would do much for his own poetic career. As he boasted to Dallas on emerging from the House of Lords following his oration, "he had, by his speech, given . . . the best advertisement for *Childe Harold's Pilgrimage*" (Dallas, *Recollections*, 204).

Byron's instincts were true. Between the 27 February speech and the 10 March publication of *Childe Harold*, his name appeared prominently in every major London newspaper. In the final days of February, the *St. James's Chronicle*, the *Morning Chronicle*, and the *Courier* all gave detailed, page-one accounts of the speech, and the 1 March issue of *Bell's Weekly Messenger* devoted half of its summary of the frame-breaking debates to Byron's oration. Perhaps most gratifying to the young lord was a *Morning Chronicle* article of 2 March, which reminded readers that he was not only an up-and-coming politician but also a respected poet: "Lord BYRON, who spoke on the Nottingham Felony Bill on Tuesday, evinced considerable eloquence.—His talents have been already established by his literary productions, but it does not always happen that able writers are gifted with the powers of elocution."

"A BOOKSELLING, BACKSHOP, PATERNOSTER ROW, PALTRY PROCEEDING"

Thus, two weeks before he supposedly awoke one morning and found himself famous, Byron was in fact one of the most talked-about figures in London. In view of the lingering circulation of *Hours* and *English Bards*, his growing presence in high society, and his widely publicized frame-breaking speech, Byron clearly had already started making a name for himself prior to the 10 March publication of

Childe Harold. Of course, it would take several more works in his new style before the Byronic brand became a fixed commodity in readers' eyes, but the rush upon bookstores in the days following *Childe Harold*'s release signals just how effective the poet, his agent, and his publisher had been in developing expectations surrounding his name.

While Byron was still a relative newcomer to the book business in 1812, his two lead partners on *Childe Harold*, Dallas and Murray, had long years of experience in the trade. Byron's senior by twenty-four years, Dallas had already lived a full life by the time the poet came of age, having played the parts of Jamaican plantocrat, London barrister, French and American immigrant, and, most recently, anti-Jacobin novelist and playwright (James Watt). A staunch pietist and confirmed conservative, Dallas was in many ways the most unlikely of mentors for the young libertine poet, entering Byron's life through a remote familial connection (Dallas's sister was the widow of Byron's paternal uncle). Yet, contrary to much of the popular and scholarly record, which follows Hobhouse's lead in portraying Dallas as a self-interested hanger-on who plagued the poet with his endless sermonizing,[24] Byron genuinely appreciated Dallas's literary and business sensibilities and displayed real warmth in his letters to him. When Dallas came into his life in early 1808, Byron had just turned twenty and was still a virtual unknown. Acting as a sort of surrogate uncle, Dallas (at least by his own account) devoted countless hours to the young man, not only imparting life advice but also donating an enormous amount of unpaid labor editing Byron's drafts and bringing *English Bards* to press (Dallas, *Recollections*, 3–67). In this light, Byron's bestowal upon Dallas of the full royalties (eventually over £1000) for *Childe Harold* I and II and *The Corsair* should be interpreted less as succumbing to the importuning of a sycophantic relation—as Hobhouse would have it (12)—than belatedly compensating a trusted mentor and advisor.

As for Murray, although only ten years older than Byron, he brought to their relationship a lifetime of involvement in the London book trade. Murray's father, also John, was a successful publisher, and upon the elder's death in 1795 the seventeen-year-old son became part-owner of the family business. In 1804, Murray took sole ownership of the firm and immediately began expanding its ambition and reach. By the time Byron came into the fold in 1811, Murray had founded the immediately influential *Quarterly Review* and forged a partnership with Archibald Constable, the powerful Edinburgh-based publisher of Walter Scott and the *Edinburgh Review*.[25] Although much of his success can be attributed to his ability to recognize and court literary genius, perhaps Murray's greatest gifts were as a salesman. From the moment he took over his father's firm, he had no illusions about a book's ability to sell itself. This is made clear in an 1806 letter to Constable in which he articulates a theory of prerelease publicity that became a hallmark of his marketing style:

> It is inconceivable how effectually the continued advertisement of a book *long* previous to publication operates upon people in the country, and upon the booksellers, who, having heard the book mentioned, and having received orders for it, subscribe voraciously; and, indeed, it occasions many people to order or buy the book immediately, who would otherwise have waited for the opinion of their Review, and, had this proved cold or unfavourable, would not have been purchasers. (Constable, 1:348)

While Murray generally remained above egregious puffery, he tirelessly marketed books he believed in. By the 1820s he was legendary for such tactics as presenting the royal family with immaculately bound display copies, commissioning and circulating paintings of his leading authors, and holding well-publicized bookseller dinners to create demand for new titles.[26]

In short, then, the Byron-Dallas-Murray partnership combined long years in the book trade with an advanced understanding of the new advertising system in general and branding in particular. Byron had already displayed a deep awareness of how authors establish and maintain their names, and, if *Don Juan* (1819–1824) is any indication—with its want-ad–mimicking invocation and frequent allusions to brand-name goods (Mozer, "I WANT")—his interest in literary and nonliterary marketing only heightened in the decade after publication of *Childe Harold*. For his part, Murray was likely even more attuned to the rise of branding and its potential implications for the book trade. While the concept of an authorial brand was relatively new in the early nineteenth century, that of branding a publisher's name was not. As Richard B. Sher has suggested, from the mid-eighteenth century forward the "publisher function" has been at least as powerful at the point of sale as Foucault's more heralded "author function" (7–8, 265–66). The ultimate goal in high-end publishing was, as it is now, to build a list of books so consistently impressive that the publisher's imprint becomes a sign of value, or, in Jerome Christensen's words, "a kind of canonical legitimation" (144).[27] That Murray was fully cognizant of the symbiotic relationship between authors' and publishers' brands was made clear in the wake of the phenomenal debut of *Childe Harold*. In a letter to Byron dated 7 September 1812, Murray imagined the potential synergy between the release of Byron's next poem, *The Corsair*, and the publicity surrounding the grand opening of his firm's Albemarle Street offices. "I am delighted to find you thinking upon a new Poem," he wrote, "for which I should be proud to give A Thousand Guineas—and I should ever gratefully remember the fame it would cast over my new establishment, upon which I enter at the close of the present month" (J. Murray, *Letters*, 8).

By Dallas's report, Murray first began following Byron's career in 1808, when *English Bards* appeared. Over the next few years the publisher occasionally mentioned to Dallas—who had himself published multiple books with the house of Murray—his potential interest in securing one of the young poet's future works. Thus, when William Miller passed on publishing *Childe Harold*, Dallas offered the poem to Murray, who promptly accepted it (Dallas, *Recollections*, 119–21). As noted above, in the months that followed, Murray and Dallas worked collaboratively to pressure Byron into, first, reconsidering his wish to publish anonymously and, second, expunging politically or religiously unorthodox passages. In Murray's initial letter to Byron, dated 4 September 1811, he obsesses over how Byron's religious skepticism and blunt critiques of Spanish and Portuguese culture will "greatly interfere with the popularity which the Poem is, in other respects, so certainly calculated to excite" (J. Murray, *Letters*, 3). Dallas seconded this sentiment in a series of long letters urging the poet to cut "free-thinking" stanzas such as the one beginning "Frown not upon me, churlish Priest! that I / Look not for Life, where life may never be." Dallas also teamed with Murray to convince Byron of the commercial wisdom of including a "hypothetical stanza," in which Harold at least entertains the reality of an afterlife (Dallas, *Recollections*, 122–26, 153–87).

Murray's and Dallas's most effectual prepublication work, however, was not in textual editing but in creating buzz surrounding the poem and its author. In hindsight, one of the more remarkable aspects of the promotional campaign they designed is how little it depended on direct advertising. In this respect, they seem to have intuited what is now recognized as a central tenet of branding theory, namely, that publicity is much more effective in establishing a brand than direct advertising (Ries and Ries, 25; see also Atkin, Stobart, and Weilbacher). While several paid notices for the poem did appear in London newspapers between 5 and 10 March, 1812,[28] Murray's account books show that the advertising expenditures for the first edition came to only £19.13s.6d. (D. Moore, 180). To put this figure into perspective, in 1813 Richard Duppa reported to Parliament that "every new book consisting of one or two 8vo. volumes is calculated to cost £30 to advertise" (21–22). By midcentury several publishing firms routinely spent over £100 to advertise each new book (Plant, 408). Therefore, even considering inflation, the expenditure of slightly less than £20 to advertise the first edition of *Childe Harold* was modest at best.

Those advertisements that did appear in the week preceding *Childe Harold*'s release are interesting principally insofar as they reveal what Murray saw as the book's most marketable features. The *Times* advertisement of 5 March is essentially identical to the advertisements that appeared in most other papers:

> Lord Byron's new Poem.—In a few days will be published, handsomely printed in 4to.
> CHILDE HAROLD's PILGRIMAGE ; a Poem: written during the Author's Travels in Portugal, Spain, Albania, and some of the most interesting parts of Greece; with notes. To which are added, a few miscellaneous Poems, and translations of modern Greek Songs, written chiefly abroad: and a short Appendix, containing observations on modern Greek Literature with a short catalogue of Romaic Authors. By LORD BYRON. Printed for John Murray, 32, Fleet-street.

Figure 3.7. Advertisement for *Childe Harold's Pilgrimage*. (*The Times*, 5 March 1812: 2.)

Along with the attempt to depoliticize the poem as little more than a travel narrative, the most striking element of this advertisement is that it both begins and ends with the poet's name, the second time in all capital letters. It was hardly uncommon to use an author's name in an early-nineteenth-century book advertisement; it was unusual, however, for a bookseller to emphasize a name as strongly as Murray does here. This emphasis on the author's name is even more striking in the *Morning Chronicle* advertisement for 5 March:

> LORD BYRON'S NEW POEM.
> On Saturday next will be published, handsomely printed in 4to.
> CHILDE HAROLD'S PILGRIMAGE: a Poem. By LORD BYRON.
> Printed for John Murray, 32, Fleet-street, London,

Figure 3.8. Advertisement for *Childe Harold's Pilgrimage*. (*The Morning Chronicle*, 5 March 1812: 2.)

The clear implication here is that the most compelling reason to purchase the book is not what it contains but who wrote it. This, in every sense of the word, is branding: the Byron sign supposedly says as much about the poem's merits as the Wedgwood imprint would say about a vase or the Warren's label about a bottle of blacking.

Again, though, these advertisements were but a small part of the multipronged marketing campaign for *Childe Harold*. While Byron did his part to attract publicity by cultivating friendships with prominent poets, joining influential social clubs, and delivering his controversial frame-breaking address, Murray and Dallas worked their trade connections to get news of the poem circulating well in advance of its release. The earliest such effort came in the late summer of 1811, when they sought the imprimatur of William Gifford, the editor of Murray's *Quarterly Review* and, with the possible exception of Francis Jeffrey, the most influential critic of the age. Despite his arch-Tory politics, Gifford had long been one of Byron's literary heroes, ranking among the select few to receive unqualified praise in *English Bards* (*CPW*, 1:228, 232 [lines 93–94], and 252 [lines 743–44]).[29] Consequently, Byron was particularly sensitive that Gifford be shown *Childe Harold* only after it was fully revised and not be coerced into praising it. In the first letter he ever wrote to Murray, dated 23 August 1811, Byron said of a Gifford review: "Now, though no one would feel more gratified by the chance of obtaining his observations on a work than myself there is in such a proceeding, a kind of petition for praise, that neither my pride or—whatever you please to call it—will admit.... Though not very patient of Censure, I would fain obtain fairly any little praise my rhymes might deserve, at all events not by extortion & the humble solicitations of a bandied about M.S." (*BLJ*, 2:78).

Much to Byron's chagrin, his request either arrived too late or was ignored altogether. As Dallas informed him on 5 September, not only had Gifford already seen the poem, but he had pronounced it Byron's best work to date and "equal to any of the present age" (*Recollections*, 157–58). Gifford's reported enthusiasm, however, did little to mollify Byron, whose spleen over what he dubbed "a bookselling, backshop, Paternoster Row, paltry proceeding" (*BLJ*, 2:105) remained high more than a month after learning of Gifford's involvement. In various letters written during September and early October 1811, Byron fantasized about "immolat[ing] the betrayer of trust" (*BLJ*, 2:105) and watching Murray drown in Paddington Canal (which he dubbed "the proper receptacle for publishers") (*BLJ*, 2:101). The issue here was not just that Byron felt disrespected by a social inferior. More important, he feared that the attempt to secure either a puff or a blurb from Gifford would be found out and, as had been the case when vigilant reviewers had exposed Cawthorn's arranged reviews for *Hours of Idleness* (Marchand, *Byron*, 1:134), he would once again be widely dismissed as a literary lightweight.

While Murray took the fall for Gifford's being shown the manuscript, it seems likely, as Andrew Nicholson has suggested (4), that Dallas played a key role in the scheme. In the midst of Byron's fury over the "paltry proceeding," Dallas was quick to point out the value of Gifford's endorsement; and after Byron's death he attributed the poem's runaway success to the fact that "the critical junto were prepared, probably through Mr. Gifford, for something extraordinary" (*Recollections*, 199). That Dallas was not beyond greasing the wheels of the reviewing system is more than evident in perhaps the most shameless episode in the build-up to *Childe Harold*. Nine days before the poem's release, on 1 March, the *Literary Panorama* published a glowing review of the poem. Byron's new work, readers were informed, was a poem "in which narrative, feeling, description, sentiment, satire, tenderness and contemplation, are happily blended" (419). "Every line of it," the reviewer concluded, "will be felt by the scholar and the man of taste" (430). As if a panegyrical review appearing days before a book's publication weren't fishy enough, any lingering doubts whether this was a bookseller's puff would have been wholly dispelled by the reviewer's byline: C. Dallas. Perhaps the casual reader would have had no idea of the connections between this "C. Dallas" and the author of *Childe Harold's Pilgrimage*, but book industry insiders would have known full well that Dallas was Byron's representative and, more important, had a sizeable financial stake in the poem's success.

Apparently, Dallas's machinations took place behind Byron's back. When the poet, who was already apprehensive about sullying his aristocratic name by joining the ranks of scribblers, learned of Dallas's puff, he panicked. Byron was versed enough in the ways of Grub Street to know that the review would easily be spotted as a puff. As Dallas himself later confessed, "it had the appearance of an eulogium prematurely hurried before the public by a friend, if not by the author himself" (*Recollections*, 220). This fact was not lost on Byron, who lamented, "I shall be set down for the writer of it" (220). Once again, Dallas went into damage control mode, insisting that the editors of the *Literary Panorama* had assured him the review wouldn't appear until after *Childe Harold*'s release. In the wake of the Gifford incident and now the bungled puff, though, Byron must have had doubts over the path he had chosen. His new world of "bandied about" manuscripts, "backshop" deals, and no-holds-barred book peddling was a far cry from the Arcadian groves of gentlemanly versifying to which he had originally aspired.

Fortunately for Byron (and Dallas), the *Literary Panorama* puff was quickly forgotten once the poem appeared and "Byromania" set in, and most of the subsequent marketing of *Childe Harold* was relatively dignified. However firmly convinced Byron may have been that Gifford himself would be asked to review *Childe Harold* in the *Quarterly*, the task fell to the esteemed gentleman-critic George Ellis, who offered a few quibbles before commending the work as a whole as one of "sterling genius" (200). Most other early reviewers, including Jeffrey in the *Edinburgh*, were similarly impressed. Tellingly, besides the *Quarterly*, none of the leading Tory, High Church, or Evangelical reviews took notice of the poem before May 1812, and many did not review it until it had gone through several editions. It seems that just as securing positive publicity was an important part of promoting Byron, so too was delaying negative reviews until the author's and the poem's reputations had been established.[30]

Cumulatively, these various attempts to put Byron's name into circulation resulted in an early brand identity that was only reinforced by *Childe Harold's Pilgrimage*, the most consciously autobiographical "nonautobiographical" poem of the nineteenth century. When they set off for bookstores on the morning of 10 March, readers may have had only a slight idea of the themes and topics they would meet with in *Childe Harold* I and II, but they had a clear sense of its author and what he represented. Although Byron's poetry would continue to evolve, the Byron brand that produced a string of best-selling poetic products and led to a host of successful spin-offs and imitations over the next decade—think Byronism and the Byronic hero—was essentially in place by March 1812. On the heels of *English Bards*, Byron's parliamentary speech, and advance reviews and rumors of *Childe Harold*, readers expected a text bearing the Byron name to juxtapose sensibility and volatility, eloquence and eccentricity, genius and heterodoxy. The sales figures of 10–12 March show that they flocked to bookstores not to buy a generic volume of poetry but a product they had been trained to ask for by name. And, thus, while a book of poems was not yet on a par commercially with razor strops or blacking paste, the age of literary branding had fully commenced.

CHAPTER 4

L.E.L., Bandwagon Marketing, and the Rise of Visual Culture

On 19 April 1827, a week to the day after George Canning was named Britain's new prime minister, his old friend William Jerdan, a fellow Tory and the editor of the widely read *Literary Gazette*, wrote to offer his services to Canning's government:

> Sir,—I occupy a singular position in the literary world .... The result is that from the highest to almost the lowest class of public writers I am of sufficient importance to possess a very considerable weight with them. From book authors, through all gradations of the periodical press, it is not a boast to assert that I could do much to modify opinions, heat friends, and cool enemies. I am on terms of personal intimacy with forty-nine out of fifty of those who direct the leading journals of the day; and I can from time to time oblige them all. (qtd. in Canning, 2:367–68)

As if there were any confusion about what he might bring to the new government, in a follow-up letter written two weeks later, Jerdan insists, "I am in a situation to render Mr. C. more efficient aid by influencing the public press than any other person whomsoever" (2:369). The role Jerdan seems to be imagining for himself in these letters is something of a cross between a press secretary and a minister of propaganda, yet no such office existed in 1827—nor would it for another century.[1] Apparently, not even Canning, the cofounder of the brilliantly propagandistic *Anti-Jacobin* and possibly the most press-savvy prime minister to that point in history, could see the possibilities of what Jerdan was proposing, for on 7 May he had his private secretary, A. G. Stapleton, send a brief and pointed letter declining Jerdan's services (2:370).

Today, William Jerdan generally comes up as, at best, a footnote in the literary history of late Romantic and early Victorian Britain; but, as his not particularly modest letters to Canning assert, he was then widely seen as one of the most influential and commercially ingenious literary figures of the age. When in June 1830 *Fraser's Magazine* launched its "Gallery of Illustrious Literary Characters"—a series that would eventually include portraits and biographies of eighty-five leading figures of contemporary British letters—it devoted the first installment to Jerdan, explaining: "With him begins our Gallery of Illustrious Portraits, because upon him depends judicially, in the first instance, the fates and fortunes of literary works. He is the grand jury, the publisher being only the committing magistrate" (Maginn, "Gallery," 605). Not only was this opinion of Jerdan widely shared in 1830, but it endured long after the *Literary Gazette*'s heyday. In June 1852, the *Ladies' Companion* recalled that in the 1820s Jerdan was a "pioneer," whose magazine produced "world-changing results." Speaking for an older generation, the *Companion*'s fictional Mrs. Smith insisted, "It must not be forgotten that the 'Literary Gazette' opened a new era in the periodical press" ("New Books," 327). William Bates offered a similar assessment in 1898, recalling: "In those old days Jerdan was a power in the Republic of Letters. Reputations were thought to depend upon his nod; he could make, or unmake, the fortune of a book; and the young Argonaut, adventuring forth on the ocean of fame, looked anxiously for 'a puff from the river Jordan' . . . to waft his bark into the haven of success" (3).

Among Jerdan's contemporaries, the general consensus was that, while he was neither an astute critic nor a great thinker, he had an unmatched sense of middle-class tastes and an even stronger knack for literary marketing. To his detractors—and there were many—he was a shameless puffer and self-publicist. At least initially, this was primarily a case of guilt by association, as the *Literary Gazette* was owned by Henry Colburn, whose name became synonymous with insider reviewing, fad publishing, and literary hucksterism over the course of the 1820s (see Chapter 5). But even as Jerdan gradually extricated the *Gazette* from Colburn's grasp, his antagonists continued to take every opportunity to cast aspersions on him and his weekly. An article on Jerdan in the *Examiner* for 20 August 1826, for instance, opens by remarking, "Our readers know something already of the ignorance and malignity of the worthless hack who conducts the *Literary Gazette*." From here it proceeds to explain that "this trafficker in puffing and abuse of books is consistent in one thing: he abuses every book connected with those to whom he is for any reason opposed—he praises every book in which his employers or his friends are interested" ("The Literary Gazette and the Novel 'Truth,'" 532). In an 1833 *National Standard* essay titled "Puffing and Fishing," William

Makepeace Thackeray sighs, "As for Jerdan, it appears that he is incorrigible, and may be given up, though he continues loudly to protest his total freedom and independence" (221). Literally dozens of similar aspersions of Jerdan's professional character appeared in the periodical press of the 1820s and 1830s, and as late as 1880 William Bell Scott could be found recording an old rumor that Jerdan was so desirous to be seen as fashionable that he was once "found running a wheelbarrow round the gravel in front of his house, to represent carriage visitors." Scott concludes, "This was, most probably, an envious jeu d'esprit, but it showed in what light it was possible to view him" (xii).[2]

While Jerdan's foes could readily list a host of lapses in professional decorum, the vast majority of published complaints centered on his tireless efforts to promote his protégée-turned-lover-and-business-associate Letitia Elizabeth Landon, or, as she was widely known, "L.E.L." These complaints certainly weren't without merit, as Jerdan used the extensive reach of the *Literary Gazette* and the full range of his marketing skills to transform Landon from a virtual unknown in 1820 into a sensation throughout much of the Western world by 1825. When the *Gazette* greeted the arrival of Landon's first major book, *The Improvisatrice* (1824), with two lengthy reviews hailing her as no less than "the English Sappho" (Review of *The Improvisatrice*, 417), it was only a matter of time before rival periodicals flagged this as an "instance of open, bare-faced puffing" (Review of *The Improvisatrice* [*Literary Magnet*], 106) and dubbed Landon "the girl the papers have been puffing so" ("The Anniversary," 204). Even *Blackwood's*, a long-time ally of Jerdan and champion of the *Gazette*, lamented, "She is one of the sweetest little girls in the world, and her book is one of the sweetest little books in the world; but Jerdan's extravagant trumpetting has quite sickened everybody" (Lockhart, "Noctes Ambrosianae, No. XVI," 237).

Undaunted by such criticism, Jerdan continued over the next decade to use every weapon in his promotional arsenal to keep Landon in the media spotlight and her books in the front windows of bookshops. The creation of L.E.L.-mania, however, was by no means a one-person production; Landon proved every bit as commercially savvy as Jerdan over time. A host of anecdotes suggests that, perhaps more than any major woman poet of the Romantic age, Landon quickly embraced market realities and set out to establish both a poetic persona that would resonate with that day's readers and a professional network that would ensure long-term success. To keep herself constantly before the public (as well as to pay her own bills and those of several family members), she composed, as she put it in 1826, "poetry 'by the pound'" (*Letters*, 33). To encourage a continuing flow of positive notices, she sent warm thank-you notes to and cultivated personal relationships with friendly reviewers and editors (26–27; Stephenson, 40). And, as both her friends and enemies reported, she had few qualms about bucking Romantic standards of poetic sincerity, even boasting at times over how contrived her poetic raptures could be. In 1826, the exasperated *Inspector and Literary Review* reported:

> This love-sighing poetess proves that there is an hypocrisy in poetical sentiment, as well as all other things. Every body, from her writings, would believe her enamoured of groves, fountains, &c.; instead of which, she is often heard to express the opinions of a tasteless, town-bred, unpoetical Miss. A friend once asked her, if she were not rapturously enamoured of rural arcades? "Pooh!" quoth she, "I never saw any other but Burlington Arcade!!"[3] ("Domestic and Literary Intelligence," 324)

This anecdote might be easily dismissed were it not bolstered by a range of subsequent reports by Landon's closest friends. Laman Blanchard wrote, "No two persons could be less like each other in all that related to the contemplation of the actual world, than 'L.E.L.' and Letitia Elizabeth Landon" (*Life*, 34). Katherine Byerley Thomson related how, much to her friends' consternation, Landon "pleaded guilty to no sentiment; she abjured the idea of writing from her own feelings" (156). And William Howitt recorded how, at a dinner party, a love-struck admirer of Landon lamented, "You never think of such a thing as love! . . . you who have written so many volumes of poetry upon it," to which Landon retorted, "with an air of merry scorn," "Oh! that's all professional, you know!" (2:154).

In many respects, then, it is not an exaggeration to suggest that the team of Jerdan and Landon was the second coming of Murray and Byron — an ambitious young publisher with control over a powerful literary periodical and a commercially-minded poet with a gift for gauging and adapting to the age's tastes.[4] While the two poet-publisher teams have rarely been compared, the similarities between Byron and Landon have been frequently noted since at least the 1840s, when Frederic Rowton dubbed Landon "the Byron of our poetesses" (424). Regularly returning to this analogy, modern Landon scholars have been divided on its merits. On the one side, Jerome McGann and Daniel Riess endorse the notion that Byron's "life and writings were the dominant influence on [Landon's] own work and career" (18), and Claire Knowles and Eric Eisner argue that, in Eisner's words, Landon's poetry "reworks and redeploys the tropes of Byronic celebrity" (Eisner, 117; Knowles, ch. 4). On the other hand, Susan Wolfson and Adriana Craciun maintain that, once their enormous popularity is removed from the equation, the comparison between the quintessential "poetess" and "that most masculine of poets" readily breaks down (Craciun, 202–4).[5]

Rather than wading into debates over just how Byronic L.E.L.'s poetry and persona may have been, this chapter will develop another comparison between the two, highlighting the extent to which Landon and Jerdan followed Byron and Murray's lead in both finding literary applications for new advertising techniques and inventing promotional methodologies of their own that would eventually cross over into other commercial sectors. Rejecting the traditional, but fundamentally flawed, explanation that L.E.L.-mania grew out of curiosity surrounding the identity of the *Literary Gazette*'s "veiled initialist," I argue that Jerdan's real masterstroke was manipulating the reading public into believing that Landon was wildly popular years before she actually was. This, in essence, was one of the first successful utilizations of the bandwagon effect, and it occurred more than a century before advertisers and social scientists coined a term for the technique. While this campaign alone would have made the Jerdan-Landon team one of the premier advertising partnerships of the early nineteenth century, it was only the beginning of their groundbreaking collaboration. When L.E.L.'s novelty began to wane in the late 1820s, Landon and Jerdan launched a new promotional strategy, built around a series of mass-reproduced portraits of the author. At once reaffirming L.E.L.'s youthful beauty and her sexual purity, these portraits represented a dramatic shift from a veiled to a thoroughly iconic Landon. The ultimate effect was to recapture her readers' imagination and, more significantly, help lay the groundwork for the great promotional phenomenon of the Victorian age: the explosion of image-based advertising.

ANONYMITY, PSEUDONYMITY, AND "THREE MAGICAL LETTERS"

In the midst of the onomastic revolution discussed in the previous chapter, and in the wake of the Byronic revolution in literary branding, Landon and other authors who came on the scene in the late Romantic age were forced to reflect carefully about the names they would use when introducing themselves to the public. Some authors, as *Chambers' Edinburgh Journal* mused in 1833, clearly came to the pitch better equipped than others. For every fortuitously named "Lady Morgan" or "Countess of Blessington," there was a score of generically christened John Smiths and, worse, disastrously named Higginbottoms and Meiklewhams. "Could the glory of a Caesar or a Napoleon," *Chambers'* asks, "be reaped under the name of Hogsflesh? Were he to affect poetry, could any new epic approaching to the Paradise Lost be published with the name Gotobed upon the title-page?" Speaking of more recent writers, the essayist opines: "Walter Scott was fortunate in his name. Had he been called Thomas Scott, or John Scott, there is a great chance of his never having arrived at the distinction he did" ("Names").[6] Much of this, of course, was hyperbole or whimsy, as a Samuel Johnson, a Charlotte Smith, or a Samuel Rogers could still have a successful career without resorting to a pseudonym or name change. Nevertheless, in an increasingly crowded print marketplace, where the odds of getting noticed grew slimmer each year, the aspiring novelist named Mary Jones or poet named William Brown was at a distinct disadvantage compared to writers with memorable names (e.g., Amelia Opie, Felicia Hemans, Washington Irving), clever nicknames (Mary "Perdita" Robinson, Anna "The Swan of Litchfield" Seward, Matthew "Monk" Lewis), noble titles (Lady Nairne, Lady Morgan, Lord Byron), or literary pedigrees (Fanny Burney, Maria Edgeworth, Benjamin Disraeli).

Predictably, as the author's name took on increased importance, the frequency of anonymous publication plummeted.[7] This trend was particularly pronounced in poetry; the percentage of books of verse published anonymously in Britain fell from 70 percent in 1778 to 36 percent in 1788 and 23 percent in 1803 (Erickson, "'Unboastful Bard,'" 269–70). While anonymity among novelists remained more common, presumably because of lingering stigmas attached to the genre, a steep decline occurred in that quarter as well. Whereas over 80 percent of British novels published between 1750 and 1790 appeared anonymously, 62 percent did so in the 1790s and less than 50 percent did in the first decade of the nineteenth century (Raven, "The Anonymous Novel," 143–45, 163–65; Mole, *Byron's Romantic Celebrity*, 10–13). The rate would climb again in the 1810s, in part because of the success of the unsigned *Waverley* novels;[8] but, even then, anonymous publication was generally more a carefully considered strategy than a routine adherence to the norm.

As was illustrated in Byron's reluctance to attach his name to *Childe Harold* (see Chapter 3), authors still occasionally had their reasons for preferring anonymity. And, just as Murray held firm in insisting that Byron's name appear on *Childe Harold*, other Romantic-era publishers (especially of poetry) strongly encouraged authors to publish under their given names. For example, in February 1800, Coleridge, in the midst of his and Wordsworth's negotiations with Thomas Longman concerning the planned second edition of *Lyrical Ballads*, reported to Robert Southey: "I find a resistance which I did not expect to the *anonymousness* of the publication. Longman seems confident that a work on such a subject without a name would not do. Translations and perhaps Satires are, he says, the only works that booksellers now venture on *without a name*" (*Letters*, 1:317). In 1819 the celebrated novelist and poet Amelia Opie got much the same response when she approached Scott's publisher, Archibald Constable, about publishing a volume of her poems anonymously. Constable advised: "With regard to the publication of the work you mention, I must tell you that I had almost determined to limit the number of my undertakings in that department of literature to those of the author of Waverley.... You are aware, perhaps, that Mr. Walter Scott's anonymous Poetry did not succeed? A good title and a popular author does much with the public" (Constable, 2:279–80).

In those cases when, even in the face of their publisher's opposition, Romantic-era authors continued to insist on anonymity, it was frequently owing to the controversial nature of their subject matter or some sense of aristocratic, domestic, or religious decorum (R. Griffin, Introduction, 7; Mullan, 6–7). Even then, anonymity was, as often as not, relatively transparent. By the mid-1810s, for instance, Jane Austen was widely known as the author of *Sense and Sensibility* and *Pride and Prejudice*. Thus, when in 1816 she published *Emma* as "By the Author of 'Pride and Prejudice,'" it was clearly a case of what Sher has called "mitigated anonymity" (150–51). Another relatively common practice was releasing a first edition anonymously but then signing subsequent editions once the book had become a popular or critical success (Erickson, "'Unboastful Bard,'" 247–49; Sher, 152).

For the purposes of the argument at hand, however, the most intriguing cases of anonymous publication during the Romantic era are those in which it was employed strategically as a promotional device. In yet another manifestation of the advertising savvy so widely found in the late-eighteenth- and early-nineteenth-century British book trade, several publishers and authors recognized that the best way to kindle readers' interest in an author's name was by making them work to discover it. As Andrew Bennett suggests, far from attempts to devalue the author's name, many modern "anonymizing and pseudonymizing gestures may in fact be seen as concentrating attention on authors, on authorialism, precisely by provoking an interest in the true originator of the text" (54). For both readers and writers alike, this catch-me-if-you-can game of veiled authorship could be enormously entertaining. Fanny Burney, one of the most obsessively anonymous writers of the era (Mullan, 59–64), brilliantly captured this dynamic in her 1779 comedy *The Witlings*. The play's second act begins with the following exchange:

> LADY SMATTER. Yes, yes, this song is certainly Mr. Dabler's, I am not to be deceived in his style. What say you, my dear Miss Stanley, don't you think I have found him out?
> CECILIA. Indeed I am too little acquainted with his Poems to be able to judge.
> LADY SMATTER. Your indifference surprises me! for my part, I am never at rest

till I have discovered the authors of every thing that comes out; and, indeed, I commonly hit upon them in a moment. I declare I sometimes wonder at myself, when I think how lucky I am in my guesses.

CECILIA. Your Ladyship devotes so much Time to these researches, that it would be strange if they were unsuccessful. (II.1.1–12)

Further evidence of the potential pleasures of anonymity comes in the Austen family's accounts of watching readers attempt to unmask the author of *Sense and Sensibility*. Mary Austen, the novelist's sister-in-law, detailed how in the resort town of Cheltenham many were attributing the novel to the Scottish writer Elizabeth Hamilton. Others reported the novel's being credited to Charlotte Smith, Catherine Dorset, and Lady Borington of Saltram. Perhaps the most amusing—or possibly infuriating—report came from Henry Austen, who recounted how one of his acquaintances declared that the novel must have had a male author, as it was "much too clever to have been written by a woman" (Mullan, 67–71).

However much curiosity the anonymous publication of Austen's early novels might have stimulated, it likely had minimal effect on her sales; and it would be a stretch to say that anonymity in this case was particularly strategic, since during the early nineteenth century many first-time novelists published anonymously as a matter of course. The most interesting cases of anonymity during the Regency and the 1820s were ones in which an author's name would certainly have resonated with readers yet was purposely left off. Of course, the *piece de resistance* of this seemingly counterintuitive marketing gambit was Walter Scott's anonymously published *Waverley* (1814). Scholars remain divided over whether this was primarily, as John Sutherland puts it, a "great sales gimmick" (*How to Read a Novel*, 106) or merely Scott's not wanting to sully his sterling reputation as a poet by slumming as a novelist. As Seamus Cooney has documented, Scott himself at various moments gave a variety of explanations that ranged from how much he enjoyed incorrect guesses to his sense that it wouldn't be "considered quite decorous for me as a Clerk of Sessions to write novels" (qtd. in Cooney, 208).

At least initially, Scott's anonymity wasn't, by most accounts, a great business decision. Five months prior to *Waverley*'s release, the printer James Ballantyne warned Scott's publisher, Archibald Constable, "I think it [the book] very clever, but anonymous things are precarious" (qtd. in Garside, 380). In the weeks following the novel's release—even while it was the talk of literary Britain—Scott insisted, "[E]very body knows that I sacrifice much money by withholding my name" (Lockhart, *Memoirs*, 1:480). What may have been a short-term risk, however, almost certainly paid dividends over the long term, as a significant subsection of Scott's readers during his thirteen years of anonymity (1814–27) recorded how speculating about the true identity of the "Great Unknown" was at the heart of their reading (and purchasing) of the book. An April 1818 article in the *Analectic Magazine* concludes that the true author of the Waverley novels is one Dr. Greenfield and reports that rumors about the author's identity have reached a fever pitch with the recent publication of *Rob Roy* (Review of *Rob Roy*, 274). A year later, Rudolf Ackermann's *Repository of Arts* conjectured that the hidden author—here "revealed" to be "the son of a Scotch baronet of the name of Forbes"—continued disguising his identity because "if the mystery were unravelled, if the solution were known, few people, comparatively, would take an interest in the novels" ("Dialogues," 146–47). As late as February 1826, fascination over the true author of the Waverley novels remained widespread enough that the Scottish man of letters Sir John Sinclair told Constable, "I am convinced that *at least* fifty thousand pounds might be made from a quarto edition of the Waverley Novels, provided there is prefixed to it the history and progress of those Novels, and an explanation of the circumstances which induced the author to decline making his name known to the public" (Constable, 2:8).[9]

Given how Landon first appeared on the scene in the early 1820s, when the publishing world was still abuzz over the brilliant marketing gambit of the Great Unknown, the natural conclusion has long been that the "L.E.L." concept was a similarly inspired experiment in promotional onomastics. The first biography of Landon to hit the bookstores after her mysterious death by poisoning in 1838 plays heavily on this theme. Written by her long-time friend and fellow poet Laman Blanchard, *Life and Literary Remains of L.E.L.* (1841) features a widely cited account of the stir created by the arrival of the mysterious L.E.L. on the literary scene:

> The three letters very speedily became a signature of magical interest and curiosity. Struck by the evident youth of the writer, by the force as well as the grace of her careless and hurried notes, by the impassioned tenderness of the many songs and sketches that, week after week, without intermission, appeared under the same signature, the public unhesitatingly recognised these contributions as the fresh and unstudied outpourings of genius; and they, by whom the loftier beauties and the more cultivated grace of the living masters of the lyre were best appreciated, at once, "with open arms received one poet more." (30)[10]

Blanchard's recollection of the immediate excitement surrounding the mysterious "L.E.L." is seemingly corroborated by Edward Bulwer-Lytton's *New Monthly*

Magazine review of Landon's first novel, *Romance and Reality* (1831). Another member of Landon's social set, Bulwer-Lytton recalled how, during his Cambridge days in the early 1820s, "there was always, in the Reading Room of the Union, a rush every Saturday afternoon for 'The Literary Gazette,' and an impatient anxiety to hasten at once to that corner of the sheet which contained the three magical letters of 'L.E.L.'" (Review, 546).

To this day Blanchard's and Bulwer-Lytton's accounts have remained foundational in Landon scholarship, repeatedly being ushered forth as evidence that the poet's use of initials was a masterstroke of literary marketing that created a groundswell of interest in her works and person between 1821 and 1824. For instance, Angela Leighton, in her pioneering reassessment of Landon in *Victorian Women Poets: Writing Against the Heart* (1992), draws heavily upon Blanchard and Bulwer-Lytton in concluding that "L.E.L.'s career began early and effortlessly," fueled in large part by the mystery surrounding her identity (46–47). Likewise, Glennis Stephenson's *Letitia Landon: The Woman Behind L.E.L.* (1995) — still the most thorough analysis of the poet's career — argues that the decision to start signing the poems "L.E.L." was "a clever marketing ploy: Landon was already packaging herself for consumption by what was soon to become a large and enthusiastic following" (25). More recently, Serena Baiesi claims in *Letitia Elizabeth Landon and Metrical Romance* (2010) that Landon's initials "immediately attract[ed] the curiosity of the reading public, which was anxious to know more about this mysterious contributor" (21). Julie Watt's new dual biography of the poet and her husband, George Maclean, argues that, like Byron, Landon "awoke one morning to find herself famous" and that her sensational popularity led to a sharp spike in the *Literary Gazette*'s circulation as early as 1823 (30–32). Rounding out the recent wave of scholarly studies, Susan Matoff's biography of Jerdan argues that as early as 1822 "L.E.L." became a widely recognized trademark and was thus "vital to the success and increased circulation of the *Literary Gazette*" (125).[11]

As compelling as this narrative might be — especially in light of the preceding chapter's account of the rising importance of authorial names in early-nineteenth-century literary marketing — it begins to crumble under scrutiny. The first major problem is that, quite simply, there was nothing remotely innovative or unusual in the early 1820s about signing a magazine poem with one's initials. In truth, appearing under real or fictive initials was rather common for Romantic-era magazine contributors of all stripes. During the autumn of 1821, when the *Literary Gazette* began regularly publishing poems signed "L.E.L.," *Blackwood's* routinely featured works by the Cockney-baiting essayist "Z." (primarily John Gibson

Lockhart) and the sentimental poet "Δ" (David Macbeth Moir). At the same time, the *London Magazine* was preparing for press the scandalous "Confessions of an English Opium-Eater" by the mysterious "X.Y.Z." (Thomas De Quincey). In the *Literary Gazette* itself, "initialists" appeared at every turn. On the very page of the 11 March 1820 issue in which Landon's first *Literary Gazette* poem, "Rome," appeared under the initial "L.," there are poems by "J.," "J.H.S.C.," "C.," and "J.F.H." In fact, in scanning the *Literary Gazette* for 1820 and 1821, one encounters a remarkable range of signing strategies, including full anonymity, onymity[12] (Bernard Barton signed his own name), pseudonymity (Charles Benjamin Tayler signed "Arthur Stanley"), pseudonymous initials ("B.C." is Barry Cornwall, the alias for Bryan Proctor), false initials ("J.L.S." is Edmund Reade), and literal initials ("L.E.L.").

The second major problem with unquestioningly rehearsing conventional narratives of Landon's overnight fame is that, setting aside the *Literary Gazette* and the misty-eyed and belated recollections of Landon partisans like Bulwer-Lytton and Blanchard, there is scant evidence that the literary world paid more than passing attention to "the mysterious L.E.L." prior to the publication of *The Improvisatrice* in the summer of 1824. If, as some have suggested, the original use of "L.E.L." was a marketing ploy modeled at least in part on Scott's "Great Unknown" and other Romantic-era experiments in veiled authorship, it can't be judged to be anything more than a half-hearted (or bungled) effort. Just weeks before her *Literary Gazette* poems started appearing under her full initials, Landon published her first book of poems, *The Fate of Adelaide*, using her full name on the title page but the initials L.E.L. in dedicating the volume to Mrs. Siddons.[13] Within the volume itself several poems are identified as having been previously published in the *Literary Gazette*. Thus, it would hardly have taken a master sleuth to ascertain the true identity of the L.E.L. whose works would soon begin appearing with some regularity in Jerdan's magazine, as it was out there for anyone curious enough to look into it.[14]

Moreover, if a cult following was indeed rising up around L.E.L. in the early 1820s, Landon and her agents would almost certainly have found a way to steer her fans toward *The Fate of Adelaide*. As is, though, the volume's sales were unremarkable, and there was never a second edition (Sypher, 52–53). Even harder to square with the narratives of instant and intense L.E.L.-mania is the fact that apparently none of Britain's major publishers displayed interest in publishing *The Improvisatrice* when Landon and Jerdan began shopping it around in late 1823. Reminiscing on her career in an 1837 letter to Samuel Carter Hall, Landon recalled: "The 'Improvisatrice' met with the usual difficulties attendant on a first attempt. It was refused by every publisher in London. Mr. Murray said peers only should write poetry; Longmans would not hear of it; Colburn declared poetry was quite out of his way; and for months it remained unpublished" (qtd. in S. C. Hall, *Book of Memories*, 267; see also Landon, *Letters*, 167–68).

If, then, British readers and critics of the early 1820s were neither keen on discovering L.E.L.'s true identity nor clamoring for a collection of her verse, one might at least expect them to have taken to the nation's dozens of literary-minded periodicals to weigh in on the new poetess who was suddenly ubiquitous in one of the age's premier magazines. Yet, when one scans periodicals published between September 1821 (the date of the first "L.E.L." poem) and July 1824 (when *The Improvisatrice* appeared) for evidence that the nation—or even London—was abuzz with talk of L.E.L., one comes up virtually empty-handed. In June 1823, the *Gentleman's Magazine* reprinted L.E.L.'s "Valedictory Lines to a Cadet on Embarking for India" from the *Literary Gazette* but neglected to offer any editorial comment on the author (636). The following January the same magazine silently reprinted "Lines on the Mausoleum of Princess Charlotte at Claremont," an L.E.L. poem that had appeared the previous month in the *Forget-Me-Not* for 1824. Digging even deeper, the 1 March 1824 issue of the *Repository of Arts* offers a brief review of John Hopkinson's *Introduction and Rondo for the Pianoforte, Composed, and Dedicated to Miss Landon*, but there is no indication whether the Miss Landon in question is, indeed, Letitia Elizabeth. Otherwise, the British periodical press was conspicuously silent on Jerdan's favorite new poet.

STAGING CELEBRITY

Of course, there was one exception to this pattern of silence surrounding L.E.L.: the *Literary Gazette*, which between 1822 and 1824 regularly noted the budding celebrity of its prized poetess. On 9 February 1822, four and half months after it published the first poem signed L.E.L., the magazine ran Bernard Barton's signed effusion, "To L.E.L. On his or her Poetic Sketches in the Literary Gazette." After opening by marveling at how L.E.L.'s briefest lyrics contained "more of Thought's best wealth, — / And Feeling's sweetest glowings" than "many a tome" (lines 3–4, 6), Barton closed the poem with the intriguing suggestion that somehow the poems' very anonymity, or "Minstrel stealth," created a powerful affective bond between poet and reader:

> I know not who, or what thou art;
> Nor do I seek to know thee,

> While Thou, performing thus thy part,
> Such banquets canst bestow me.
> Then be, as long as thou shalt list,
> My viewless, nameless Melodist.
>
> (lines 13–18)

At first blush, there's nothing particularly suspicious about this poem, as it falls into the time-honored tradition of one minor poet celebrating another. Even more reassuringly, Barton was widely known as "the Quaker poet," as he was the rare member of the Society of Friends willing to risk ostracism within his congregation by publishing verse. Yet, contrary to his public reputation as a courageous and deeply moral poet, Barton's correspondence from the early 1820s shows him to have had few scruples about bending industry ethics and protocols in his quest to trade his dreary life as a Suffolk bank clerk for that of a literary celebrity. During the winter of 1820 he repeatedly wrote Jerdan, whom he had never met, praising the *Literary Gazette* and imploring its editor to notice his new volume of poems in the magazine (Jerdan, *Autobiography*, 3:113–18). At the same time he was pestering Robert Southey to use his connections at the *Quarterly* to secure him a positive review from a "poetical Critic in Gifford's corps" (*Literary Correspondence*, 42). Most audaciously, in January 1822 Barton wrote Taylor and Hessey, publishers of the *London Magazine*, suggesting that he himself might review his poems in their magazine if they couldn't find another for the task. "The fact is," he explained, "that one half of the Critiques of my Poetry have contain'd little more than extracts from my own Notes sent with said Poetry to this, that or the other Journal; and such transplantation of ones [sic] own ideas might almost warrant any Poet in being his own Reviewer" (58). When Taylor declined this offer, Barton wrote Southey, with whom he had begun a correspondence, suggesting that his "best chance of fame" now lay in Southey's finding a way to make an "incidental allusion" to Barton's verse in his works. Seemingly cognizant that he was stooping to new lows, he closed the letter, "thus contingent are the opportunities a Minor Poet has of being famous" (60).

In this increasingly dispiriting period of Barton's life, Jerdan was the lone member of the London literary establishment to consistently take him and his works seriously. On 22 April 1820, the *Literary Gazette* published an effusive, nine-column review of Barton's *Poems*; and six months later, on 4 November, Jerdan ran an equally warm, five-column review of the poet's *A Day in Autumn*. Even more generously, in the 9 December 1820 issue of the *Literary Gazette*, Jerdan included a panegyric by the poet "X." titled "To Bernard Barton. On the publication of his last Poem, 'A day in Autumn.'" In the years to come, Jerdan continued feeding Barton's insatiable need for attention, prominently reviewing and advertising his new works, printing several of his original poems, and treating him as one of the *Gazette*'s house poets.

Not surprisingly, then, Barton felt deeply obligated to Jerdan. Add to this the fact that Barton and Jerdan are known to have carried on an extensive correspondence about the *Literary Gazette* during these years (Jerdan, *Autobiography*, 114–20), and there is ample reason to suspect that the "Quaker Bard's" querulous title, "To L.E.L. On his or her Poetic Sketches in the Literary Gazette," was more than a little staged. While Barton may indeed have greatly admired Landon's verse—the two soon became close friends and regular correspondents—it seems highly unlikely that he wouldn't have known even the gender of Jerdan's new poet when he wrote his poem in "his or her" honor. A clearer signal that Barton's poem may be more than just one poet's spontaneous and disinterested celebration of another is how Jerdan used its publication as the occasion to finally break his editorial silence regarding the *Gazette*'s new poetess. Jerdan appends Barton's poem with an exuberant response to its titular query about L.E.L.'s gender: "We have pleasure in saying that the sweet poems under this signature are by a lady, yet in her teens! The admiration with which they have been so generally read, could not delight their fair author more than it has those who in the *Literary Gazette* cherished her infant genius."

If we read this, as I suggest we should, as the first major advertisement of L.E.L.'s career, we can quickly discern that Jerdan is employing two techniques that were already relatively common in early-nineteenth-century literary advertising: the puff and the ruse of veiled authorship. What makes this poetical advertisement truly noteworthy, though, is its employment of a third, and much more original, technique: the bandwagon effect. While bandwagon marketing—or stimulating demand by creating the illusion that everyone in the know is buying a particular product—is a staple of modern advertising, it was rarely practiced and generally untheorized in the nineteenth century. In the 1890s, American journalists and politicians began speaking of "hopping on the bandwagon" for a certain candidate; but it wasn't until the 1940s that sociologists, psychologists, and political scientists identified the "bandwagon effect" and began seriously studying its impact on social behavior.[15] And yet, here we see Jerdan using the technique in 1822, to full effect. Simply put, the ultimate function of Barton's poem and Jerdan's editorial aside was less to represent, in high Romantic fashion, the private experience of a single reader than to cultivate the collective fervor of the general readership of the Literary Gazette. If we take the editor's report of the "admiration with which [L.E.L.'s poems] have been so generally read" at face value, the humble Quaker poet has given voice to a passion experienced by throngs of readers.

What Jerdan seems to have grasped at this early moment in Landon's career was that the mirage of literary celebrity could be every bit as effective at selling books and magazines as real celebrity. As a result, in the two-plus years between the publication of Barton's ode to L.E.L. and the July 1824 publication of *The Improvisatrice*, Jerdan regularly took to the pages of the Literary Gazette to propagate the fiction that a swarm of readers was clamoring for more works by the magazine's retiring poetess. On 15 February 1823, for instance, Jerdan published a second poem titled "To L.E.L.," this one signed "W.L.R."[16] The new poem features an aged speaker whose "wither'd heart" is stirred for the first time in years by L.E.L.'s "plaintive lyre." Perhaps consciously echoing Barton's line on the poetess's "witching melody," W.L.R. muses, "And when thy strain is o'er, I feel / As if some 'witching dream had vanish'd" (lines 13–14). The poem concludes by attempting to voice the collective experience of L.E.L.'s admirers:

> Long may the sorrows of thy song
> Be to thy guileless heart unknown;
> And whilst thou melt thy readers' hearts,
> May ev'ry bliss reign in thine own!
> (lines 21–24)

Rather than leaving it here, Jerdan once again felt the need to add his own editorial testament. "It is something like self-praise," his footnote to the poem demurely begins, "to admit into our columns any thing complimentary to what has appeared in them; but the many tributes we receive to the genius addressed in these lines will escape the censure, when we acknowledge them as due to a young and a female minstrel, and expressive of feelings very generally excited by her beautiful productions."

In the months that followed, Jerdan continued publishing Landon's poems in nearly every issue of his magazine, and on 6 December 1823 he proudly announced the imminent arrival of *The Improvisatrice*, a new collection of verse "by our own delightful minstrel L.E.L." As Landon's agent and confidante, he obviously was aware of the difficulties she had experienced finding a publisher for the volume, yet he persisted in his use of the bandwagon technique, once again rehearsing the fiction of a book-buying public clamoring for her works. He proclaimed, "The multitude of correspondents who have addressed us on the subject of collecting the poetry under the signature of L.E.L. into a volume, will thus shortly enjoy the gratification of an original poem from this admired writer, with other new compositions and selections" ("Periodical Publications," 781).

As the actual date of *The Improvisatrice*'s release approached, the puffery and bandwagon rhetoric only intensified. On 3 July 1824—five days before newspapers announced the book's publication and a week before any other periodical reviewed it—Jerdan devoted the first three pages of his magazine to an encomiastic review that boasts, "We can adduce no instance, ancient or modern, of similar talent and excellence" (Review of *The Improvisatrice* [*Gazette*], 417). Beneath this claim Jerdan inserted a seemingly random footnote reminding rival editors to be sure to note that L.E.L.'s verses originally appeared in the *Literary Gazette* when they inevitably quote from them in their reviews of *The Improvisatrice*. The note explains,

> The compositions of L.E.L., as they have appeared in the *Literary Gazette*, have been most universally copied to adorn their pages; and while our Journal alone was concerned, we were not over-desirous that they should quote the original: but now when the writer comes forward in her own person, justice, gallantry, and honour, demand that tribute which we are confident will be generally and cheerfully paid. (417)

At first glance, this is little more than an arcane reminder of industry courtesies; in reality, though, it is a stunningly audacious con. With the exception of the two poems reprinted in the *Gentleman's Magazine* (only one of which had originally appeared in the *Literary Gazette*), no major British periodical had reprinted or even mentioned L.E.L.'s magazine poems prior to this moment. Jerdan would have been fully cognizant of this fact, of course; he had no compunctions, however, about carrying forward the fiction that his colleagues had somehow flagrantly and "universally" extracted L.E.L.'s poems from the *Literary Gazette*.

In the week that followed, this ruse only intensified. As if on cue, just days after Jerdan's initial review appeared, Landon's publishers, Hurst and Robinson, began running newspaper advertisements for *The Improvisatrice* built almost entirely around one of the most effusive paragraphs from the *Literary Gazette*'s review of the book (see Figure 4.1). In this context, the words of Landon's discoverer, mentor, and principal cheerleader are allowed to function as an essentially objective endorsement of the book. As if this weren't enough, Jerdan saw fit to devote five more columns in the 10 July issue of his magazine to further extracts from and comments on L.E.L.'s poem. Once again, the dominant theme was that readers and reviewers everywhere were finding themselves caught up in L.E.L.-mania.

> This Day is Published, in foolscap 8vo. with Plates, price
> 10s. 6d. boards,
> THE IMPROVISATRICE, and other Poems.
> By L. E. L.
> "It will be expected from us that we speak of this volume in terms of the warmest admiration; because, if we had not thought very highly of the genius of its author, the pages of the Literary Gazette would not have been enriched with so many of her compositions. But indeed we are enthusiastic in this respect; and as far as our poetical taste and critical judgment enable us to form an opinion, we can adduce no instance, ancient or modern, of similar talent and excellence. We do not hesitate to say, that in our judgment this volume forms itself an era in our country's bright cycle of female poetical fame. What may spring from the continued cultivation of such promise it is not easy to predicate; but if the author never excels what she has already done, we can confidently give her the assurance of what the possession of such talents must most earnestly covet—immortality."—Literary Gazette, July 3.
> London: printed for Hurst, Robinson, and Co. 90, Cheapside, and 8, Pall mall. Of whom may be had,
> Watts' Poetical Sketches, 3d edition, 8s. boards.

Figure 4.1. Advertisement for *The Improvisatrice*. (*New Times*, 8 July 1824: 1.)

Jerdan rejoiced, "So far the public opinion has coincided with ours upon the genius of the author and the merits of this volume; for on the first day of its appearance nearly the whole of a large impression was rapidly disposed of, and other editions, we have not the slightest doubt, will follow in quick succession" (437). Given market realities, not to mention Jerdan's history of hyperbole when it came to Landon, the claims here invite skepticism. From the sluggish sales of *The Fate of Adelaide* and the fact that most of the day's major publishers apparently had questions about the demand for a book by L.E.L., it is doubtful that the original print run was as large as this account suggests. Moreover, if, as Jerdan reported, the first edition of *The Improvisatrice* nearly sold out on the day of publication, a second edition would most certainly have been ready in weeks, not the two and a half months it eventually took.[17] After all, in relatively recent memory, Murray had been able to supply Byron's frenzied readers with seven editions of *The Corsair* within a month and Constable had printed an enormous 5,000-copy second edition of Scott's *Guy Mannering* within three weeks of the book's original release.

When other periodicals began noticing *The Improvisatrice* in the ensuing weeks, they generally praised the poet's precociousness, sweetness, and feminine sensibility, and briefly mused on her semi-anonymity. (An amusing exception was *John Bull Magazine*, which in its July 1824 issue spoke knowingly of "Miss

Sandon's [sic] long promised poem" ["Prose Postscript," 38]). Only in the reviews published in late July and August—some weeks after Jerdan had declared Landon to be the talk of London—does one start to get a sense that the poet was indeed becoming a *cause de célèbre*. When reviews published during this span do acknowledge a prior familiarity with L.E.L., there's no suggestion she had already become a cult favorite through her mysterious initials and her seemingly ubiquitous poems in the *Literary Gazette*. In some cases, in fact, reviewers signal mild befuddlement over why Jerdan had so frequently given pride of place in his magazine to so unestablished a poet. In its otherwise positive review of *The Improvisatrice*, for instance, the *Literary Chronicle* wonders aloud whether L.E.L. had "written too much," as a result of being "overvalued" by the *Literary Gazette*, and confesses to having "trembled for the poetical reputation of L.E.L. . . . when we found her so frequently before the public" (Review of *The Improvisatrice* [*Chronicle*], 435). Even more stinging is a *Literary Magnet* review from late July, which blasts Jerdan for turning the genuinely promising L.E.L. into an overhyped sideshow. Rather than being a grassroots sensation with inherent popular appeal, it observes, L.E.L. had entered the public consciousness solely through "bare-faced puffing, and undisguised partiality" (Review of *The Improvisatrice* [*Magnet*], 106).[18]

All told, then, our standard notions that *The Improvisatrice* was, from the day of its release, one of the age's great literary sensations need serious qualification. With aggregate sales of more than 10,000 copies, the volume did eventually rank among the top twenty best-selling poetry books of the Romantic period (St. Clair, *Reading Nation*, 218, 615); but, outside the pages of the *Literary Gazette*, there is no evidence that the volume was either widely anticipated or immediately snatched up. In short, the popularity of both L.E.L. and her breakout book were widely reported fictions before they became reality. Accordingly, they represent remarkable early instances of successful bandwagon marketing and the manufactured media event.

L.E.L.'S VISUAL TURN

For Landon and Jerdan, the year following the release of *The Improvisatrice* must have felt like something out of a fairy tale. As if by magic, the make-believe world of swooning admirers, enraptured critics, and eager publishers they had long been pantomiming for readers of the *Literary Gazette* had suddenly become reality. If anything, sales of *The Improvisatrice* accelerated throughout the fall of 1824 and winter of 1825, with a total of six editions appearing within a year. At the same time, poems commemorating the beauties of L.E.L.'s verse were for the first time surfacing in magazines besides the *Literary Gazette*,[19] and rumors began surfacing of L.E.L. impostors attempting to capitalize on her fame.[20] Perhaps most tellingly, British wags and wits began making L.E.L. a punch line in their squibs on the fashions of the day. In their popular satirical collection *Odes and Addresses to Great People* (published in February 1825), Thomas Hood and John Hamilton Reynolds lumped the L.E.L. craze with the age's other great fads, asking "And, truly, is there such a spell / In those three letters, L. E. L., / To witch a world with song?" ("Ode to Mr. Graham, The Aeronaut," lines 127–29). The following August the *London Magazine* published a 96-line mock-ode to the "LYRIC encomiast of Love," contrasting the airy visions and "bedazzled" vistas of L.E.L.'s verse with the humdrum realities of industrial London ("Ode to L.E.L."). More splenetically, in the 10 May 1826 issue of the *Star Chamber*, the young Benjamin Disraeli groused that, after failing under her own name, Landon resorted to the gimmickry of initials and thus became "a sub-urban Sappho, foundress of the INITIAL SCHOOL, the pet-lamb of Magazinery, and the peculiar poetess of sentimental ladies'-maids" (82).[21]

Not surprisingly, given Jerdan's recurring descriptions of her nubile beauty and the poet's self-representation as a lovelorn nymph, much of this first wave of L.E.L.-mania took on thinly veiled sexual overtones. As Anne Mellor, Richard Cronin, and Patrick Vincent have observed, Landon's poems openly invited the male gaze, and gaze they did (Mellor, 107–21; Cronin, 82–92; Vincent, 110). In *Blackwood's*, the amorous Irishman William Maginn—who by some reports was so smitten with Landon that he spontaneously proposed to her in the early 1820s (Sypher, 63, 66)—used his review of *The Improvisatrice* as occasion to further his flirtations. Near the outset Maginn teases, "Now it is not because she is a very pretty girl, and a very good girl, that we are going to praise her poems, but because we like them" (190). After insisting that she was "the cleverest girl in print," he closed by hoping that "all the *bon-bons* which have been distributed to her with unwonted liberality by the stern censors of books, will not spoil her" (193). Later in the same issue, *Blackwood's* semifictional editor, Christopher North, announced that he was pulling his Irish staffer, Morgan Odoherty (another semifictional creation), off the Landon review, as one couldn't expect a clear-eyed assessment from a critic who was "half in love with the damsel concerned" (Lockhart, "Noctes Ambrosianae No. XVI," 238). Even more over-the-top is the *Attic Miscellany*'s review of *The Improvisatrice*, in which the critic takes on the persona of an "old and hoary-headed" man who, despite his diminished virility, finds himself "no more able to resist the seductions of her style than the attraction of her eyes." After being wooed by Landon's "voluptuous music" and luxuriating in her "sails purpled and perfumed," the reviewer is too sexually spent to offer anything but generic praise for this "charming young lady, whose poetry is as liquid and flowing as her name" (Review of *The Improvisatrice* [*Attic Miscellany*], 150).

It wasn't only besotted reviewers, however, who came to view Landon as a sex symbol. In the mid-1820s the poet apparently had to endure several would-be wooers who had fallen in love with her L.E.L. persona. On Christmas Day of 1825, she bemusedly wrote her friend Katherine Thomson about the discomposing effect her presence had had on one of her young admirers at a recent dinner party. "I acted upon him like an air-pump," she chuckles, "suspending his very breath and motion; and my asking him for a mince-pie, a dish of which I had been for some time surveying with longing eyes, acted like an electric shock—and his start not a little discomposed a no-age-at-all, silk-vested spinster, whose plate was thereby deposited in her lap." She goes on to report taking particular delight in sensational accounts of her romantic conquests: "One young lady heard at Scarborough last summer, that I had had two hundred offers; and a gentleman at Leeds brought an account of three hundred and fifty straight from London. It is really very fortunate that my conquests should so much resemble the passage to the North Pole and Wordsworth's Cuckoo, 'talked of but never seen'" (qtd. in Blanchard, *Life*, 46–47).

By today's standards, Landon's honeymoon period with readers and reviewers was relatively long, lasting through the protracted media campaigns for *The Improvisatrice* and *The Troubadour* (published in July 1825). By the autumn of 1826, however, as she prepared to release her fourth book of poems, *The Golden Violet*, there were signs that the previously successful promotional blend of puffery, bandwagoning, and sex appeal was wearing thin. In its 22 October 1826 review of the *Forget Me Not* for 1827, an annual gift book featuring Landon and other popular writers, the *Atlas* complained that the L.E.L. gambit increasingly felt mercenary and even tawdry. In a remarkable passage that warrants quotation in full, the critic laments that L.E.L. has become so completely commodified that there is no longer even a veneer of artistic integrity about her and her work:

> We wish to say nothing harsh of a female, and she too a female of talent; it is likewise hard that a lady should suffer for the indiscretions of her friends. But, for interested purposes, the modicum of talent which Miss LANDON possesses has been so puffed and placarded, that she must pardon us if her very initials warn us off her game like notices of "men-traps and spring-guns." For her own

sake, she should not only husband the power she has, but she should withdraw herself, if possible, from the retailers of small verse, who, to sell their wares, are for ever puffing the inventor of the article. It is the practice of the tradesman who takes up a "patent" commodity, to be for ever advertising [to] the world of the wonderful ingenuity of the patentee. It may be not disagreeable to the man who renders a hat impenetrable to rain to see his praises plastered at the top of every other man's head; or to Mr. Hodges or Mr. Deady, the compounders of the cordial British gin, which far surpasses all other genera of gin, to be lauded by drunken tipplers in dram-shops; but to a young lady like Miss L.E.L., it must be odious to be bedaubed by the venal and dirty paragraphs of ****** and *******. Another melancholy thing as regards L.E.L. is, that she is stimulated to write when she is written out—to pump up not merely the last dregs of her poetry, but to destroy the very engine itself, by pumping a vacuum. (Review of *Forget Me Not*, 362)

This caustic assessment of what the once vibrant L.E.L. was fast becoming set the tone for several subsequent reviews of *The Golden Violet*. Seizing upon the *Literary Gazette*'s recent boast that in the early 1820s Landon had single-handedly revived poetry at a time when even "the writings of Byron himself were published without exciting a nine days' sensation" (Review of *The Golden Violet* [*Gazette*], 785), the *Inspector* argued that L.E.L. was, in fact, the most generic, monotonous, and ephemeral of contemporary poets. "She writes too fast and too much to write for posterity," the reviewer insists, and "nobody remembers a line of [her poems] next week" (Review of *The Golden Violet* [*Inspector*], 244). The *Monthly Review* concurred, suggesting that her poems were increasingly marked with "a sameness, a monotony of sighs and lamentations, which has become perfectly irksome" (Review of *The Golden Violet* [*Monthly*], 60). In 1827 the satirist Robert Montgomery dubbed her "the verse-manufacturer for every magazine, review, and journal" (*The Age Reviewed*, 147), and a year later a newspaper wag included in his list of recent bankruptcies a notice for "Miss Landon, dealer in lines, Literary Gazette. Solicitor, Wm. Jerdan" ("Bankruptcies Extraordinary," 37).

Clearly, then, as the 1820s wore on, it was time for a rebranding of the L.E.L. franchise and a corresponding overhaul of its long-time advertising strategies. One of the most basic shifts Landon made was diversifying her publication venues and genres. In yet another display of her (and likely Jerdan's) commercial savvy, Landon was one of the earliest poets to go all-in on what would become the most successful site for original poetry of the late 1820s and 1830s, the illustrated annual. If during the first half of the 1820s L.E.L. was metonymous with the *Liter-*

ary Gazette, during the ensuing decade she became the face of the annuals and gift books phenomenon, penning dozens of original poems for various editions and eventually editing four separate annuals (*Fisher's Drawing Room Scrapbook, The Easter Gift, Heath's Book of Beauty*, and *Bijou Almanac*). Beyond this, as the market for single-authored collections of verse steadily eroded in the wake of the Crash of 1826, Landon began refashioning herself as a society novelist, publishing *Romance and Reality* in 1831, *Francesca Carrara* in 1834, and *Ethel Churchill* in 1837.

In terms of image management, however, Landon's most original move during the latter half of her career was morphing from the mysterious poetess perpetually hidden behind her initials into a bona fide icon whose likeness was scattered far and wide throughout the empire. In effect, Landon ditched veiled authorship, a stratagem somewhat tired (in the wake of Scott and a host of imitators) and only marginally effective (in that there was never a great deal of speculation over L.E.L.'s true identity), in favor of the much fresher, more inventive approach of catering to an increasingly visual society.

As many cultural, literary, and art historians have documented, the early nineteenth century saw remarkable shifts in the availability of and emphasis on visual images. Of course, the "birth of visual culture" occurred only after a long gestation period, highlights of which include the often ingeniously illustrated broadsides of the English Civil War and the Hogarthian prints and woodcut and copper engravings of the early eighteenth century.[22] On the heels of these key developments, the Romantic Century witnessed an explosion of visually oriented entertainments, exhibitions, and publications. In London alone, this era saw the opening of the British Museum (1759), Christie's auction house (1762), the Royal Academy (1768), the British Institution (1805), and the National Gallery (1824) (Simonsen, 13; Rovee, ch. 2). For the down-market crowd, there was everything from Madame Tussaud's to Punch-and-Judy shows to the "Belzoni's Tomb" exhibition of recently exhumed Egyptian mummies (G. Wood, 1–7). Even the pornography industry, it seems, is an invention of this era, as it was only in the 1820s and 1830s that, in Bradford Mudge's words, "graphic images or narratives" were "mass-produced for the sexual use of their consumers" (para. 3; see also McCalman, 205–20).

Perhaps the strongest indications of British society's visual turn, however, came in the world of print. Employing copperplate engraving techniques, the *Observer* utilized illustrations more extensively and effectively than any previous newspaper, reaching particular heights in the early 1820s with its depictions of Queen Caroline's trial and George IV's coronation. In 1832 George Knight brought illustrated journalism to the masses with his wildly popular *Penny Magazine*, and in 1842 the *Illustrated London News* achieved the previously unthinkable in commissioning, creating, and printing highly topical woodcuts within a twenty-four-hour news cycle (M. Jackson, 77–78; Tucker, 111; Brake and Demoor, 1–3). Reflecting on this revolution, Andrew Wynter remarked in 1868, "Thirty years ago Cruikshank's capital woodcut of the cat seeing herself reflected, and spitting at the boot [see Chapter 3], stood almost alone; but now the country papers teem with woodcuts in the advertising department" ("The Art," 735).[23]

However rapidly illustrations evolved in mid-nineteenth-century periodicals, the most technologically advanced images of the era came in art books, annuals, and illustrated editions of novels and verse, which used such recent innovations as stereotyping, steel-plate engraving, mechanical papermaking, and the steam-powered press to produce high-quality images at a relatively reasonable price (Thomas, 354–55). These advances, combined with the number of preeminent artists who tried their hand at illustrating books, led the historian of illustration Edward Hodnett to call the early nineteenth century "the great period of English book illustration" (107). So prevalent did illustration become in the world of letters, in fact, that several major writers—including Wordsworth, Lamb, and Southey—expressed fears that, for the average reader, the image was supplanting the word as the principal selling point of a book. As numerous scholars have suggested, the Romantics, at least partly in reaction to this threat, crafted an aesthetic that was wary of, if not outright hostile toward, visual experience (Galperin, 19–25; G. Wood, 6–7, 171–72; Simonsen, 1–16; Thomas, 354–55).

At the same time that many of her poetic peers were subscribing to the Wordsworthian notion that the eye is the "most despotic of our senses" (*Prelude* [1805], 11:171–76), Landon was taking an entirely opposite tack, embracing visual culture more enthusiastically than perhaps any other major literary figure of the late Romantic age. From the very beginning of her career, she had showed an intense fascination with the visual arts. In fact, skimming through her early magazine poems, one finds as many ekphrastic musings on classical statues and contemporary portraits as lyrics on disappointed love. If anything, as McGann and Riess have pointed out, "Landon specialized in writing 'poetical sketches' for the *Gazette*—that is, poems on the subject of paintings and mass-produced engravings of contemporary artists" (12). Moreover, this interest in art wasn't just professional or opportunistic; whenever possible, even when traveling outside the capital, Landon sought out portrait shows (*Letters*, 32–35), and in July 1826 she confided to Thomson that, should she ever become independently wealthy, she would take up portrait-painting (30). Indeed, so deep was Landon's interest in the visual arts that by the mid-1820s Jerdan had apparently designated her the *Literary Gazette's* chief art critic, a remarkable opportunity for a Romantic-era woman (and one in her early twenties, at that) (Sypher, 60).[24]

Given how immersed Landon was in the visual culture of her age, it is little surprise that when the veiled poetess stratagem started to lose its novelty she and Jerdan began exploring iconographic means of reclaiming the public's interest. The result was a remarkable series of portraits of her, many widely reproduced as prints and engravings. These disseminated carefully staged and highly symbolic likenesses of Landon far and wide between the late 1820s and the early 1840s.[25] The first known portrait of the poet was painted by the well-known artist H. W. Pickersgill at the peak of Landon's early fame and was being exhibited at the Royal Academy in the late spring of 1825. It is unclear exactly how this painting came about, but, given Pickersgill's longstanding interest in poetic subjects—among his best-known paintings at the time were portraits of Hannah More and George Crabbe and scenes from Robert Bloomfield and Walter Scott—it is likely that he approached Landon rather than vice versa. Apparently, Landon and Jerdan didn't initially conceive of the portrait as an advertisement, for the painting was never engraved until after Landon's death, when Henry Robinson issued a considerably altered version of Pickersgill's original (see Figure 4.2).[26] That said, appearing as it did when the initial wave of interest in *The Improvisatrice* and its semi-mysterious poet remained strong, the painting attracted unusual attention in the British press. The *Literary Chronicle* for 14 May 1825 was pleased with the "touch of the romantic in her appearance" and confessed, "we should have been half angry had we found that the fair minstrel looked like a demure dowdy" ("Exhibition," 318). Two weeks later, the *Literary Gazette* hailed the portrait as "among the happiest efforts of the truly able artist's pencil" ("Fine Arts," 347). Even the *Literary Magnet*, which had led the charge against Jerdan's puffing of L.E.L., conceded: "The absence of all affectation in the portrait of a successful author is by no means an usual circumstance. We had expected something that would remind us of the 'love-lost Sappho,' or the fancifully vivid looks of Mrs. Tighe, but were agreeably disappointed" ("Fine Arts: Exhibition at Somerset House," 45).

Ironically, the first widely published portrait of L.E.L. was not part of a carefully staged promotion but was a thoroughly imaginary, unauthorized engraving that appeared as the frontispiece to Richard Ryan's 1826 collection, *Poets and Poetry: Being a Collection of the Choicest Anecdotes Relative to the Poets of Every Age and Nation* (see Figure 4.3). Reviewing Ryan's volume in the *Literary Gazette* for 31 March 1827, Jerdan complained: "We must remonstrate against the

Figure 4.2. Henry Robinson's engraving of H. W. Pickersgill's 1825 portrait of Landon. The ostentatious hat is apparently Robinson's addition. (Frontispiece to vol. 3 of the *Autobiography of William Jerdan*.)

pseudo portrait of L.E.L. as a frontispiece to one of the volumes. It is a sheer invention, and must belong, if to any one, to some other lady. It was wrong to palm, for the sake of attraction, so gratuitous a forgery upon the public" (Review of *Poets and Poetry*, 197–98).

While neither of the two L.E.L. portraits from the 1820s, then, was produced at the poet's behest for promotional purposes, Jerdan and Landon must have taken their commission and reception as indications of a public appetite for images of the poet. Consequently, beginning in the early 1830s, they began actively working to make L.E.L. iconic in the broadest senses of the word. To begin with,

Figure 4.3. Adam Buck's "pseudo portrait" of L.E.L (1826). (Frontispiece to vol. 2 of Richard Ryan's *Poets and Poetry*.)

Landon sat for a second portrait by Pickersgill. Little is known of this painting, as it appears to have disappeared until an engraving of it by a C. Cook appeared in *Bentley's Miscellany* in 1848 (see Figure 4.4).

It was during this period that Landon met Daniel Maclise, the up-and-coming Irish painter who, over the course of the 1830s, would do more than any other artist to establish an iconography surrounding L.E.L. Soon after the twenty-one-

Figure 4.4. C. Cook's engraving of H. W. Pickersgill's second portrait of Landon. (*Bentley's Miscellany* 23 [1848]: 532.)

year-old Maclise came from his native Cork to London in 1827, he fell in with S. C. Hall, William Maginn, and other members of Landon and Jerdan's circle of Tory artists, writers, and socialites. The poet and the painter quickly bonded, and in the summer of 1830 Maclise unveiled his first portrait of her at the Royal Academy. The painting, which has apparently since been lost, failed to impress the critic at the *Belle Assemblée* magazine, who complained that it "convey[ed] the idea of a figure of almost twice the dimensions of L.E.L." ("Fine Arts Exhibitions," 40). The *Dublin Literary Gazette*, however, praised the portrait for uniting "delicacy and strength" ("Lady's Letter," 315), and, not surprisingly, the *Literary Gazette* warmly complimented both the painter and his subject. "Merely as a work of art," Jerdan's magazine opined, "this drawing would do great credit to the artist; but it is much more: it is a faithful resemblance of one whose genius, whether displayed in the descriptive, the imaginative, or the philosophical, has held captive the attention, and elicited the admiration, of all who are capable of feeling the beauties of fine poetical composition" ("Fine Arts: Exhibition of the Royal Academy," 402–3).

By far the most important portrait of Landon from the early 1830s, however, was a Maclise sketch that appeared in *Fraser's* "Gallery of Literary Characters" in October 1833 (see Figure 4.5). Being commissioned by Maginn, *Fraser's* de facto editor, to draw the eighty-one portraits in this series was Maclise's big break, and his perceptive and highly individualized depictions of virtually every major literary figure of the day warrant recognition as the highpoint in late-Romantic literary iconography.[27] In each case, Maclise's portrait accompanied a brief prose sketch, most of which were written by Maginn in his trademark irreverent style. For whatever reason, Landon's was one of the five life sketches Maginn delegated to his and Maclise's fellow Corkonian Francis Mahony (Higgins, 66–70). Clearly, though, Mahony, who had arrived in London only months earlier, took guidance from Maginn on his description of Landon, as the sketch in many ways reads like a sequel to the flirtatious review of *The Improvisatrice* Maginn had written for *Blackwood's* nearly a decade earlier. Although now thirty-one years old, Landon is presented as still being in the full bloom of youth and, despite her immense fame, is said to remain "a very nice, unbluestockingish, well-dressed, and trim-looking young lady." Rejecting critics' complaints about the sameness of Landon's poetry, Mahony's piece argues that she chose wisely in sticking to love: "Can there be too much of love in a young lady's writings? . . . Is she to write of politics, or political economy, or pugilism, or punch? . . . [S]he does right in thinking that Sappho knew what she was about when she chose the tender passion as the theme for woman" (Mahony, 433).

Maclise's sketch corresponds exactly with this description. The nearly middle-aged Landon here appears positively girlish, with radiant eyes, delicate hands and feet, a waspish waist, and such emblems of polite adolescent recreations as a ballroom glove, a well-bound book, and a sprig from a nearby bouquet. Years later, Dante Gabriel Rossetti, a fervent admirer of Maclise, marveled at how in this portrait the artist "allow[ed] himself to render character by playful exaggeration of the most obvious kind." Rossetti went on to note how "the kitten-like *mignonnerie* required is attained by an amusing excess of daintiness in the proportions, with the duly charming result nevertheless" (Rossetti, 218). By portraying Landon as this paragon of youthful charm, beauty, and innocence, Maclise not only indulged in bit of flattery toward his friend (and possible lover[28]), but he also offered a direct riposte to two sets of malignant rumors about Landon.

Figure 4.5. Daniel Maclise's second portrait of Landon. (*Fraser's* 8 [October 1833]: 433.)

The first of these was that the long ballyhooed beauty of L.E.L. was actually something of a sham and that in reality, as one rumor reported in the *Dublin Literary Gazette* had it, she was rather "ugly" ("Original Correspondence," 157). James Hogg, a literary veteran whose personal experiences left him as aware as anyone of the frequent gap between what magazines reported of an author and the truth, confessed to having held similar doubts about Landon's actual beauty before meeting her. By S. C. Hall's account, when Hogg was first introduced to Landon, he looked her over for half a minute before bursting out: "Eh, I didna think ye'd been sae bonnie! I've said many hard things aboot ye. I'll do sae nae mair" (*Book*, 273).

More important than substantiating Landon's beauty, though, was portraying her as such a paragon of virginal femininity that readers could never imagine her being guilty of the sexual libertinism with which she was frequently charged by her and Jerdan's enemies. Rumors about alleged affairs dogged Landon from the mid-1820s forward, and she and her friends vehemently proclaimed her innocence. Twentieth-century scholars almost unanimously took Landon's side, portraying her as the victim of a venal press hunting for scandal and finding an easy target in an attractive young woman whose recurring themes were passion and remorse (Stephenson, 36; Mellor, 120–21). Since 2000, however, when Cynthia Lawford published compelling evidence that Landon and Jerdan did indeed carry on a fifteen-year-long affair that resulted in at least three carefully concealed children, these rumors have taken on much more credence ("Diary").

The earliest known published hints of a Landon-Jerdan affair came in the *Sunday Times* for 5 March 1826, which reported that "a well-known English Sappho" had not only been "detected in a *faux pas* with a literary man" but had apparently given birth to his child (qtd. in Sypher, 81–82). Later that year the *Wasp* reported that Landon had mysteriously left town and returned several months later considerably thinner (qtd. in Stephenson, 36). The most extensive attacks on Landon's reputation, however, came in the *Royal Lady's Magazine*, a monthly specializing in, of all things, horticulture and fashion. In its "Editor's Room" column of February 1831, the magazine alleges: "Miss Letitia Elizabeth Landon was not only cradled in the *Literary Gazette*, but has been dry-nursed by it, ever since her poetic birth. Moreover, the said young Lady, and the Editor of the *Literary Gazette*, have occasionally written desperate verses to each other in its columns" (107). The attacks became even more pointed in December 1831, when the *Royal Lady's* mused, "It is very strange (and we only mention it on that account), but it *is* very strange (and therefore we cannot help mentioning it), that L.E.L. and Mr. Jerdan should be so fond of writing about scandal and little children" ("Titled Authors," *1831*, 343). Finally, in June 1832, the magazine sunk to a new low with "The Lament: A Poetical Dialogue between L.E.L. and W. Jerdan, in the Manner of Both." In her portions of the dialogue, L.E.L. complains of the heartbreak she has endured in forsaking the children her "Willy" has given her. Touched by his beloved's sighs, Jerdan promises:

Then grieve no more—for here I swear—
(Nay, smile, my love, you must—)
I'll give again whate'er I've given,
As freely as at first.
                              (Coppinger, lines 21–24)[29]

So widespread was gossip about Landon and Jerdan's affair that even foreign periodicals began taking their shots. In 1834, for instance, drawing upon news just in from Captain John Ross's Arctic expeditions, the *North American Magazine* ribaldly quipped:

> A lake and a river having been discovered in the Polar Regions by Captain Ross, he named the one Lake Landon, after Miss L.E.L., and the other Jerdan River, in compliment to William Jerdan, of the London Literary Gazette. Jerdan River runs into Lake Landon. Captain Ross should have known that his nomenclature had been anticipated, and that his discovery in the Arctic Circles was, long ago, known in England. ("Table Talk," 358)[30]

Needless to say, after a series of such gibes, any attempt to restore Landon's maidenly reputation via visual advertisements would require more than just a single magazine portrait. Consequently, in the years following Maclise's *Fraser's* sketch, Landon and Jerdan commissioned several additional portraits, all of which laid heavy emphasis on her youth, beauty, and innocence. For her 1835 collection of poems, *The Vow of the Peacock*, they for the first time decided to include a likeness of her as a frontispiece, commissioning Maclise again for the task. Maclise's new portrait (Figure 4.6) picked up right where his 1833 *Fraser's* illustration left off in imbuing L.E.L. with all the trappings of conventional maidenhood. As before, she comes off as dainty, demure, and significantly younger than her actual age (then 33), but, if anything, there's a heightened emphasis on her thoroughgoing modesty. In contrast to the fashionably low necklines and bare shoulders featured in her earlier portraits, here Landon wears a billowy, floor-length gown and a full-sized bonnet. While with her long neck and hourglass figure she remains conventionally attractive, the portrait conveys an unmistakable message about the poet's wholesomeness and virtue.

Another portrait from this period is Henry Weekes's medallion keepsake of the poet (see Figure 4.7). If Maclise's Landon is a model of sexual modesty, Weekes's verges on sexual apathy. Dressed far less elegantly than in her earlier portraits and offering little more than an indifferent stare, the demure poet here displayed

Figure 4.6. Daniel Maclise's frontispiece to Landon's *Vow of the Peacock* (1835).

bears no resemblance to the promiscuous and coquettish L.E.L. of the gossip columns. While John William Wright's 1837 portrait for the *New Monthly Magazine* (see Figure 4.8) imbues Landon with a bit more energy and style, there is again a clear sense of reserve. Slightly older than previous L.E.L.s, Wright's version conveys placidity, wisdom, and tenderness.[31] Perhaps thinking these likenesses had gone too far, reducing Landon to something of a cipher, Maclise made what turned out to be a final image of the poet in 1837 (see Figure 4.9). One of the great literary portraits of the era, this engraving showcases both the artist's skill and the subject's spirit. Although more elaborately attired than in Maclise's previous portrait, Landon is again fully covered, showing a minimum of skin. The

Figure 4.7. Henry Weekes's medallion portrait of L.E.L. (Courtesy of the New York Public Library's Digital Gallery [ca. late 1800s].)

conventional modesty ends there, however; with her cocked right arm and firm gaze, this is a woman fully at ease with herself and in control of her world. This image was quickly embraced as the definitive likeness of Landon, and to this day it remains the most widely reproduced image of the poet.[32]

Tallying it up, then, while only two portraits (one unauthorized) of Landon appeared in the 1820s, at least six were commissioned in the 1830s, leaving little doubt that she and Jerdan consciously pursued this new promotional strategy as her career wore on. Although Landon certainly wasn't the first author to use her likeness as an advertising tool—think of Byron's Albanian portrait or Mary Robinson's "Perdita" images—arguably no author to this point in literary history

Figure 4.8. John William Wright's portrait of Landon. (*New Monthly Magazine* 50 [1837]: 78.)

showed so clear an awareness of the power of iconography in self-promotion. Moreover, Landon was on the cutting edge not only of literary marketing but of advertising in general. Prior to the repeal of the stamp taxes in the 1850s and 1860s, British advertising remained overwhelmingly verbal (Nevett, *Advertising*, 44; Elliott, 170–71). As the *Westminster Review* lamented in 1830, American newspapers, unburdened by advertising and paper duties, were far outpacing their British counterparts in visual advertising: "In the American papers scarcely an advertisement appears without some engraving of a character adapted to the nature of the announcement, and the practice, although not very chaste to us, who are accustomed to see advertisements set in the smallest type, and crowded together so as to be almost lost, is found to be very useful to the advertiser" (Merle, 101). To some extent, British advertisers were able to overcome these restrictions by using trade cards, handbills, and street posters. Tellingly, though, what is usually considered the first great visual advertising campaign in British history—the brilliantly illustrated advertisements for Pears' soap—did not arrive until late in the Victorian age (Elliott, 174).

Figure 4.9. Daniel Maclise's final portrait of Landon (1837). (From G. N. Wright, ed., *The Gallery of Engravings*, vol. 1 of 3, London: Fisher, Son, and Co., between pp. 18 and 19.)

Thus, Landon and Jerdan were well ahead of the curve in embracing graphic advertising. That this fact wasn't lost on the satirists of their age is evidenced in a long-forgotten volume titled *The Poetical March of Humbug!* Stealing a page from William Frederick Deacon's *Warreniana* (see Chapter 3), this satirical volume pretends to publish applications for the open position as chief writer of advertising jingles for Warren's Blacking. Alongside parodic submissions from Wordsworth, Coleridge, Southey, Caroline Norton, and other famous poets is one titled "The False Hussar. By L.E.L." The volume's first mention of L.E.L., however, comes several pages earlier, in the second stanza of its opening parody, "The Omnipresence of Humbug. By Robert Montgomery, Esq." Mimicking the scorched-earth style of Montgomery's satire, the poem proclaims:

> Chief in the ranks of Humbugs and Empyrics,
> Tall Jerdan stands who wrote low "London Lyrics;". . . .
> Arch puffer, hail! and with thee, L.E.L.,—
> For who'd of one without the other tell?—
> 'Tis hard to say where greater store you set,
> Upon her,—in thy study or Gazette;—
> Since, puffed on canvas and on paper too,
> Her verses here, her picture there we view.
> (*Poetical March*, lines 13–14, 19–24)

This point about the puffing of L.E.L. "on canvas and on paper too" is driven home later in the volume in Robert Seymour's illustration "The Editor of the Literary Gazette and L.E.L., or, 'Puff' and His Protégée" (see Figure 4.10).[33] Set in Jerdan's study, the great man of letters is seen engaging in his three favorite pursuits: puffing a cigar, puffing his poet, and ogling a portrait of L.E.L. Surprisingly, Jerdan took this portrait in good fun. In a generally admiring review of *The Poetical March of Humbug!* in the 11 August 1832 number of his magazine, he suggested that the only fault in the book was that "the Editor of the *Literary Gazette* is represented as a great smoker of cigars and a worshipper of pretty portraits; whereas, to our knowledge, he abhors tobacco in any of its forms, and prefers fair originals to the most beautiful pictures" (Review of *Poetical March*, 505).

Perhaps by this point Jerdan had given up rebutting the accusations of puffery and may even have started to embrace his reputation for being more gifted as a promoter than as a man of letters. Fittingly, the last essay Jerdan published in his long and colorful career was a testimonial to the powers of advertising. Appearing in the March 1869 number of *Fraser's*, just months before he passed away at the age of 87, Jerdan's "The Grand Force!" begins with a parable in which a respected professor of engineering is stumped when asked to name a mechanical force that is at once "substantial without weight," "capable of moving all creation," and "magical and cabalistic." Much to the professor's consternation, the answer is not steam, wind, or water, but "THE ADVERTISEMENT!" This distinctively modern power, the article insists, "can sell millions of yards of shoddy for honest broadcloth," "cleanse the Augean stable of millions of boxes and bottles of quack medicine," and "keep up, for hundreds of nights without intermission,

Figure 4.10. "The Editor of the Literary Gazette and L.E.L." (*The Poetical March of Humbug!*, [1832], 13.)

the heaviest tomfoolery and outrageous performances at the theatres" (380–81). "Ten thousand pounds spent on advertising," Jerdan proclaims, "is the way to make twenty thousand," and all great merchants would do well to adopt the Macbethean motto, "Double, double, puff and bubble, / Well will it repay the trouble!" (382).

CHAPTER 5

Puffery and the "Death" of Literature in Late-Romantic Britain

In 1822 one of America's most outspoken nationalists, James Kirke Paulding, published *A Sketch of Old England, by a New England Man*. Conceived as a rejoinder to British travel narratives that routinely characterized the United States as backward and lawless, Paulding's *Sketch* portrays England as a fallen titan whose industry, government, and culture are in shambles. Emblematic for Paulding of the Old Country's demise is the moral decay of the literary book trade. Once the nation's proudest cultural institution, literature, as Paulding saw it, has become merely another branch of British industrial manufactory, slavishly devoted to the bottom line and "overstocked with workmen." "It is inconceivable," his Yankee traveler sneers, "what a vast literary taste there is in England, that is to say, a taste for literary scandal, tittle tattle, reviewing, and magazining" (2:87). Of all the corrupt branches of Britain's literary system, Paulding casts book reviewing as the blackest. Nine of ten reviews in British periodicals, he reports, "originate in personal, political, and religious antipathies or attachments" (2:88). That such shameless practices thrive in the Old Country is astonishing enough, but what most appalls Paulding's narrator is that "they don't mind these things here, where it is almost as common for an author to puff his own book in the magazines, as for a quack doctor to be his own trumpeter in the newspapers" (2:88).

Given Paulding's pronounced Anglophobia, it is obviously tempting to dismiss his report as little more than spirited jingoism; yet several of his allegations, specifically those concerning book reviewing in the mother country, are consonant with what many Britons themselves were saying during the Romantic period. In his introductory essay to the *Watchman* (1796), for instance, Samuel Taylor

Coleridge lamented: "So many and so varying are the writers employed by the proprietary Booksellers, that it is hardly possible for an author, whose literary acquaintance is even moderately large, to publish a work which shall not be flattered in some one of the reviews by a personal friend, or calumniated by an enemy" (15). A year later the *Telegraph* published a list of forty-two authors, politicians, and socialites—including, most notably, Mary Robinson and William Beckford—who "pay to have themselves puffed in the Newspapers" ("List"). And in 1826 the pseudonymous author "One Master Trimmer" bluntly proclaimed, "Reviews . . . are nothing now but vehicles for puffing off trash books" (4).

While several literary historians have studied the role of puffery in eighteenth-century British culture (see Chapter 2), relatively little scholarly notice has been paid to its proliferation in the early nineteenth century and to its wide-ranging commercial and cultural consequences. At least part of this neglect can be attributed to the more generalized neglect of Romantic-era book reviewing. In recent decades, scholars such as Jon P. Klancher and Mark Parker have rigorously explored the cultural importance of late-eighteenth- and early-nineteenth-century literary periodicals, and several others have provided detailed studies of individual journals like the *Edinburgh Review* and the *Quarterly Review*.[1] Still, John O. Hayden's *The Romantic Reviewers, 1802–1824* (1969) remains the only book-length attempt to provide a systematic overview of early-nineteenth-century reviewing practices. And, like most less-comprehensive studies, Hayden's book provides only brief glimpses of the underworld of Romantic reviewing, generally adopting an apologetic stance toward the subject rather than "indulg[ing] in undue condescension" (3).[2] Elsewhere in scholarly studies of High Romanticism one occasionally encounters references to isolated cases of insider reviewing, but even the most skeptical scholars often treat the average review article from this era as inherently objective, and few show an awareness of how deeply ingrained puffery had become in early-nineteenth-century literary culture.[3]

The aim of this chapter is to redress this gap in the scholarly record, offering both a general overview of the "age of puffery," as the *Westminster Review* took to calling the era ("Puffing, and *The Puffiad*," 441), and an analysis of puffery's wide-reaching impact on literary production and consumption in the latter half of the Romantic Century. In effect, what follows serves as both a sequel to Chapter 2, which chronicled the mid- and late-eighteenth-century rise of puffery, and a companion piece to Chapters 3 and 4, which recounted the early-nineteenth-century book trade's pioneering work in branding, bandwagon marketing, and visual advertising. At the same time, this chapter breaks from the preceding two in focusing less on new experiments in literary advertising and more on the refinement and eventual naturalization of already existing practices. This, in essence, is the story of how the puff became British Romanticism's dirty little secret, alternately derided and employed by hack and lion alike. As the pages below document, pick a name from the firmament of great Romantics and, with enough digging, you're likely to discover her encouraging a friend to review a new release, standing by idly as a publisher arranged puffs, or, in the most egregious cases, deciding to review his new book himself. So pervasive, in fact, had insider reviewing become by the late 1820s that a number of poets, critics, and cultural commentators identified puffery as the principal cause of the collapse of the publishing industry and, more significantly, the recent demise of the literary arts in Britain.

"CHEATS AND DUPES"

When John Newbery died in 1767, England lost not only one of its most prominent booksellers but one of the age's great advertising theorists and practitioners. The void wasn't easily filled. A number of potential candidates rose up, including the London booksellers John Trusler (H. J. Jackson, 23–27) and James Lackington (see Figure 5.1). But if any one late-eighteenth-century figure can be said to have inherited Newbery's mantle it was William Lane, the legendary owner of the Minerva Press and publisher of gothic novels and other modes of low-brow fiction. As E. J. Clery has noted, Lane was the publishing industry's answer to Josiah Wedgwood, mastering all of the new techniques and technologies of marketing in order to make his products a staple in middle-class homes (135). Lane's genius lay less in concocting new promotional schemes than in taking preexisting tactics to an entirely new level. While several publishers, intent on extending a book's shelf life, would routinely post-date new offerings by a few weeks, Lane was known to post-date his publications by an entire year. Hence the *Critical Review* could complain of Lane's title *The Minor*, "On this day, the first of April, 1787, we peruse a book of 1788" (Review of *The Minor*, 307); and, while other publishers would frequently advertise their books as "new" for a year or two after publication, Minerva Press novels were on several occasions announced as "just published" a decade after their release. In one particularly egregious case, Lane continued to advertise *The Beau Monde* (1809) as "new" fourteen years after its initial publication (Blakey, 104; Jacobs, 171–75).

In her still-definitive 1939 study of the Minerva Press, Dorothy Blakey traces the elaborate devices Lane used to make Susannah Gunning's *Anecdotes of the Delborough Family* a bestseller in 1792. Capitalizing on the high-society author's widely reported separation from her husband, Lane ran a series of stories in the *Star*—a

Figure 5.1. With a manuscript labeled "PUFFS & LIES for my Book" in his pocket, the London bookseller James Lackington uses a make-shift platform of religious tomes to ascend into his fashionable carriage on the occasion of his third marriage. At his feet a dog defecates on a copy of Lackington's recently published (and generally self-congratulatory) memoirs. (Frontispiece to Peregrine Pindar, *Ode to the Hero of Finsbury Square: Congratulatory on His Late Marriage, and Illustrative of His Genius as His Own Biographer* [1795].)

newspaper he had purchased in 1788 primarily as a medium for puffing his own titles—insinuating that the titular Delborough family was a thinly disguised version of Gunning's marital home. Another series of articles expressed outrage that some readers would dare question Gunning's authorship of the book, challenging naysayers to come see the manuscript, written in Mrs. Gunning's hand, at the Minerva Press's offices. Hoping to keep this "scandal" alive for yet another week, Lane later ran a testimonial, signed by twenty-four responsible citizens, proclaiming that the *Anecdotes of the Delborough Family* was indeed the work of Susannah Gunning.[4]

Perhaps Lane's most shameless commingling of the worlds of publicity and literature came in *The Follies of St. James's Street*, a society novel his firm published in 1789. Midway through the tale, the character Miss Mortimer recounts the travails she experienced on her path to becoming a professional novelist. After being summarily rejected by one Paternoster Row publisher after another, she finally took her manuscript to the Minerva Press's Leadenhall Street headquarters, where she found William Lane to be a gentleman who was "liberal in his ideas, and equally polite in his manner, who, not only with spirit receives these kind of light airy readings, but, in a manner that does honour to his publications, introduces them to the world" (2:17). Despite being deluged with dozens of other worthy manuscripts, the story recounts, Lane still gave Miss Mortimer's work his full attention and eventually saw fit to publish it. The chapter ends with the authoress imploring other "young and timid adventurers for fame" to "present the offsprings of their genius, to Lane's Literary Repository," a series featuring "James Wallace, Village of Martindale, Welch Heiress, Duke of Exeter, and other Novels that are universally read and esteemed" (2:18–19). While it is hard not to imagine such brazen self-congratulation alienating readers, Lane's blend of hucksterism, iconoclasm, and astute market analysis proved immensely successful over the long haul, and at his death in 1814 this son of a Whitechapel poulterer left behind an estate worth some £17,500 (Blakey, 23, 97–100).

As Lane's career exemplifies, the commercial culture of Britain circa 1800 bore little resemblance to that of 1700, and one of the most significant developments in the interim was the ubiquity and temerity of advertising. If anything, the rate of growth even hastened in the first half of the nineteenth century. By T. A. B. Corley's estimates, gross advertising expenditures in Britain tripled between 1800 and the 1840s, soaring from £160,000 to £500,000 per annum (161). Signaling the extent to which familiarity with major advertising campaigns was becoming a central element of cultural literacy, the *Times* for 25 January 1816 included several advertising-related questions in its "Parody of a Cambridge Examination Paper."[5] Question #16, for instance, asks: "When was Sprying and Marsden's Lemon Acid invented? Distinguish between this and Essential Salt of Lemons? Enumerate the principal Patentees, especially those of Liquid Blacking." The ensuing question makes a nod to the popularity of advertising verse:

> 17. Scan the following Lines—
> But for shaving and tooth-drawing,
> Bleeding, cabbaging, and sawing,
> Dicky Gossip, Dicky Gossip is the man!

That by 1840 it was no longer a matter of whether to advertise but how aggressively to do so is evidenced by the spread of such commercial aphorisms as "Early to bed, early to rise, / Stick to your work, and advertise" and "Advertising is to business what steam is to machinery, the grand propelling power."[6]

Whereas reserve and humility had characterized most early-eighteenth-century advertisements, a century later bombast and extravagance were quickly becoming the norm. Early-nineteenth-century visitors from the Continent marveled at how oblivious most Britons seemed to the stunning levels of puffery going on all about them. William Hazlitt, for instance, reported that Coleridge, upon returning from a trip to Italy, lamented "how all the people abroad were shocked at the *gullibility* of the English nation, who on . . . every . . . occasion were open to the artifices of all sorts of quacks" (2:317). The French writer Flora Tristan, a frequent visitor to England, wrote, "The puff is so much a part of English life that one encounters it everywhere" (295). Domestic critics concurred, as witnessed in the *Quarterly Review*'s assessment that the English "consisted of only two classes— cheats and dupes" (Wynter, "Advertisements," 202).[7]

If England had indeed become a nation of quacks, then few groups were as responsible for this development as the writers and sellers of books. At the heart of the most important essay on British advertising from the first half of the nineteenth century, Abraham Hayward's 1843 *Edinburgh Review* article "The Advertising System," is a detailed list of those professional groups most given to puffery. After chronicling the exploits of quack medicine dealers and auctioneers, Hayward laments: "It is a humiliating confession to make, but Authors undoubtedly come next; and we are by no means sure that they would not take precedence of even quack-doctors and auctioneers, if the amount of charlatanry were estimated by either the money or ingenuity expended on it" (13). A year earlier, *Ainsworth's Magazine* had voiced similar views regarding the book trade's preeminence in puffery, observing, "For copiousness of fancy, daringness of inference, and well-turned periods, [booksellers] are unapproachable by all the rest of the [puffing] craft" ("A Paper on Puffing," 42–43).

Especially in their ingenuity in securing positive reviews, writers and booksellers of the early nineteenth century outpaced all other trade groups. It is not surprising, of course, that book trade insiders, more than any other group, recognized the magic of print and exploited it to their own ends. In 1822 Hazlitt explained: "There is a wonderful power in words, formed into regular propositions, and printed in capital letters, to draw the assent after them, till we have proof of their fallacy. The ignorant and idle believe what they read, as Scotch philosophers demonstrate the existence of a material world, and other learned propositions, from the evidence of their senses" (2:306). Reiterating this sentiment, the *Westminster Review* suggested in 1828 that the public "believes two thirds of what it reads in print in honour of typography" ("Puffing, and *The Puffiad*," 441). In earlier stages of print culture even more than today, print held such power over the average reader that he or she was inclined to trust the expertise and objectivity of any news item, commentary, or review unless compelled to believe otherwise. Only slightly overstating the case, *Ainsworth's* opined that "nine-tenths of what is facetiously called the 'reading' (in contradistinction, as we imagine, to the 'thinking') public always build up their critical judgment on the foundation of the journal or periodical which forms one of their *Penati*" (i.e., household gods) ("A Paper on Puffing," 46).

Generally speaking, authors and publishers, whether wildly successful or commercially frustrated, tended to agree with this sentiment. In 1807 Wordsworth, whose poems had yet to find a wide audience, lamented how "the immediate sale of books is more under the influence of reviews than is generally supposed" (Wordsworth and Wordsworth, *Letters*, 2:155). Six years later Byron, at the height of his post–*Childe Harold* glory, dubbed the *Edinburgh* and the *Quarterly* "monarch-makers in poetry and prose" (*BLJ*, 3:209). In 1817 Coleridge went so far as to maintain, in the *Biographia Literaria*, "To anonymous critics in reviews, magazines, and news-journals of various name and rank, and to satirists with or without a name, in verse or prose, or in verse-text aided by prose-comment, I do seriously believe and profess, that I owe full two thirds of whatever reputation and publicity I happen to possess" (48). And Edward Moxon, the publisher of Wordsworth, Percy Shelley, Charles Lamb, and several other important Romantics, avowed that "a review, even with a sprinkling of abuse in it, is, in my opinion, worth a hundred advertisements" (qtd. in Merriam, 78).

Few recognized the innate credibility of the printed word as fully as did Henry Colburn, the most notorious publisher of the later Romantic era and a man whom *Fraser's* once dubbed the "Prince Paramount of Puffers and Quacks" (Maginn, Review of *The Dominie's Legacy*, 320). From the time he set up as a publisher and bookseller in the mid-1810s, Colburn began aggressively buying up literary journals for the expressed purpose of guaranteeing positive reviews of his books.[8] In an 1816 letter to Lady Morgan he boasts, "No one bookseller, I am certain, takes the tenth part the pains I do in advertising, and in *other* respects I do not think any one will *in future*, cope with me, since, from January next, I shall have under my sole control *two journals*, viz., the *New Monthly*, which flourishes as well as possible in England, and my new forthcoming *weekly* literary journal [the *Literary Gazette*], which is to be sent *free by the post* instantly all over the country like a *newspaper*, and to foreign parts" (Morgan, 2:52). By 1831 Colburn would own shares in the two periodicals his letter mentions plus three others—the *Court Journal*, the *Sunday Times*, and the *United Service Journal*—all of which he used to praise his own works and denounce those of his competitors (Review of *A Journal*, 517). In 1830 the *Athenaeum* computed that of the one hundred books included in the *New Monthly Magazine*'s list of forthcoming works, ninety-five were Colburn titles ("The Literary Gazette," 556n). A year later the same magazine conjectured that if one were to "examine five hundred columns of reviews in the *Literary Gazette*, one half will be found filled with the praise of works published by Colburn" (Review of *Memoirs of Celebrated Sovereigns*, 705). That Colburn remained unreformed in 1843 is evidenced in a letter from Thomas Hood, editor of the *New Monthly*, to Miss H. Lawrance, who had inquired about reviewing for the magazine: "I undertook to review all books except Colburn's own, with the puffing of which I of course desired to have no concern. They are *done* by the persons of the Establishment, Patmore, Williams & Shoberl. If you see the Magazine you will know what wretched things these reviews are" (qtd. in Jerrold, 369–70).

"PUFF ME, COLERIDGE!"

It was not only publishers like Colburn, however, who manipulated reviews in order to sell their books, for authors themselves were often just as gifted in the arts of puffery. A generation before Walt Whitman famously penned his own laudatory reviews of *Leaves of Grass* (1855),[9] self-reviewing was widely practiced across the Atlantic. In August 1831 *Fraser's Magazine* published a roll call of contemporary British authors who were given to praising their own works in print:

> Bulwer, for example, always reviews himself in the *New Monthly*; Croker criticises his speeches in the *John Bull*; Collier comments on his "Theatrical Annals" in the *Morning Chronicle*; Williams considers his "Sir Thomas

Lawrence" in the *Times*; Mrs. Charles Gore explains the merits of her comedy in the *Court Journal*; Hogg's tales are critiqued by himself in *Blackwood*; Johnson's pamphlets are extolled by their author in the same periodical; Westmacott eulogises "Nettlewig Hall" in the *Age*; Croly descants on his "Tales of the Great Saint Bernard" in the *Monthly*; Campbell's praises are sung by his own disinterested mouth in the *Metropolitan*; Sir James Mackintosh assures the public that his History is something quite transcendental through the *Edinburgh*; Wakley puffs the editor of the *Lancet* in the *Ballot*; Basil Hall does himself the kind office of being reviewatory on his "Travels" in the *Quarterly*; and so forth. (Maginn, "An Apology," 3)

To this seemingly comprehensive catalogue of now mostly obscure writers, *Fraser's* might well have added the names of more revered Romantics who either wrote reviews of their own works or stood by approvingly as their books were, in *Blackwood's* terminology, "buttered." Examples from the waning years of the eighteenth century include Hugh Blair urging his friend Archibald Allison to "give some account" of his new volume of sermons "in some of the Periodical Publications" (qtd. in Sher, 138); Mary Robinson being puffed almost daily in Daniel Stuart's *Morning Post*, a reformist newspaper to which she regularly contributed (Pascoe, 171–72); and Mary Wollstonecraft reviewing her own translation of Jacques Necker's *De l'Importance des Opinions Religieuses* for the *Analytical Review* (De Brouwer, 212). With the dawning of the nineteenth century, the Lake Poets got in on the act, publicly lamenting the corruption of literary criticism while privately angling for friendly reviews from literary and political allies. In his 1807 *Letters from England*, Southey, under the guise of a Portuguese visitor to London, comments, "England is but a little country; and the communication between all its parts is so rapid, the men of letters are so few, and the circulation of society brings them all so often to London, as the heart of the system, that they are all directly or indirectly known to each other;—a writer is praised because he is a friend, or a friend's friend, or he must be condemned for a similar reason" (346). A year later, Southey returned to this theme in a letter to Coleridge, in which he complains that his poetry "gets reviewed by enemies who are always more active than friends." As if at last giving up the fight, Southey pleads, "Puff me, Coleridge! if you love me, puff me! Puff a couple of hundreds into my pocket!" (*Life and Correspondence*, 3:134).

For his part, Coleridge had a life-long aversion to the reviewing system, frequently recording his disdain for institutionalized criticism. In an epigram titled "Modern Critics," first published in the *Biographia Literaria*, he lumped together

Figure 5.2. Robert Seymour's depiction of the Lake Poets' all being in the same boat. (*The Poetical March of Humbug!*, [1832], p. 18.)

all critics as "Disinterested thieves of our good name— / Cool, sober murderers of their neighbours' fame!" (2:109).[10] A few years earlier, in a long, moody letter to Daniel Stuart dated 12 September 1814, Coleridge declared that he had had enough of the "hootings and pelting" of the critical establishment; he grumbled about false friends at the *Quarterly* who hadn't sufficiently promoted him in their reviews, and he pledged to expose the perfidy of modern reviewing in "two long satires, in Drydenic verse, entitled 'Puff and Slander'" (*Letters*, 3:532; *Poetical Works*, 2:1133). What is perhaps most remarkable about this rant is that it was touched off not by some partisan hatchet job in the radical press but by the *Quarterly*'s mixed yet ultimately complimentary review of Coleridge's new closet drama, *Remorse*. The review in question not only praises the play's "rich and glowing poetry," "loftiness and purity of sentiment," and "luxuriance of fancy" (187) but, as it turns out, was written by the poet's nephew, John Taylor Coleridge (Reiman, Part A, 2:818). Apparently, though, the family connection here wasn't close enough for Coleridge; a few years later he enlisted an even more closely related reviewer to assess his intellectual skills—himself. In the thirteenth chapter of the *Biographia Literaria*, Coleridge prefaces his now-legendary discussion of the respective powers of the fancy and the imagination with an anonymous letter from "a friend, whose practical judgement I have had ample reason to estimate and revere" (1:300). While this "very judicious letter" urges the poet to be less abstruse in his philosophizing, it repeatedly praises his original imagination and dazzling intellect (1:304, 301). Had this letter indeed been written by a "friend," reprinting so flattering an assessment of his own genius would have been in questionable taste; but when we discover Coleridge subsequently boasting to his publisher that this "letter addressed to myself as from a friend . . . was written without taking my pen off the paper except to dip it in the inkstand" (*Letters*, 4:728; Engell and Bate, lvii and 300n), it becomes clear that even this dedicated opponent of insider reviewing wasn't beyond the occasional puff.

And he had exalted company. William Wordsworth—that famed champion of high literary principles—couldn't help but encourage his allies as they buttered his works. A case in point occurred in 1814, when his old friend Charles Lamb reviewed *The Excursion* in the *Quarterly*.[11] As we might expect, Lamb's review was rhapsodic, claiming of the poem's fourth book, "It stands without competition among our didactic and descriptive verse" (106) and later declaring, "Those who hate the Paradise Lost will not love this poem" (111). That the Wordsworth family was fully aware in advance of Lamb's puff is evidenced in a letter from Dorothy to her sister-in-law Priscilla Wordsworth, where, speaking for both herself and William, she complained that the *Quarterly*'s editor, William Gifford, had so deformed the original of this review that "not even the skeleton of Lamb's production remains." The letter continues with the strikingly blunt admonition that authors ought "never to employ a friend to review a Book unless he has the full command of the Review" (Wordsworth and Wordsworth, 3:207). In Dorothy's and William's ethical system, it seems, personal loyalties almost invariably trump fealty to one's profession. And, hence, when in October 1798 Southey published an unsympathetic review of the *Lyrical Ballads* in the *Critical Review*, Wordsworth, in a letter to Joseph Cottle, seethed: "He knew that money was of importance to me. If he could not conscientiously have spoken differently of the volume, in common delicacy he ought to have declined the task of reviewing it" (1:267–68).[12]

THE COCKNEY SCHOOL OF PUFFERY

A similar spirit of critical *comitatus* carried over into the second generation of Romantic poets, where coterie puffery quickly became naturalized. As Jeffrey N. Cox has argued, the Cockney School of writers—centered around Leigh Hunt and including such notables as Keats, the Shelleys, Hazlitt, and, at times, Byron—represents a remarkable site of resistance to this era's ascendant ideology of solitary literary production (*Poetry and Politics*, 6–7, 62). The Cockneys wrote, traveled, philosophized, and fought together. They also collaborated on poems and articles, on the establishment of the *Examiner* and the *Liberal*, and, as it turns out, in trumpeting one another's—and occasionally their own—works. In browsing the earliest reviews of the Cockneys, one finds Hazlitt reviewing his own *Characters of Shakespear's Plays* in the *Edinburgh Magazine* (Hayden, "Hazlitt"), Percy Shelley drafting a laudatory review of his wife's *Frankenstein* for the *Examiner* (St. Clair, *Reading Nation*, 188 and 318), and Mary Shelley in turn anonymously puffing her father's *Cloudesley* in *Blackwood's*.[13] Not to be outdone, Charles Lamb, an adjunct member of the Hunt circle, contrived to review his own collection of *Album Verses* in the *Englishman's Magazine*. In an 1831 letter to his publisher, Edward Moxon, Lamb jauntily announced: "Dear M.,— I have ingeniously contrived to review myself. Tell me if this will do. Mind, for such things as these . . . I do not charge '*Elia*' price" (*Letters*, 5:267).[14]

Perhaps the most interesting study in critical contradictions among the frequently high-minded Hunt circle was Hunt himself. Hunt first made a name for himself in 1806, when he burst upon the scene as the straight-talking, brashly independent theater critic for his brother John's weekly paper, the *News*. This was an era, Hunt would later recall, when "puffing and plenty of tickets were . . . the system of the day. It was an interchange of amenities over the dinner-table; a flattery of power on the one side, and puns on the other; and what the public took for a criticism on a play, was a draft upon the box-office, or reminiscences of last Thursday's salmon and lobster-sauce" (*Lord Byron*, 402). Refusing to sink into this mire, Hunt insisted on paying for his seats at performances and avoided forming close relationships with actors and theatre managers. In the *News* he skewered his fellow critics in essays like "Rules for the Theatrical Critic of a Newspaper," and he fearlessly denigrated the elocutionary style of no less than John Kemble, the leading actor of the age (Holden, 28–29). Hunt's recent biographer, Anthony Holden, only slightly overstates the case when he asserts, "As theatre critic for the *News*, Hunt pioneered the art of objective, disinterested theatre criticism as we now (for the most part) know it" (28).

This stance of stubborn critical independence carried over into the *Examiner*, the weekly paper Leigh and John Hunt founded in 1808. In the prospectus to the new periodical, Leigh famously declared, "NO ADVERTISEMENTS WILL BE ADMITTED in the EXAMINER." The statement continues:

> [Advertisements] shall neither come staring in the first page at the breakfast table to deprive the reader of a whole page of entertainment, nor shall they win their silent way into the recesses of the paper under the mask of general paragraph to filch even a few lines: the public shall neither be tempted to listen to somebody in the shape of a wit who turns out to be a lottery-keeper, nor seduced to hear a magnificent oration which finishes by retreating into a peruke or rolling off into a blacking-ball. (*Prospectus*, vi–vii)

As Strachan points out, this idealistic stance quickly gave way to the realities of running a paper, and within five years advertisements began appearing in the *Examiner* (*Advertising*, 66–67). In addition to these paid notices, Hunt also began slipping in unpaid advertisements in the form of glowing reviews for his friends' new books. By the late 1810s, Hunt, the one-time scourge of insider reviewing within the theater community, was routinely running reviews of one Cockney by another. Between 1816 and 1818 alone, Hunt himself wrote and published a lengthy announcement of the arrival of Keats, Shelley, and Reynolds on the literary scene, a two-part essay on Hazlitt's *Lectures on the English Comic Poets*, separate three-part reviews of Shelley's *Revolt of Islam* and Keats's *Poems*, and a comparatively modest one-part review of Shelley's *Rosalind and Helen*. During the same period, he allowed Shelley to review his mentor and prospective father-in-law, William Godwin; Reynolds and Lamb to effusively praise their friend Keats; and Keats, in turn, to laud Reynolds's *Peter Bell* parody (1819).[15]

The most remarkable quality of the puffery by Hunt and his comrades may be how unabashed it all was. In reading the correspondence of the Hunt circle, one gets little sense that they saw anything ethically remiss in reviewing one another's works. On the very day that Reynolds's review of Keats's 1817 *Poems* appeared anonymously in the *Champion*, Keats, obviously aware in advance that his friend was writing it, wrote to thank him: "Your kindness affects me so sensibly that

I can merely put down a few mono-sentences—your criticism only makes me extremely anxious that I should not deceive you" (*Letters*, 13–14). A year later, on the eve of the publication of *Endymion*, Benjamin Bailey offered his puffing services to Keats's publisher, John Taylor, writing: "You know, as far as I am able, I shall be most happy to answer any attack upon [Keats]. Or, if required, I will write a Review of Endymion. If I can serve you, command me" (Rollins, 1:20). In the ensuing months, Bailey sent puffs for Keats to a wide range of periodicals, landing some in an Oxford newspaper but generally meeting with rejection.

In defense of such cronyism, Cox suggests that "what might seem to be coterie puffing was a way of combatting a world of hostile, politically driven reviewing" (*Poetry and Politics*, 63; see also Newlyn, 24–26). This certainly is true of much Cockney School insider reviewing, which was clearly intended to counterbalance the merciless attacks on Keats, Hazlitt, and others in Tory journals. Yet in Keats's case, well before he was attacked in *Blackwood's* (in October 1817) and the *Quarterly* (in April 1818), his friends were working diligently to puff him to fame. As early as March 1817 Reynolds, writing for the *Champion*, ranked Keats's sonnets right behind those of Wordsworth and Milton and predicted that the young poet would one day eclipse Byron, Thomas Moore, and all other poets of the age. The *Examiner*'s promotional campaign for the poet started even earlier, commencing with Hunt's "Young Poets" essay on Shelley, Keats, and Reynolds (1 December 1816) and continuing in the three-part review of Keats's *Poems* the following year (in the 1 June, 6 July, and 13 July 1817 issues). Thus, several months before conservative critics assailed Keats, the liberal press had done its best to herald his arrival.

This fact was not lost on the editors of *Blackwood's*, who, upon being accused of sending the poet to an early grave with their "Cockney" slurs, responded, "Long before any Tory Review whatever took notice of Keats, he had not merely been puffed in the Examiner, but he had put forth sonnets upon sonnets of his own, in honour of Leigh Hunt . . . ; and, in short, had identified himself in a hundred different ways, with all the bad political principles, as well as with all the bad poetical taste, of the Cockney school" (Maginn and Lockhart, 226). Although obviously one-sided, this defense complicates the notion that *Blackwood's* attacks on Keats were purely political. Without question, the poet's rough treatment at the hands of Tory reviewers was partly owing to his liberal affiliations, but it would seem that equally offensive to the *Blackwood's* circle was the shameless manner in which they saw him being puffed in the *Examiner* and elsewhere. Taking this into consideration, we can say that our conventional histories of the persecution of Keats seem to stop short of the mark. More than just the victim of partisan politics, Keats was also the victim of his own acquiescence to the puffing machine of his age.

SCOTT ON SCOTT

While many of the aforementioned instances of Romantic-era puffery have long been known to literary scholars, they have generally been dismissed as isolated and harmless pranks or (as with Keats) well-intentioned if ultimately misguided attempts to rectify the imbalances of a deeply partisan reviewing system. This pattern of explaining away even the most egregious puffs also characterizes much of the critical discussion surrounding Walter Scott's 1817 self-review of *Tales of My Landlord*, a review which John O. Hayden has called "undoubtedly the most famous instance of anonymous self-criticism in the history of periodical reviewing" ("Hazlitt," 20). The well-known story here, as most thoroughly told by Martin Lightfoot, is that Scott undertook the review in large part to convince his publisher, John Murray, who also published the *Quarterly Review*, that he had nothing to do with the Waverley novels. "I have a mode of convincing you," Scott wrote to Murray in December 1816, "that I am perfectly serious in my denial—pretty similar to that by which Solomon distinguished the fictitious from the real mother—and that is, by reviewing the work, which I take to be an operation equal to that of quartering the child" (Lockhart, *Memoirs*, 2:26).

The clear implication in Scott's letter was that no true gentleman of letters would ever consider reviewing his own work. Yet, given how thoroughly normalized puffery was in Romantic-era reviewing, it is highly unlikely that either Scott would have been naïve enough to really believe this or, more to the point, that he would have thought Murray, who had literally spent his entire life in the book trade, would have taken a review as a de facto disavowal of authorship. What this amounted to, then, was an elaborate game of chicken between the author and his new publisher. Scott, of course, was not beyond playing mind games with even the most powerful of publishers. In 1809, for instance, he trumped up charges against Constable and the *Edinburgh Review* to justify his own disloyalty in setting up a rival firm (Ballantyne and Company) and periodical (the *Quarterly*); during this period he also stole Constable's idea of founding a historical almanac to compete with the *Annual Register* (Sutherland, *Life*, 135–36). Basically, the self-review of *Tales of My Landlord* seems a case of Scott testing whether Murray would have the audacity to directly accuse him of authoring the Waverley novels, and of Murray, in turn, gauging whether Scott would have the pluck to actually allow the self-review to appear.

Neither blinked, and the unusually long review, which manuscript evidence suggests was written primarily by Scott but with contributions from William Erskine and William Gifford (Lightfoot, 152–60), immediately went to press. Given the *Quarterly*'s long history of praising Scott—who was, in fact, its original guiding spirit—the irony of this self-review is that it likely turned out to be more equivocal in its praise of the author and his *Tales* than the journal's review would have been had it been assigned to one of Scott's cronies.¹⁶ Scott actually takes himself to task at certain points, suggesting that his plots might be less haphazard and his heroes more memorable. At the same time, though, he praises the Waverley novels collectively for their brilliant pictures of real life, maintaining that the huge sales of the volumes are owing to their genuine literary merit. And along the way he also manages to include such knowing asides as "none have been more ready than ourselves to offer our applause" and "few can wish [the author's] success more sincerely than we do" (Review of *Tales*, 431).

It didn't take long for news of Scott's authorship of the review to leak out. On 23 May 1817—less than a month after the self-reviewal appeared—the *Morning Chronicle* reported: "Mr. WALTER SCOTT is said to be the author of the critique on *Tales of my Landlord*, in *The Quarterly Review*, and it is insinuated in the concluding paragraph, that his brother is the writer of the Novels that have made so strong an impression on the public mind. This has long been suspected, and we hear that another is on the anvil, under the title of *Rob Roy*" ("The Mirror of Fashion," 3). This report was promptly reprinted in a number of British and American newspapers, including the *Caledonian Mercury*; and, much as Scott had hoped, it helped dampen rumors that he had authored the Waverley novels. By 1827, however, as Scott prepared to unveil the true identity of the Great Unknown, it became expedient to distance himself from his earlier self-reviewal. And thus, in the introduction to *Chronicles of the Canongate*, he suggests that William Erskine "reviewed with far too much partiality the Tales of my Landlord, for the Quarterly Review of January 1817" (1:xix). Not surprisingly, in his biography of Scott, the novelist's son-in-law, John Gibson Lockhart, kept up this fiction, expressing "his conviction, that Erskine, not Scott, was the author of the critical estimate of the Waverley Novels" (*Memoirs*, 2:27n).

By the time Lockhart's *Life of Scott* appeared, in 1837, however, various magazine articles and an 1835 edition of the *Periodical Criticism by Sir Walter Scott* had substantiated that the review's manuscript was largely in Scott's hand (19:1). Perhaps inured to puffery by this point, the British press remained relatively neutral about this discovery, more or less buying into the notion that it was intended more as a prank than an attempt to ward off criticism or stimulate sales. The

American journal the *Knickerbocker*, however, would have none of this, using Scott's self-reviewal as Exhibit A in its argument that he was at once "full of talents, worldly prudence, [and] management," but also "false principles, insincerity, mystification, and moral fraud" (Review of *Memoirs of the Life*, 351). Were this a one-time lapse, the *Knickerbocker* argued, it might be forgiven, but the reality was that time and again Scott had stooped to self-promoting ploys that were "worthy of a Grub-Street hack" (353). In the paper's view, whether it was Scott's founding of the *Quarterly Review* as an organ for puffing his friends and pet political causes or his repeatedly lying to the public about his authorship of the Waverley novels, he represented the worst of a debauched British literary culture. In short, the *Knickerbocker* argued, it would "require the credulity of a believer in Animal Magnetism, or in Mormonism, to think [Scott] a man of high moral sensibilities, upright mind, simple practices, or ingenuous habits" (356).

Obviously, the rhetoric here is a bit overheated, but the basic argument merits consideration. One of the *Knickerbocker*'s strongest points—and one consistently overlooked in most commentaries on Scott's self-reviewal of *Tales of My Landlord*—is that this was not the first time he had taken the occasion to review his own works. Seven years earlier, while serving as the de facto editor of the *Edinburgh Annual Register* (Curry, 3), Scott had anonymously published in that periodical a lengthy survey entitled "Of the Living Poets of Great Britain." The article's central claim was that three contemporary poets stood head and shoulders above their peers: Thomas Campbell, Robert Southey, and, of course, Walter Scott. After reviewing Southey's and Campbell's respective strengths and limitations, Scott began the section on his own narrative poems by critiquing their loose plots and flat characters (424). He then insisted, however, that these shortcomings were more than counteracted by the poems' stunning descriptions and vivid action sequences. In such moments, Scott argued, this poet was unrivaled, excelling first in "the art of . . . rivetting the attention of the audience" and second in capitalizing on his remarkable "knowledge of the manners of the time in which his scenes are laid" (425).[17]

Even if Scott's assessment of his own strengths and weaknesses was eventually confirmed by the critical consensus, it was, like Coleridge's "letter from a friend" in the *Biographia*, in decidedly poor taste to devote twenty-six pages to arguing one's own superiority over all but two of one's peers. Scott himself seems to have recognized this. In an all too credible scene from his *Anecdotes of Scott*, James Hogg reports being so incensed at his erstwhile friend Scott's article, which treated Hogg as an unequivocally minor poet who suffered from "a vulgarity of conception and expression" (Scott, "Of the Living Poets," 442), that he scribbled out a rejoinder that was published in what would prove to be the final issue of his own periodical, *The Spy*. Hogg's witty rebuttal of 24 August 1811 reads in part:

> Since it is of late become fashionable for some great poets to give an estimate of their own wonderful powers and abilities in periodical works of distinction, surely others have a right to give likewise their own estimates of the works of such bards. It is truly amusing to see how artfully a gentleman can place himself at the head of a school, and make himself appear as the greatest genius ever existed. (*The Spy*, 517)[18]

Rather than seeing this as the payback it was and taking it in stride, Scott worked himself into a lather over Hogg's essay. In fact, the next time he saw the "Ettrick Shepherd," Scott reportedly declared, "Mr. Hogg I am very angry with you . . . and I think with good reason. I demand sir an explanation . . ." (Hogg, *Anecdotes*, 20). When Hogg retorted that he was merely responding to Scott's own provocations in the *Edinburgh Annual Review*, Scott unflinchingly swore it was Southey, not he, who had written the piece. With this assurance, Hogg let the matter rest, but, in recounting the incident several years later, he couldn't help but note, "Mr. Southey subsequently told me that he believed Scott to have been the author of that paper" (20).

THE DEATH OF LITERATURE

At the end of the day, given the evidence put forward in all the preceding pages, a good argument could be made that the ubiquity of puff reviewing during the Romantic period has been the single most underreported story of that era in literary history. Far from some fringe practice encountered only on the dark side of Parnassus, puffery could be found in all sectors of the literary book trade—high and low, fiction and poetry, male and female, liberal and conservative, aristocratic and plebeian, metropolitan and provincial. And, situated as it was at the crossroads of literary production, distribution, and reception, the system of puff reviewing affected everything from writerly strategies for conceiving and crafting marketable tales to readerly habits in purchasing and evaluating texts.

The lack of previous scholarly attention to puffery is surprising, given how poorly hidden so much of the age's insider reviewing was and continues to be. If puffery is the great skeleton in the closet of Romantic literature, the closet hasn't exactly been locked. To begin with, virtually every publisher's archive from the era preserves letters detailing the arranging of puffs; and several editors— including those at the *Monthly*, *Blackwood's*, the *Quarterly*, and the *Examiner*—

left behind meticulous contributors logs and account books laying bare instances of insider or self-reviewing. Moreover, outside the private archive and in the full sunlight of print, one can find scores of pamphlets, periodical essays, and poems from the Romantic Century chronicling instances of puffery. While many of these exposés came from shadowy figures like "Anti-Puff" and "Antipuffado,"[19] a number were by such leading men of letters as Fielding, Johnson, Sheridan, Coleridge, Hunt, Carlyle, and Macaulay.

From the earliest published complaints about puffery in the 1730s through the mid-1820s, most critics of the practice followed Fielding's and Sheridan's leads in finding it a source of amusement and mild irritation rather than full-blown angst. For the average late-eighteenth- and early-nineteenth-century commentator, the impulse to puff one's wares was a quintessentially modern vice but no worse than a host of other sins, and best dealt with through satire rather than sermonizing. Typical of the Horatian attitude toward puffery that endured into the early nineteenth century is a series of squibs published in the *Satirist* between 1807 and 1810. In the first of these, a piece titled "Comparative Criticism," the magazine sardonically surveys five recent instances in which a journal on one end of the political spectrum heralded a new work as an instant classic while one at the other end dismissed it as execrable trash. So patently absurd had modern reviewing become, the writer of this piece guffaws, that no less than the *Edinburgh Review* had recently hailed a book as "exceedingly valuable" before confessing, "We have not had the advantage of consulting this work" (93).[20] Subsequent articles in the *Satirist*, such as 1809's "Puff Extraordinary" and 1810's "Specimens of Puffing," adopted a similar tone, tending more toward bemusement than hysteria over the depths to which modern marketing had sunk. Such is the case also in the *John Bull Magazine*'s 1824 squib "The Rhyming Review," where the poet jests that all modern reviews are merely advertising pages for their sponsoring publishers:

> Who thinks that cross Gifford would venture to worry
> A quarto, red-hot, from the counter of Murray;
> That Campbell would treat a smart novel from Colburn,
> As if it were printed by Benbow, in Holburn[?]
> (lines 25–28)[21]

If anything, though, "The Rhyming Review" was a bit of a throwback; by the mid-1820s, British society's once whimsical attitude toward puffery was turning increasingly hostile. In many respects, *Blackwood's* attacks on Keats during the late 1810s and 1820s represented something of an early salvo against literary graft, and by the late 1820s a loose collective of reform-minded authors and critics had declared outright war on puff reviewing. Despite the rapid expansion of the reading public and new printing and papermaking technologies that drove down production costs, a doomsday mentality suffused much of literary Britain between 1825 and 1835. Much of this gloom was related to the fiscal crisis that gripped the publishing industry during these years. As has been widely documented elsewhere, the recession that followed the stock market collapse and bank panic of late 1825 had a particularly devastating effect upon the book trade. During what is generally referred to in publishing history as "the Crash of 1826," two publishing giants, Constable and Ballantyne, went under, and a third, John Murray, nearly capsized under the burden of staggering losses.[22]

In the view of many observers at the time, the economic downturn would pass, but a much more serious problem—a dearth of literary genius—would remain in its wake. The poet, in particular, seemed an endangered species. In 1826 John Wilson declared in *Blackwood's* that poetry was "by universal consent exploded" (99). Two years later the *London Weekly Review* lamented: "Whatever may be the cause, the fact seems to be undeniable, that poetry is now become a very degraded thing among us. Every body writes, but nobody reads it: it is out of fashion" (Review of *The Poetical Album*, 717). In much the same vein, a *New Monthly Magazine* essay, "Literature in 1834," pronounced:

> The state of English literature, at this moment, seems to us to be anything but progressive. In the department of poetry we have had nothing for several years worth mentioning. A desultory effusion now and then finds its way into the periodical journals, as if to show that the fire of genius is not as yet wholly extinct amongst us. But no poem of any length or character has lately seen the light in this country. (S. C. Hall, "Literature in 1834," 498)

Finally, in 1835 *Tait's Edinburgh Magazine* delivered what amounted to a post mortem for verse: "Poetry will not do, the world has outgrown it: there is no relish for it: the very sight of verse is a kind of *noli me legere*" (or, touch me not) (Tait, 15).[23]

What is most remarkable in reading these and the many other accounts of the "demise" of poetry and, more generally, of literature itself is the cause-and-effect thinking often on display. One might expect to find causal narratives such as "the Crash of 1826 so discouraged authors that quality suffered" or "the Crash only accelerated the demise of literature already under way." Instead, one finds that, among authors and critics, perhaps the single most widely credited cause of literature's supposed ruin was not the recession generally or the failure of Ballantyne and Constable specifically but the rise of puffery in the book trade. Thomas

Carlyle, for one, on several occasions in the early 1830s cast blame for his stagnant literary career on puffery, which he held directly responsible for what he regarded as the collapse of the publishing industry. In an 1832 letter to his brother John, he asserted, "One thing I imagine to be clear enough: that *Bookselling*, slain by Puffery, is dead, and will not come alive again, tho worms for some time may live on the carcase. What method writers (who have some thing to write) shall next take is now the question" (*Collected Letters*, 6:195).[24] A year later Carlyle confided to John Stuart Mill: "Bookselling even Effingham Wilson [a prominent publisher] finds to be about *dead*—of Puffery. I do not think *it* will ever revive" (7:25). In the years to come, Carlyle would increasingly go public with his rants against the evils of modern advertising, his most famous commentary coming in *Past and Present* (1843), where he thunders out: "the Quack has become God. Laugh not at him, O reader; or do not laugh only. He has ceased to be comic; he is fast becoming tragic. To me this all-deafening blast of Puffery, of poor Falsehood grown necessitous, . . . sounds too surely like a Doom's-blast!" (122).

However distinctively Carlylean in tone, these jeremiads were actually somewhat derivative, drawing much of their content and spirit from the assaults on puffery that had been a staple of several literary magazines since the late 1820s. As is most thoroughly documented in two seminal early-twentieth-century studies, Miriam M. H. Thrall's *Rebellious Fraser's* (1934) and Leslie Marchand's *The Athenaeum* (1941), the reform era saw the formation of an unofficial consortium of supposedly independent journals—including, most notably, the *Athenaeum*, *Fraser's*, *Blackwood's*, and the *London Magazine*—devoted to salvaging the credibility of literary criticism.

Despite their divergent political agendas—the Tory *Blackwood's* and the Whig *London* in particular had a long history of hostile relations—these magazines collectively set out to unmask and debunk the nation's most notorious puffers, chief among whom was Henry Colburn. Particularly intent on thwarting Colburn was the *London Magazine*, whose editor, Henry Southern, penned a series of exposés in 1825 and 1826 on the "Colburniana" that were appearing weekly in the rogue publisher's various journals and newspapers.[25] Three years later, *Fraser's* and the *Athenaeum* joined in, with William Maginn in *Fraser's* nominating Colburn to head the guild of "literary puffers and trumpeting booksellers" (Review of *The Dominie's Legacy*, 319) and an *Athenaeum* reviewer in September 1829 accusing him of "plac[ing] literature on a footing with Liquid Blacking" ("The Divan," 599).

The intensity of such attacks on Colburn grew out of a widely shared belief that the very survival of literature was at stake. In calling out Colburn, Maginn lamented, "We feel that the world of every-day literature cannot wag on as it has been wont to wag for some time past" (Review of *The Dominie's Legacy*, 318). More pointedly, an 1830 *Athenaeum* review explained: "Ten thousand times more mischief is done by puffing and commendation than by all the weapons of ridicule that critic ever wielded. The slow ripening of genius—the indefatigable perseverance of learning, have no chance in this age" (Review of *A Journal*, 517). One of the most detailed explanations of how Colburn's tricks could have so pernicious an effect on the whole of British literature came in *Blackwood's* July 1826 installment of "*Noctes Ambrosianae.*" John Wilson, under the guise of the magazine's fictional editor, Christopher North, suggested that Colburn's style of marketing, which drew upon all the tricks of the quack medicine dealer and the blacking manufacturer, robbed literature of its aura and reduced a work of art to a mere commodity. Of Colburn's advertising system Wilson prophesied: "Were it to become general, [it] would sink the literary character into deep degradation, till the name 'Author' would become a by-word of reproach and insult; and the mere suspicion of having written a book, be sufficient ground for expulsion from the society of gentlemen" (98).

A year later the bookseller Thomas Cadell argued that the effect of Colburn's books, which were heavy in hype but light in content, was to "satiate the Publick and prevent really good Books experiencing that quick & extensive sale to which they are entitled" (Besterman, 77). Cadell was suggesting that puffery, with its tendency to wax more euphoric the worse a book was, vitiated the public's taste, leaving the common reader unable to discern between works of genuine genius and the tripe flowing from Colburn's press. Theoretically, the major reviews existed in order to combat Colburn and his ilk, pointing readers toward the next Milton or Byron; but it seemed quite clear that in the late 1820s no periodical could claim to be untainted by puffery. As the pseudonymous "One Master Trimmer" lamented, all of Britain's major review publications at one point or another had submitted to the impulse to puff. Boasting behind-the-scenes experience in major publishing houses, the "Trimmer" revealed: "It is no uncommon thing to hear publishers of the present day boast that they can make '*almost any thing go down*' . . . . The first thing to be fixed upon is a good catch-penny title. An imposing advertisement is sent forth—the reviewer has had his cue; and an inviting current, from the puffing pump, flows in a thousand directions" (4–5).[26]

The most extended broadside from this period on the ruinous effects of puffery is Robert Montgomery's 1828 Popean mock epic *The Puffiad*. The "Introductory Epistle to an Eminent Puffer," addressed to those booksellers responsible for popularizing puffery, charges, "By undesignedly giving birth to an universal system of Puffery, you have inflicted a lasting injury on the literature of the country, and given it a venal character as disgraceful as it is injurious" (6). It goes on to link this rise of puffery directly to the emergence of print culture:

> Perfect critical independence, perhaps, never existed in any age; but, certainly, there was never so much critical prostitution as is now daily exhibited. There is no sort of trash—no insipid verse—no crude prose—no species of dulness, which may not find a critic ready to fire away his triumphant Puffs in its support; and such is the magic of print, that, though his very quotation give the lie to his verdict, the common reader is caught, and the splendid volume must be purchased. (15)

Montgomery's basic argument here and elsewhere is that, as a result of print's sway over the average reader, well-written puffs in the pages of a literary review all but ensure a book's commercial success. And since publishers of third-rate novels tended to have fewer scruples than others in the book trade, they had been the true beneficiaries of the rise of puffery, refining their skills to such a degree that they could pass off the most foppish of novel-writing dunces as the greatest writers of the age. From Montgomery's perspective, the declining popularity of poetry and the rising popularity of the novel were not due to improvements in printing technology, the death of the major poets, or even cyclical public tastes; quite clearly, the enemy of poetry and champion of the novel was the system of puffery.[27]

Taken on its own terms, *The Puffiad* offers useful insights on the connections between print and puffery, but the real beauty of this work lies in one marvelous bit of irony: its author, Robert Montgomery, was generally considered the most shameless puffer among the poets of his age. In literary circles it was held as something of a truism that Montgomery's *The Omnipresence of Deity* (1828) had quickly reached a twelfth edition on the wings of puffery rather than of poesy ("Puffing, and *The Puffiad*," 449–50; "Landon's and Montgomery's Poetry," 160, 165–66; *The Poetical March of Humbug!*, 5–9). In fact, perhaps the most famous essay on early-nineteenth-century puffery is Thomas Babington Macaulay's 1830 *Edinburgh Review* article entitled "Mr. Robert Montgomery's Poems, and the Modern Practice of Puffing." In this piece, Macaulay seems either to have been unfamiliar with *The Puffiad* or unaware that Montgomery was its anonymous writer. It is interesting, however, that Macaulay's general thesis echoes that of Montgomery in *The Puffiad*: "The puffing of books is now so shamefully and so successfully practised, that it is the duty of all who are anxious for the purity of the national taste, or for the honour of the literary character, to join in discountenancing it" (Macaulay, 196).[28]

The problem, as Macaulay explained it, was that with the shift of power from the patron to the publisher, the literary world had merely exchanged one evil for another: "Men of letters have . . . ceased to court individuals, and have begun to court the public. They formerly used flattery. They now use puffing" (196). Macaulay observed that nine out of ten readers were "ashamed to dislike what men, who speak as having authority, declare to be good" (199). As a result, any well-written puff could have a significant impact on the sales of a book. In the end, Macaulay took comfort in what he saw as the test of time's ability to distinguish between fleeting sensations and genuine classics. But his ultimate fear was that puffery would prove the death of British literature, in that talented, honest authors would be discouraged from entering a marketplace where only the unscrupulous prospered (200). His conclusion, then, is a call-to-arms for ethical critics to stand up against the puffing machine: "If our remarks give pain to Mr Robert Montgomery, we are sorry for it. But, at whatever cost of pain to individuals, literature must be purified from this taint" (210).

Given the dire predictions Macaulay and others of his generation made about the long-term impact puffery would have on literature, we should consider whether duplicitous reviews from the era still affect the study of early-nineteenth-century literature. While Wordsworth famously argued that the great authors of his age were responsible for creating the tastes by which they would be enjoyed in posterity ("Essay, Supplementary," 654), their success during their own lifetimes was largely in the hands of reviewers. Quite clearly, a series of well-placed puffs could greatly increase a book's sales and, by extension, elevate its author considerably in the mind of the public. As Catherine Gore put it in 1840: "Puffed therefore, and praised on all sides, [the author's] writings first attract notice, and finally command attention. The public is convinced that *all* the weekly, monthly, and three-monthly critics cannot be in the wrong" (165). Still, puffery's long-term effects on canon formation are more difficult to gauge. Undoubtedly, some traces of original assessments endure in contemporary critical tastes, but overall the reputations of most major Romantic-era writers have undergone so many revaluations over the past two centuries that one would be hard-pressed to argue that we are still laboring under illusions of a literary work's greatness that were cast by an early puff.

A more productive lesson to be learned from all I've cited above is that we should redouble our caution when working with reviews from this, or really any, era. One of the dangers, of course, in chronicling the explosion of puffery that occurred in the Romantic age is going too far and casting aspersions on all of the age's reviewers. To be fair, many critics from this age earnestly aspired to what Matthew Arnold would, a generation later, call "disinterestedness," and several periodicals took pains to maintain their independence from booksellers. The *Edinburgh Review*, for instance, was founded on the premise that it would best serve the public by keeping booksellers at arm's length, and magazines like the *Athenaeum* and *Fraser's* often wearied readers with obsessive reaffirmations of their critical neutrality. More generally, at least in theory, the entire industry retained the system of anonymous reviewing because it allowed critics to speak their minds without fear of retribution from publishers and fellow authors (Shattock, 4–17).[29]

As we have seen, though, critical anonymity quickly became widely abused, and it seemed to facilitate crooked reviews as often as objective ones. Just how compromised the era's major reviews were is either widely misunderstood or willfully ignored in a good deal of today's scholarship. Even in a skeptical age, we routinely proffer generalizations about the critical reception of a particular author or work that fail to consider the potential links between the author and his or her reviewers. While most scholars grow suspicious about scathing reviews of now-canonical works, crediting the critic's spleen to personal or political animosity, they tend to be much less leery of reviews that correspond to the critical judgments of their own time. A case in point is how we have come to treat the earliest reviews of Keats's poetry. Although one might reasonably argue that the *Examiner*'s puffs represent a greater breach of critical ethics than the *Blackwood's* attacks do, over the past century most scholars have found the *Examiner*'s reviews considerably more palatable than those in *Blackwood's*.

The solution, I would argue, is not to disregard Romantic-era reviews altogether, as in doing so we would push some of the best and most woefully neglected writing of the age even further into the shadows. At the very least, though, we need to be more informed and resistant readers of reviews, training ourselves and our students never to take reviews at face value and always to do basic "background checks" of reviewers before citing them in our scholarship. While a large number of reviewers from the era continue to remain stubbornly anonymous, resources like the *Wellesley Index to Victorian Periodicals* and contributors' indexes for the *Monthly Review* and *Blackwood's* have vastly simplified the process of discovering the authorship of many reviews. Moreover, the ongoing digitalization of Romantic-era books, letters, and manuscripts has made sleuthing out instances of puffery easier than ever. In short, there's never been a better moment to begin applying the same critical rigor to reviews that we've long applied to poems, novels, and other literary texts.

CONCLUSION

The Art of Advertising

Given the evidence ushered forth in the preceding chapters, there should be little question that British advertising was thoroughly transformed between 1750 and 1850. To be sure, promotional theories and methods have continued evolving, especially with the explosion of printed media, the rise of data-driven marketing, and the dawn of electronic and digital communications. But, as we have seen, many of the core techniques of modern marketing—branding, product placement, market saturation, bandwagoning, visual rhetoric, disguised advertisements, and so forth—were thoroughly understood and widely practiced prior to the Victorian era.

If there is any lingering doubt about the scale of British advertising by the late Romantic age, one need only consider John Orlando Parry's 1835 watercolor *A London Street Scene* (see Figure C.1). In Parry's London, the eye is seized less by the dome of St. Paul's than by ubiquitous street posters advertising politicians, opera halls, haberdasheries, and pubs.[1] It is easy to understand why Caroline Alice White suggested in 1849 that advertisements had come to function as "the social history of the times" (42) and *Fraser's Magazine* would maintain three years later that "Catholic Emancipation, Reform Bills, and a few trifles of that sort, will be thrust back into the second rank: but steam locomotion and the puff-advertisement system will stand forth as the grandest of world-phenomena—as the symbols of the strides which society has made during the past quarter of a century" (Francis, 90). Even more pointedly, the *London Society* magazine for August 1863 proclaimed:

> "Nothing is done now without advertising" has become an indisputable statement in relation to almost every trade where there is any possibility of competi-

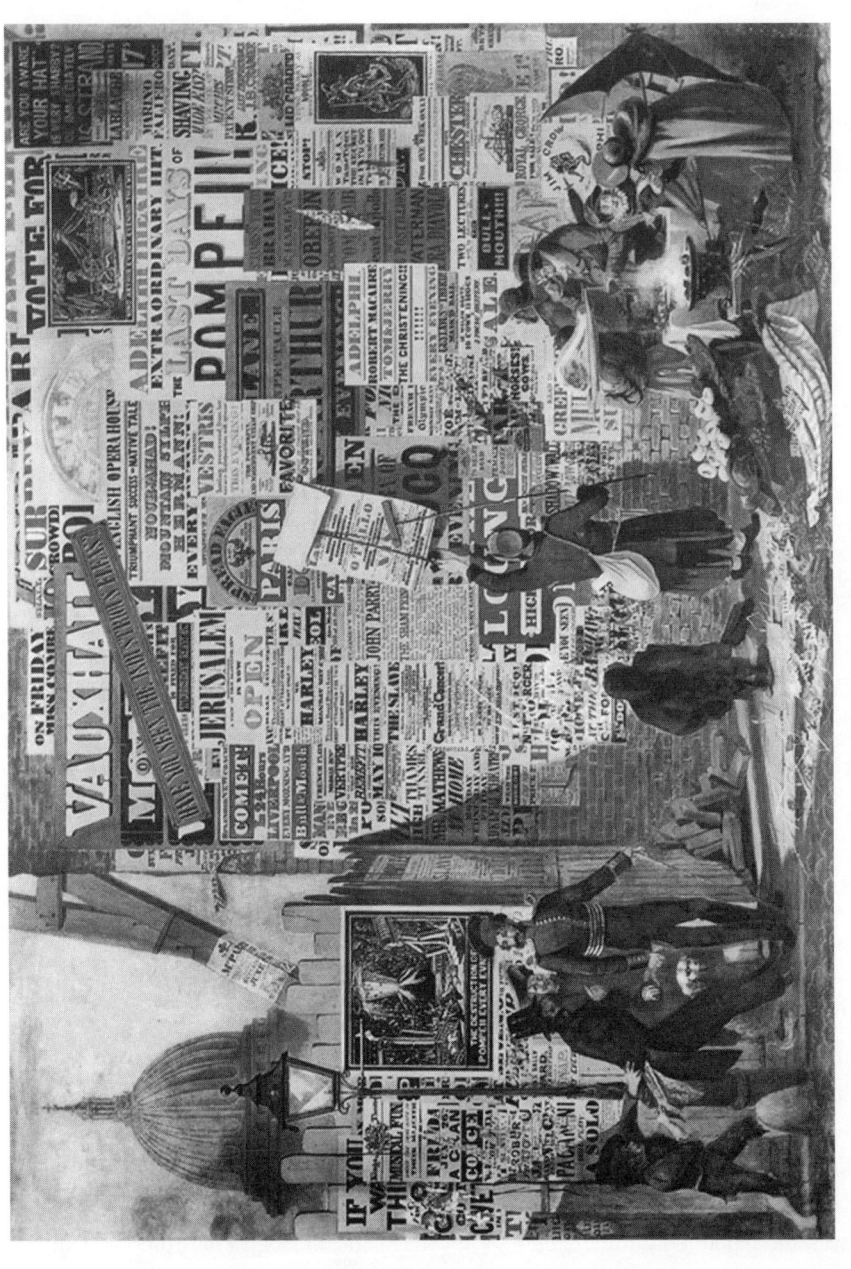

Figure C.1. John Orlando Parry, *A London Street Scene* (1835). (Courtesy of the Alfred Dunhill Museum and Archive.)

CONCLUSION: THE ART OF ADVERTISING   145

tion; and even the quietest, sternest representatives of the quiet old steady-going men of business, who rejoiced in their scorn of a puff, and long held fast to the proverb, that "Good wine needs no bush"—have latterly been compelled to adopt the new method which has been introduced by the revolution effected through advertisements. ("The Modern Art," 188)

As this book has chronicled, British advertising and literature share a common genealogy, their family lines routinely intersecting and occasionally merging over the course of the Romantic Century. On the one hand, the rise of advertising had an enormous impact on Romantic-era literature in Britain. New advertising technologies and practices catalyzed such crucial components of the modern literary system as institutionalized criticism, the celebrity author figure, and the unprecedented hyping of new titles. At the same time, men and women of letters had a profound impact on late-eighteenth- and early-nineteenth-century advertising, pioneering many of the age's most groundbreaking marketing methods. At the turn of the nineteenth century, puffery, product placement, and special-offer schemes were largely associated with the book trade, and the decades that followed would see writers and publishers outpacing professionals in virtually every other field in their pioneering uses of group-think psychology, appeals to celebrity, and visual marketing.

Perhaps nothing better illustrates just how tight the kinship of literature and advertising had become in this era than a phenomenon with which I'd like to close—namely, the "art of advertising" debates of the middle decades of the nineteenth century. While, in the midst of the eighteenth-century explosion of advertising, the occasional writer noted the artistry of particular advertisements,[2] it wasn't until the second quarter of the nineteenth century that the British press began recurrently asking a previously unthinkable question: could advertising legitimately be considered a branch of the literary arts? Among the earliest noteworthy treatments of the question is a July 1824 *Westminster Review* article in which the writer, since revealed as John Hamilton Reynolds, half-jestingly notes how, in the absence of first-rate living bards, the Warren's blacking lyricist (see Chapter 3) had emerged as Britain's most influential and popular poet ("Professor Wilson's *Danciad*," 213). Seven months later Reynolds's satirical partner, Thomas Hood, linked advertising and art even more explicitly in his parodically titled *London Magazine* squib, "The Art of Advertizing Made Easy. With Specimens of the Most Approved Kinds. For the Use of Tradesmen and Others. By a Lover of the Fine Arts." After opening by declaring, "Advertizement writing is an art in itself" (246), Hood went on to suggest that any catalogue of the age's great writers must include the likes of such renowned advertisers as Alexander Rowland (of Macassar Oil fame), James Atkinson (the James Street perfumer), and, of course, Robert Warren (of Warren's Blacking) (247).[3]

The real turning point in British discourse regarding the "art of advertising," however, came in 1835, when for the first time a major magazine article was able to consider the topic without smirking. *Tait's Edinburgh Magazine*'s landmark essay "On Advertisements; and Advertising, Considered as One of the Fine Arts; in Which the Theory and Practice are Combined" asserts unequivocally that "Advertising is now one of the Fine Arts; and, moreover, the one which is most extensive in its use, influence, and personal profit" (575). Anticipating the late-twentieth-century arguments of Colin Campbell and others (see Chapter 1), the anonymous writer goes on to argue that advertising, like poetry, is essentially an exercise in that most fundamentally Romantic trait: imagination. "The chief thing in every business," aspiring entrepreneurs are counseled, "is the Art of practising gracefully upon the corporal sense through the imagination of the Public, by the exercise of your own imagination, combined with factual experience. Without this, capital and industry are utterly thrown away" (575). Advertising, in other words, is an exercise in the yoking of imaginations, with the writer seizing the reader's imagination via the skillful projection of his or her own.

By the 1840s and 1850s, variations on the theme "the art of advertising" began routinely appearing in British periodicals. Abraham Hayward's landmark survey of "The Advertising System" (1843), for instance, asserts, "On the whole, there is no denying that Advertisements constitute a class of composition intimately connected with the arts" (4). A year later, Thomas Hood expanded his earlier musings on the art of advertising in a new essay, titled "The Advertisement Literature of the Age." While Hood remained to the end a satirist, there's at least a glimmer of earnestness in his contention that

> the advertisement has long since become an independent department of literature, subject to its own canons of criticism, having its own laws of composition, and conducted by a class of writers, who though they *may* (we do not assert that they *do*) acknowledge their inferiority to the great historians, poets, or novelists of the day, would nevertheless consider themselves deeply injured were we to hesitate to admit them into the corporation of the *"gens de lettres."* (111)

Three further contributions to the national conversation on the "art of advertising" came in 1855. Most prominently, the *Quarterly Review* said of the recently deceased auctioneer and puff-writer George Robins: "His advertisements were really artistically written. Like [the British painter John] Martin, he had the power of investing every landscape and building he touched with an importance and majesty not attainable by meaner hands. . . . [W]hen he died the poetry of advertising departed" (Wynter, "Advertisements," 110). For James Dawson Burn, however, Robins was hardly Britain's last great poetical puffer. In his manifesto on modern advertising, *The Language of the Walls*, Burn argued, "The polite literature of puffing in the present age engages a considerable amount of talent; and there is also much ingenuity employed both by the various classes of quacks and those who are in the legitimate trade" (113). Adding to Burn's witness, another treatise of 1855, the anonymous pamphlet *Puffs and Mysteries* insists, "Puffing is a delicate art, not to be acquired without study, or practised with any high degree of success by the unlearned. Even those 'Professors' who have raised the wind most successfully by puffing, will admit that the practice of the art becomes every day more difficult" (viii).[4]

Possibly the most intriguing mid-century discussion of the literariness of advertising, however, comes in an 1844 *Chambers' Edinburgh Journal* essay entitled "Advertising Considered as an Art." Taking as its point of departure Samuel Johnson's 1759 claim that "the trade of advertising is so near to perfection, that it is not easy to propose any improvement" (*Idler* #40), this essay aimed to demonstrate "the high condition to which modern literary skill [had] brought" advertising in the eighty-five years since Johnson's remark (401). The essay begins by marveling at the celebrity-producing power of brand-name advertising, pointing out how the names of such blacking manufacturers as Day and Martin had become "quite as well known to the public at large as Scott of Abbotsford, and Wellington of Waterloo" (401). Admittedly, a large part of this fame resulted from the blacking companies' enormous advertising budgets, yet, to produce truly memorable advertisements, "literary resources of a high character are necessary" (402). In an extraordinary passage that might easily be mistaken for an excerpt from Coleridge's *Biographia Literaria*, Shelley's "Defence of Poetry," or any number of High Romantic treatises on the powers of the poet, *Chambers'* goes on to insist that the expert writer of advertising copy must possess "ingenious inventive powers, an unbounded play of fancy, and a subtilty of contrivance, which few branches of the literary art require in so high a degree" (402). In essence, *Chambers'* here effects the full apotheosis of the oft-maligned ad-man, lifting him from the garrets of Grub Street to the pinnacle of Parnassus and classifying him as a close cousin of that most estimable of writers, the Romantic poet.

This transmogrification of Sheridan's Mr. Puff into the full-blown Romantic genius received an even more vivid treatment seventeen years later in Anthony Trollope's *The Struggles of Brown, Jones, and Robinson*. First published serially in *Cornhill Magazine* in 1861 and 1862, Trollope's novel centers around three businessmen who, despite their starkly different commercial philosophies, pool their capital and talents to found a clothing shop named "Magenta House." While Brown preaches the necessity of carefully guarding one's capital and Jones the importance of polished salesmanship, Robinson insists that the only path to fame and fortune in the modern economy is artful advertising. As the novel progresses, we learn that Robinson was born into poverty and thus forced at an early age to find work as a bill-sticker. Rather than being ashamed of these roots, he boasts that it was through poring over the posters he was paid to hang that he learned to read and write: "From studying the bills which he carried, he soon took to original composition; and it may be said of him, that in fluency of language and richness of imagery few surpassed him." Before long, the autodidact Robinson aspires to earn his own place in the pantheon of advertising writers, and he soon thereafter "establish[es] himself as an author in his own line" (20).

That Trollope lacks Robinson's enthusiasm for advertising is evident at every turn, yet he chooses to cast his protagonist as a talented professional who takes his art seriously rather than as a hopelessly confused drudge. Like the pitchman-poet envisioned by *Chambers'*, Robinson is a direct descendant of the Romantic author figure, working in solitude and awaiting inspiration from the muses of marketing. Eventually the literary advertisements Brown posts in Magenta House's front windows become required reading for London's citizenry, leading him to lament in a melancholy hour: "There is nothing so fickle as the taste of the public. The most popular author of the day can never count on favour for the next six months" (87). Having become one of London's most widely read "novelists," Robinson fears his fate will be that of other acclaimed authors whose genius is initially admired only to be later ignored by an unfaithful reading public. In essence, the depiction of the clothier as a novelist is an inversion of Trollope's famous analogy of the novelist and the shoemaker. Here it is not the novelist going about his task in the workmanlike way of the tradesman, but the tradesman turning the dull life of selling clothes into a career that requires the imagination and genius of an author figure.

What *The Struggles of Brown, Jones, and Robinson* offers is a clear-eyed vision of a world where advertising serves as the principal vehicle for both the aestheticization of commerce and the commercialization of the aesthetic. For better or worse, the once daunting gulf between advertising and literature had been effectively bridged. From there, it was a short leap—or perhaps no leap at all—to William Stead's 1899 pronouncement that "ordinary persons cannot write advertisements any more than they can write poetry" (62) or Raymond Williams's 1980 claim that advertising functions as "the official art of modern capitalist society" (184). While there remains a certain iconoclasm to such blunt amalgamations of the putatively high (the literary) and low (huckstery), there really should be little shock value left in such claims. We are, after all, embarking on our fourth century since advertising and literature began functioning as, to a large degree, co-productive systems.

Notes

INTRODUCTION: ENTANGLED HISTORIES

1. For more thorough overviews of *Blackwood's* early years, see Finkelstein, Mason, and Oliphant.

2. See Oliphant, 1:270–71, and Strout, 96, for fuller histories of this incident.

3. While, as of yet, no major publisher has been caught overloading Amazon's system with puffs, a similar scandal rocked the movie industry in 2001, when two employees in Sony's advertising department were discovered to have invented "David Manning of *The Ridgefield Press*," a fictional critic who provided enthusiastic blurbs for many of the studio's most widely panned films (Horn).

4. See the winter 2000 issue of *European Romantic Review*, which features essays by Susan Wolfson, Claudia Johnson, Anne Mellor, Peter Manning, William Keach, and William Galperin on the notion of a "Romantic century."

5. Barthes, "Rhetoric of the Image" and "The New Citroen"; R. Williams, "Advertising: The Magic System"; and Hebdige, "Object as Image: The Italian Scooter Cycle."

6. See also William Stead, Jr.'s 1899 book *The Art of Advertising*, which proclaims: "Advertising is universal, and must necessarily be so. It has always existed; but it is only in the last decades of the present century that it is being systematised and treated in an intelligent fashion" (17).

7. Mui and Mui, *Shops and Shopkeeping in Eighteenth-Century England*; Briggs, "'News from the little World'"; James Raven, *Judging New Wealth* and *The Business of Books*; Jill Campbell, "Domestic Intelligence"; and Cynthia Sundberg Wall, *The Prose of Things* (esp. 158–66).

8. For examples of studies on the Romantic-era book trade that touch briefly upon advertising, see Erickson, *The Economy of Literary Form*; Jordan and Patten, eds., *Literature in the Marketplace*; Clery, Franklin, and Garside, eds., *Authorship, Commerce, and the Public*; and St. Clair, *The Reading Nation*.

9. There have also been two somewhat recent doctoral dissertations on Romantic-era advertising by Hadley J. Mozer and Andrea Bradley.

CHAPTER 1. ADVERTISING IN THE ROMANTIC CENTURY

1. The six installments of Francis's "The Age of Veneer" appeared in the September 1850, October 1850, February 1851, April 1851, September 1851, and January 1852 numbers of *Fraser's*. Francis's authorship of these anonymously published essays is

confirmed in his 1866 obituary in *The British Controversialist and Literary Magazine* ("Literary Notes," 320). While "The Age of Veneer" is largely forgotten today, in the first two decades after its publication it resonated broadly, with many commentators adopting the essay's title as their preferred label for the era. Early reflections on Francis's series appeared in forums as varied as *Chambers' Edinburgh Journal* ("Mahogany," 183) and *The Medical Times and Gazette* ("To Correspondents"). Most famously, Dickens took up the metaphor of veneering in *Our Mutual Friend*, where it serves as both a key plot device and a running typological motif. For an analysis of Dickens's likely borrowings from the *Fraser's* series, see Owen Knowles.

2. The rumored employment of leading poets by Packwood, Warren, and other manufacturers is described at length in Chapter 3 of this book.

3. The most authoritative histories of British advertising to date are Nevett and Elliott. See also Sampson, Presbrey, E. S. Turner, Gloag, and Schuwer.

4. Mulrooney estimates that most Romantic-era newspapers devoted 50–70 percent of their column space to advertising (359–60).

5. "Advertise," def. 6, and "Advertising, *ppl. a.*," def. 2, *The Oxford English Dictionary Online*.

6. The Latin translates, "His ashes are here, his fame everywhere." A number of nineteenth-century sources reproduced this epitaph after it was originally brought to the general public's attention in the December 1821 issue of the *Gentleman's Magazine* (see Q.B.). The earliest known mention of the inscription, though, comes in the 1813 collection *The Beauties of England and Wales* (Nightingale, Part 2, 235).

7. For an excellent contemporary take on the advertising tax and its impact on circulation, see Lockhart, "Noctes Ambrosianae, No. XVI," 232–34.

8. The point of origin for most contemporary scholarship on the historicity of literature is the late 1970s, when Raymond Williams published *Keywords* (1976) and René Wellek summarized several years of reflections on the subject in his essay "What Is Literature?" (1978). The most widely read work in this vein is Eagleton's *Literary Theory: An Introduction*, which draws heavily upon Williams's *Keywords* and *Marxism and Literature*. Perhaps the most extensive treatment of the subject, however, comes in Peter Widdowson's *Literature*.

9. For studies on the emergence of British copyright, see Rose, *Authors and Owners*, "The Development of the Author's Copyright in Britain" and "The Author as Proprietor"; St. Clair, *The Reading Nation*, 51–65; Raven, *The Business of Books*, 230–38; and Mazzeo, 10–12. For scholarship on the evolution of the literary canon, see Patey, "The Eighteenth Century"; Guillory; Kramnick; Terry; Bonnell; Ross, *The Making of the English Literary Canon*; St. Clair, *The Reading Nation*; and Cox, "The Living Pantheon." For accounts of the rise of national literatures, especially in Britain, see Crawford, Court (esp. ch. 1), and Trumpener. For studies of the creation of the Romantic author figure, see Haynes, A. Bennett, Foucault, and Barthes, "The Death of the Author."

CHAPTER 2. THE PROGRESS OF PUFFERY

1. As Feather points out, Continental booksellers began circulating trade catalogs in the late fifteenth century, nearly a full century before the practice became common in England (*English Book Prospectuses*, 22–23).

2. Among the most insightful studies of eighteenth-century quack medicine ads are Porter, Doherty, Styles, and Curth. Quack medicine advertising is also covered in most general histories of advertising.

3. Briggs explores this passage from Defoe at some length in "'News from the little World,'" 32–33. See also M. Wood, 26–27.

4. The apparently common practice of reissuing older books as new is described at length in the July 1791 issue of the *Monthly Review* (Review of *Labyrinths of Life*). See also Zachs, 36.

5. For contemporary exposés on postdating, see Review of *The Minor*, 307, and Review of *The Happy Release*, 391.

6. See also A. Forster, *Index to Book Reviews*, 5.

7. Upon encountering this "free book" advertisement, the waggish editor of *The World* professed to being so touched by Newbery's generosity that he promised to give away the first three volumes of his periodical "GRATIS at every bookseller's shop in town, to all sorts of persons, *they only paying* NINE SHILLINGS for the BINDING" (E. Moore, 688 [corrected page number; mispaginated in original]).

8. The house of Newbery would print at least eight editions of Dr. James's *Dissertation on Fevers and Inflammatory Distempers* between 1748 and 1778.

9. For more on Newbery's involvement in the patent medicine trade, see Dobson, 129–31; Buck, 203–8; Mounsey, 92–94; and Branch, 139–42.

10. Despite the straightforward nature of the vast majority of seventeenth-century advertising, scholars have identified several instances when writers and publishers found creative ways to promote their books. In 1647, for instance, Henry Walker's newspaper *Perfect Occurrences of Every Dayes Journall in Parliament* ran a puff piece reporting widespread clerical enthusiasm for a new book by one of Walker's friends, *The Divine Right of Church-Government* (Presbrey, 41–42). In other cases, hype occurred within books themselves; publishers would often preface the main text with "commendatory verses" testifying to the genius or eloquence of the book's author (F. Williams, 1–2). And in the late seventeenth century the bookseller John Dunton went so far as to found periodicals for the explicit purpose of having a convenient medium in which to promote his books (Graham, 227). Instances such as these, however, are noteworthy primarily for their avant-garde quality, as they were well outside the norms of mainstream seventeenth-century publishing.

11. Theodore Sedgwick Fay offered a similarly pointed definition in 1825, asserting that a "puff" is "an author's opinion of his own works, expressed in a daily paper, by himself or his friends" (255).

12. Another potential point of origin for the term "puff" is gambling. In its 13 January 1721 exposé on London's gambling dens, the *London Journal* reported that "a Puff" was slang for someone who "has Money given him to play to decoy others" (*London Journal*, 3). The card-playing puff, then, resembles the literary puffer in being paid to decoy others.

13. The prefatory pages from *Pamela*'s second edition are reproduced in volume 1 of Keymer and Sabor, eds., *The Pamela Controversy*.

14. For other commentaries on the emergence of institutionalized criticism, see Habermas, ch. 5; Eagleton, *The Function of Criticism*, ch. 1; and Basker, "Criticism and the Rise of Periodical Literature."

15. The few known details from Griffiths's life prior to the founding of the *Monthly* are summarized in Antonia Forster's entries on the publisher in the *Dictionary of Literary Biography* and the *Oxford Dictionary of National Biography*.

16. For detailed accounts of the founding of the *Monthly*, see Forster, "Review Journals," and Roper, 19–21.

17. Other noteworthy attacks on Griffiths and his journal include John Free's *The Monthly Reviewers Reviewed by an Antigallican* and John Shebbeare's *Lydia, or Filial Piety* (3:237).

18. Smollett's prospectus for the *Critical Review* first appeared in the *Public Advertiser* for 30 December 1755. It is reprinted in full in Knapp, *Tobias Smollett*, 171–72. For more detailed accounts of Smollett's attacks on the *Monthly*, see Basker, *Tobias Smollett*, 36–38; Forster, *Index*, 6–7; and Donoghue, 25–32.

19. For early instances of negative reviews of Griffiths titles in the *Monthly*, see "Review of *The Ligature Preferable to Agaric*" and "Review of *An Address to Dr. Huddesford*."

20. See, for instance, Griffiths's January 1750 review of Mary Collier's *Felicia to Charlotte* and his December 1753 review of Cleland's *The Dictionary of Love*.

21. For the publication history of *Fanny Hill*, see Sabor's introduction to the Oxford World's Classics edition of the novel. See also Knapp, "Ralph Griffiths," and Fader and Bornstein, 34–37.

22. For fuller accounts of the impact of late-eighteenth-century review criticism, see Roper, 24–27; Donoghue, 3–7; and Basker, "Criticism," 329–30.

23. See also Mullan, 184–86, which documents how, during the latter half of the eighteenth century, Smollett, James Boswell, Henry Fuseli, and Charles Burney all published self-reviewals in journals to which they had connections.

24. Noteworthy late-eighteenth-century complaints against critical corruption include Crabbe's *The News-Paper: A Poem* (esp. lines 355–400); Lloyd's "The Puff: A Dialogue between the Bookseller and Author"; Wolcot's *A Poetical, Supplicating, Modest, and Affecting Epistle to Those Literary Colossuses, the Reviewers*; Dudley's *The Dramatic Puffers*; and the anonymous satires *The Town* and "Song 202."

25. Charles Beecher Hogan records how late-eighteenth-century theater managers ensured positive reviews by making direct payments to newspapers. At one point the proprietors of Covent Garden paid an annuity of one hundred pounds to the *Times* to guarantee strong reviews. Hogan also suggests that puffery became so common that discriminating readers were inclined to pass off any marginally favorable review as a puff (176–79).

26. While certainly the best-known taxonomy of puffery, Sheridan's was not the first. The earliest known such list is in the anonymous 1765 pamphlet *The Art of Puffing, An Inaugural Oration*, which introduces the categories of the "puff oblique" and the "puff direct" (12).

27. Taxonomies of puffery became a regular feature of books and articles on the subject in the nineteenth century. *The Puffiad: A Satire* (1828), by Robert Montgomery, lists twenty-nine categories of puffs, including the "The Puff Mendacious," "The Puff Impudent," "The Puff Stupid," "The Puff Tremendous," and "The Puff Astounding" (113–25). An equally detailed taxonomy appears in the anonymous *Puffs and Mysteries; or, The Romance of Advertising* (1855), which includes such new categories as "The Puff Boomerang," "The Puff Infantile," and "The Puff Interjec-

tional" (vii). See also *The Modern Puff* (1849) by the pseudonymous "Anti-Puff" and John Fisher Murray's 1841 *Blackwood's* retrospective on the prescience of Sheridan's Mr. Puff (486–89).

CHAPTER 3. BUILDING BRAND BYRON

1. For Odoherty's claim to have penned the Day and Martin's jingles, see Lockhart, "*Noctes Ambrosianae*, No. I," 369.

2. See also John Galt's "Tit for Tat" (*The Autobiography*, 2:189) and the 1832 collection *The Poetical March of Humbug!* The latter of these begins with the claim, "We all know that the notorious Warren keeps a poet, whose Heliconian effusions are sufficiently known to the public through the medium of newspapers" (4). Apparently there was at least some truth to the notion of Warren's "keeping" a poet. In 1823 the Scottish writer Alexander Kemp confessed to Walter Scott that he had written some two hundred Warren's Blacking advertisements (Partington, 9). Another account from the era suggests that, as a boy, Jesse Boot, the founder of the British pharmacy chain Boots, "once won 10s. in a competition to promote Day and Martin's blacking by rhyme" (Waller, 330).

3. However gifted Linnaeus may have been as a taxonomist, he was possibly even more talented as a self-promoter. In his autobiography, written in the third person, Linnaeus says of himself, "No one before him had . . . been a great botanist or zoologist . . . written more books, more correctly . . . listed so many animals—yes, as many as all the others put together" (qtd. in Yoon, 45). As for the *Systema*, he obviated the need for others to blurb the book when he himself touted it as "a masterpiece that no one can read too often or admire too much" (qtd. in Yoon, 50).

4. As Edward Mars Elmhirst has documented, while branding did not become common until the eighteenth century, manufacturers had used trademarks to distinguish their products since at least the thirteenth century.

5. The earliest examples I have found of branding outside the medicine trade come in advertisements for blacking. The "Boots and Shoes" box in the John Johnson Ephemera Collection at Oxford's Bodleian Library contains a 1735 advertisement for "Kirby's New German Blacking Balls" and a 1736 advertisement for "Mawtass's Italian Balls for Shoes." These instances of branding appear to be isolated ones, however, since newspapers did not regularly carry advertisements for brand-name household products until several decades later.

6. Advertisements for these products appeared, respectively, in the *Morning Post* (13 January 1779), the *Edinburgh Advertiser* (6–9 June 1780), the *Morning Herald and Daily Advertiser* (10 January 1787), and the *London Recorder, or Sunday Gazette* (31 March 1793). For additional examples of early branded goods, see Corley, 159.

7. McKendrick quotes several of these dialogues in their entirety in "George Packwood," 153–56, 166–68.

8. Strachan records how books of advertisements such as *Packwood's Whim* became so common in this period that they acquired their own genre label, the "ana" (*Advertising*, 50).

9. The Warren's outfit for which Dickens worked was run by Jonathan Warren, who founded his business to capitalize on the fame of his cousin Robert, the propri-

etor of the original Warren's Blacking. See Dickens's account of his days at Warren's in John Forster's *Life of Charles Dickens*, 1:21. Dickens later alluded to blacking advertisements in *Pickwick Papers*, *Hard Times*, and, most prominently, *The Old Curiosity Shop*, in which Mr. Slum is a composer of blacking jingles.

10. The blacking industry became one of the first battlegrounds of modern branding for several reasons. In an era when the shine of one's boots was readily equated with moral rectitude and city streets were generally filthy—recall Swift's "Description of a City Shower," in which the roadways are filled with a confluence of "dung, guts, and blood" (line 61)—most fashionable city-dwellers considered blacking a necessity. Moreover, blacking proved an ideal commodity for national distribution, as it was relatively affordable and easy to ship (Davis, 30).

11. Many historians credit Warren with inventing both the advertising jingle and the corporate emblem. See Presbrey, 85–87; Gloag, 167; Strachan, Introduction, xii–xiii; Davis, 29–30; and Wicke, 21–22.

12. Graffiti for Warren's was apparently still visible on Pompey's Pillar in 1877. An article that year in *The Champion Journal for the Boys of the United Kingdom* noted: "Like all other monuments to which the genuine cockney can, thanks to cheap travelling, gain access, this venerable column's base is covered all over with names and inscriptions, among which . . . [is] the painted name of 'Warren's Blacking.' This is cockneyism with a vengeance" ("Pompey's Pillar," 79).

13. "Sir W.S." is Sir Walter Scott; "Lord B" is Byron; "S.T.C." is Samuel Taylor Coleridge; and "W.W." is William Wordsworth.

14. On the poem's success being based in its timeliness, see, for instance, Chew, 9–10.

15. On the commodification of Byron, see also Elfenbein, 47–89.

16. In 1812 fifty shillings would have been roughly half of the average gentleman's weekly income. Thus *Childe Harold* I and II could not have been an impulse purchase for the vast majority of the book-buying public. On the expensiveness of the volume, see St. Clair, "The Impact of Byron's Writings," 2–6, and St. Clair, *The Reading Nation*, 195–96.

17. See also "When to their airy hall," another Byron poem from this period.

18. Byron added his name and a preface to the second edition of *English Bards*, published in May 1809 (less than two months after the first edition).

19. Just how steep the odds were against becoming a famous poet is borne out by St. Clair: "For the period between the 1780s and the 1830s, we have records of about 5,000 new books of verse, 10,000 new editions, written by about 2,000 living poets, as well as of a vast amount of reprinting of old-canon poetry written earlier. About fifty poets, it was believed at the time, made some money from their writings" (*Reading Nation*, 172; see also 169). The edition count for *English Bards* might have been even higher had Cawthorn not printed an unusually large first edition of 1,000 copies (see *BLJ*, 1:192, 248). For a concise publication history of *English Bards*, see McGann's notes in Byron, *CPW*, 1:392–98.

20. The original quotation, which Byron slightly altered, is found in Boswell's *Life of Samuel Johnson*: "Johnson praised the Earl of Carlisle's Poems, which his Lordship had published with his name, as not disdaining to be a candidate for literary fame. My friend was of opinion, that when a man of rank appeared in that character, he

deserved to have his merit handsomely allowed" (2:397). For more on how Byron's rank affected his reception, see Elfenbein, 51.

21. Another valuable reading of Byron's early iconography comes in Mole, *Byron's Romantic Celebrity*, ch. 5.

22. For an insightful discussion of Byron's career-long indecisiveness about anonymity, see Mullan, 237–43.

23. Years later, Rogers reported that Byron used this dinner not only to repair relations but also to further his reputation for eccentricity. When dinner was served, he successively refused soup, fish, mutton, and wine, explaining that he ate "nothing but hard biscuits and soda water." "Some days after," Rogers recounts, "meeting Hobhouse, I said to him, 'How long will Lord Byron persevere in his present diet?' He replied, 'Just as long as you continue to notice it'" (Byron, *His Very Self*, 41).

24. For pejorative accounts of Dallas and his relations with Byron, see Hobhouse, 1–2, 11–15; "Dallas's *Recollections*," 529–31; and Eisler, 142, 296.

25. For a succinct history of the publishing house of Murray, see Schmidt.

26. Manning, 183–84; Mole, *Byron's Romantic Celebrity*, 22; S. Bennett.

27. The brand value of a publisher's imprint is also explored in Schoenfield, 83–97, and Joseph.

28. In an unfootnoted passage, Marchand claims that the first advertisement for *Childe Harold's Pilgrimage* appeared on 1 March 1812 (*Byron*, 1:325). Manning, however, maintains that the first advertisements did not appear until 5 March (183). My research supports Manning's date, as I have located no advertisements earlier than 5 March.

29. Byron also praises Gifford in *BLJ*, 1:174.

30. For more on the practice of strategically withholding review copies, see Reiman, Part B, 1:234.

CHAPTER 4. L.E.L., BANDWAGON MARKETING, AND THE RISE OF VISUAL CULTURE

1. The first official press secretaries for the Crown, the White House, and Downing Street were named, respectively, in 1918, 1929, and 1931.

2. The literary veteran Henry Fothergill Chorley shared a similar opinion in 1874, suggesting that Jerdan "was the puppet of certain booksellers, and dispensed praise or blame at their bidding, and it may be feared 'for a consideration'" (Stoddard, 8). Not surprisingly, both in the *Gazette* and in his autobiography, Jerdan frequently and vehemently denied being guilty of puffery and other lapses in literary or commercial ethics. "The tricks of the trade are bad enough in chandlery and petty-huckstering," he wrote in 1853, "but in Letters, *absit omen* [let there be no evil here], misrepresentation, envy, depreciation, malice, detract perniciously from the glory of pursuits which should refine and elevate the souls of its professors" (*Autobiography*, 4:67). A series of 1819 letters in the Blackwood papers at the National Library of Scotland, however, shows Jerdan and William Blackwood negotiating a quid-pro-quo endorsement of each other's favored authors. If *Blackwood's* will favor Barry Cornwall "with an early and kindly review," Jerdan promises it "will confer an obligation on me which I shall be at any time happy to requite, in any other or in the same manner, that is by

bringing before the public as taste & justice will admit any work in which you feel a warm interest" (10 May 1819, #163). Part of this letter is quoted in St. Clair's *Reading Nation*, 574.

3. Burlington Arcade is a fashionable shopping center in London's West End.

4. In a June 1826 letter to her friend Katherine Byerley Thomson, Landon revealed the extent to which she credited Jerdan with making her the success she was: "Your own literary pursuits must have taught you how little, in them, a young woman can do without assistance. Place yourself in my situation. Could you have hunted London for a publisher; endured all the alternate hot and cold water thrown on your exertions; bargained for what sum they might be pleased to give; and, after all, canvassed, examined, nay quarreled over accounts the most intricate in the world? And again, after success had procured money, what was I to do with it?" (qtd. in Blanchard, *Life*, 49; see also P. Vincent, 143–44).

5. Wolfson's unpublished remarks on the Landon-Byron comparisons are quoted on page 204 of Craciun.

6. One has to suspect that Walter Scott's attribution of his *Tales of My Landlord* series to "Jedediah Cleishbotham" was, at some level, a gibe at the increased importance of authors' having marketable names.

7. Until the turn of the seventeenth century, anonymity was so naturalized that no English word had yet been needed to describe the condition. It was only around the year 1600 that "anonymous"—derived from the Greek for "no name"—started to take hold in the English language (Ferry, 194–95; Mullan, 296). Over the next century and a half, writers began to think more reflectively about the value of attaching their name to a text, but it's still rather striking how many now-canonical works of English literature from the Restoration and eighteenth century were initially published without the author's name. In fact, with such available titles as *Absalom and Achitophel*, *The Rape of the Lock*, *Robinson Crusoe*, *Gulliver's Travels*, *Joseph Andrews*, and "Elegy Written in a Country Churchyard," one could easily construct an entire syllabus out of "masterpieces" of this era that originally appeared anonymously.

8. In the May 1822 installment of *Blackwood's* "Noctes Ambrosianae," the magazine's fictional editor, Christopher North, quips that, on the heels of the *Waverley* novels, "every body writes books in our days, and nobody owns them" (Lockhart, "Noctes Ambrosianae, No. III," 601).

9. See also R. F. St. Barbe's 1821 *Blackwood's* essay "Semihorae Biographicae, No. III." After beginning with an account of a friend who "was uneasy till he could assign nameless works," St. Barbe satirically evaluates rumors that the Waverley novels were written by writers ranging from Charles Maturin to Leigh Hunt to *Blackwood's* own Christopher North.

10. The concluding phrase in Blanchard's quotation is line 142 of Pope's "Epistle to Dr. Arbuthnot."

11. From the early 1990s, a common thread in Landon scholarship has been how thoroughly (and cynically) commodified the "poetess" and her works were from the outset. In Anne Mellor's reading, "Landon constructed both her life and her poetry as an embodiment of Burke's female beauty" (110); for Linda H. Peterson, she allowed herself to become a model "of the poetess as a performer who strikes a pose for the pleasure of her audience but to her own detriment" ("Rewriting," 121); and for Rich-

ard Cronin, her works consciously and cannily "dissolve the distinction between poet and poem, so that she becomes herself the object of the reader's admiring attention" (90). See also McGann and Riess, who suggest that Landon developed a "totally self-conscious style of writing that often—especially in the later work—comes inflected with a disturbing mood or tone of bad faith" (22–23), and Lootens, who warns against too readily embracing the notion that Landon was "a competent literary business-woman, but emotionally disingenuous" (249).

12. "Onymity" is Gerard Genette's useful term for cases where an author's name is affixed to the text. "As always," Genette observes, "the most ordinary state is the one that, from habit, has never received a name, and the need to give it one responds to the describer's wish to rescue it from this deceptive ordinariness" (39).

13. See *Romantic Theatricality: Gender, Poetry, and Spectatorship*, where Judith Pascoe draws similar conclusions about the half-hearted attempts to keep Landon's identity secret in the early 1820s (238).

14. Even when L.E.L. at last garnered the attention of the literary world, speculation surrounding her "mysterious" identity was short-lived. Less than a month after her initial blockbuster, *The Improvisatrice*, appeared in early July 1824, *John Bull Magazine* spoke openly of the new "volume of poems by pretty Miss Landon" ("The Rhyming Review," 77) and, in a review titled "Miss Landon's Poetry," *Blackwood's* went so far as to provide readers not only with Landon's full name but her home address as well (Maginn, 190).

15. For one of the first major studies of the bandwagon effect, see Leibenstein.

16. Odes to L.E.L. eventually became ubiquitous. Indeed, "writing a poem to L.E.L. became a rite of passage for numerous early nineteenth-century readers and writers, women and men alike" (McGann and Riess, 16).

17. The earliest advertisements for the second edition of *The Improvisatrice* appeared on 17 September 1824.

18. Illustrating the depths to which Jerdan would stoop to puff L.E.L., the review in the *Literary Magnet* goes on to recount: "We remember that sometime since, a report was spread of the premature death of this same interesting young lady, and the *Literary Gazette* joined in the solemn foolery, lamenting her timeless decease, as if it really happened" (Review of *The Improvisatrice* [*Literary Magnet*], 108). In my research, I have found no other reports of this rumor, including in the *Literary Gazette*, but such a stunt likely wouldn't have been beyond the pale for Jerdan.

19. Barton published a second panegyric titled "To L.E.L." in the *Literary Magnet* for July 1824, and "Sonnet to L.E.L." (signed "J.W.C.") appeared in the 4 December 1824 issue of the *Mirror of Literature, Amusement, and Instruction*.

20. The 1 January 1825 issue of the *Literary Gazette* warns readers, "If any Mrs. Tucker gives herself out to be the writer in the *Lit. Gazette*, under the signature of L.E.L., she is an impostor: no such person is at all known to the *Lit. Gaz.*" ("To Correspondents," 14). More credibly, *Oxberry's Dramatic Biography* for 2 April 1825, referring to a particular poem, cautioned, "The person who has borrowed the initials of L.E.L. is miserably deceived if he (or she) hopes to impose trash upon us as the production of Miss Landon. That lady's splendid talents are more profitably employed than in writing eulogistic stanzas to such an actor as Young" ("Notices," 249–50).

21. This notion that Landon had founded the "initialist school of poetry" would be

repeated frequently—sometimes in earnest, sometimes in jest—in the years to come. See, for instance, Review of *The Golden Violet* (*Gentleman's Magazine*), 239–40, and "Libraries and Catalogues," 13.

22. For a good summary of the gradual emergence of visual technologies, see Tucker, 111–12. For a more detailed account of eighteenth- and early-nineteenth-century developments in engraving and printmaking, see G. Wood, ch. 2.

23. The painter W. P. Frith commented on this subject in his 1889 essay "Artistic Advertising," calling the shift from simple woodcuts to elaborate illustrations "the great change which has shown itself in the modern system of advertising—a change which calls upon the advertiser to spend enormous sums in producing pictorial representations" (421).

24. For extended treatments of Landon's relationship to the visual arts, see Peterson, "Rewriting," 117–22, and Hoagwood, Ledbetter, and Jacobsen's introduction to their *Romantic Circles* edition of the *Keepsake for 1829*.

25. What follows in the text is greatly indebted to F. J. Sypher's outstanding catalogue of Landon portraits in his 2009 biography of the poet (310–23).

26. Of this posthumous engraving, the *European Magazine* wrote: "Pickersgill, a man of undeniable talent, has one picture—Miss Landon—which is quite unworthy of him. He has made a modest and retiring young lady a virago-looking Amazon in a Spanish hat, which unquestionably the improvisatrice never wore; and although he has succeeded in communicating an idea of her talent, she may fairly complain that he has also succeeded in omitting every trait of her beauty" (qtd. in Whitley, 89). Pickersgill's original is reproduced as the frontispiece to McGann and Riess's edition of Landon's poems.

27. For a fuller study of *Fraser's* Portrait Gallery, see Latané.

28. One of the many rumors surrounding Landon in the 1830s was that her and Maclise's friendship had taken a sexual turn. By some accounts, reports that Landon had been sleeping with Maclise ultimately caused John Forster to break off his engagement to the poet in 1835 (Higgins, 70–72; Hoagwood and Ledbetter, 56–60). According to some scholars, Maclise's amorous sketch "Meet Me by Moonlight Alone" (first published in 1836 in *The Reliques of Father Prout*) depicts the painter wooing Landon (Sypher, 320–21).

29. While, at least in print, Landon generally stayed above the fray, she was irritated enough by the *Royal Lady's* ongoing smears that she chose to fight back in her first novel, *Romance and Reality* (published December 1831). Midway through the novel, Landon inserts the following dig at the fashion sensibilities of the *Royal Lady's* and its readers: "Two daughters followed, who looked as if they had just stepped out of the Royal Lady's Magazine—that is, the prevailing fashion exaggerated into caricature. Their bonnets were like Dominie Samson's ejaculation, 'prodigious!'—their sleeves enormous—their waists had evidently undergone the torture of the thumb-screw—indeed they were even smaller—and their skirts had 'ample verge and space enough' to admit of a doubt whether the latitude of their figure did not considerably exceed the longitude" (2:257).

30. For evidence that Captain Ross did, indeed, name a lake in honor of Landon, see Huish, 604. I have found no evidence corroborating the existence of the Jerdan River.

31. By Blanchard's account, Landon was less than pleased with how this likeness turned out, complaining that "the painter, or the engraver, had magnified her ears... in a most libellous manner" (*Life and Literary Remains*, 239).

32. Shortly after Landon's death, her friend Anna Maria Hall, in a critique of various portraits for the *Art-Union*, remarked how this portrait "so forcibly recalls to our remembrance the highly gifted and amiable woman of genius . . . : it seems to us now so much truer a likeness than we thought it when it first met our eye; and is, at the same time, so agreeable a memory of her eloquent countenance, that we strongly recommend it to all who enjoy her works" (3). It is worth nothing that, of all Maclise's portraits of Landon, the one that has received the most critical attention in recent years is "Regina's Maids of Honour." First appearing in the January 1836 issue of *Fraser's*, the picture shows Landon (seated to the left with her back to the viewer) alongside several of Britain's leading literary ladies. For commentaries on "Regina's Maids of Honour," see Hoagwood and Ledbetter, ch. 3; Higgins, 69–72; Peterson, *Becoming a Woman of Letters*, ch. 1.

33. While the sketches in *The Poetical March of Humbug!* are anonymous, Seymour is identified as its illustrator in an advertisement for the volume that appeared in the *Athenaeum* for 7 July 1832 (445).

CHAPTER 5. PUFFERY AND THE "DEATH" OF LITERATURE IN LATE-ROMANTIC BRITAIN

1. See especially Shattock and the articles in Demata and Wu's *British Romanticism and the* Edinburgh Review: *Bicentenary Essays*. The general shortage of critical studies on Romantic-era periodicals has been partially compensated for by the numerous reference works available on the topic, most notably Donald Reiman's indispensable *The Romantics Reviewed*.

2. Hayden's refusal to indict the rampant puffery of this age is all the more curious given how many instances of insider reviewing he alludes to over the course of his study.

3. One noteworthy exception is Marjorie Morgan's *Manners, Morals, and Class in England, 1774–1858*, which includes several excellent passages on the influence of advertising in general and puffery in specific on the late-eighteenth- and early-nineteenth-century book trade (see esp. 36–40, 112–15).

4. In another remarkable example of his marketing genius, Lane managed to mention nearly forty Minerva Press titles in the course of one seven-page chivalric tale (Sadleir).

5. The *Times* printed a slightly abridged version of this *jeu d'esprit* nearly ten years later, in its 17 January 1825 number. For a reading of this later printing, see Strachan, *Advertising*, 72–73.

6. Alfred Bird, the renowned maker of baking and custard powders, is said to have coined the "early to bed" rhyme (see J. R. Turner). The earliest known British use of the "advertising is to business" line comes in the 5 September 1840 issue of the *Preston Chronicle and Lancashire Advertiser* ("Varieties," 2), where the quote is attributed to an "American paper." By the late Victorian age, however, the British had come to claim the quote as their own, routinely attributing it to either Macaulay or Gladstone.

7. *The Trifler* for 12 June 1796, in regards to medical ads, quips, "A foreigner, from perusing our daily newspapers, if he took time to read the specious advertisements with which the newspapers abound, would be struck with astonishment at hearing such a thing as death talked of in this part of the world" (Maw-Worm, 167).

8. Although no book-length study of Colburn exists, several scholars have documented his puffing acumen at some length. See especially Sutherland, "Henry Colburn"; Marchand, *The Athenaeum*, 97–165; and Rosa, 178–206.

9. For an excellent treatment of Whitman's self-promotional gambits, see David Haven Blake's *Walt Whitman and the Culture of American Celebrity*.

10. For a fuller reading of Coleridge's "anxiety of reception," see Newlyn, ch. 2.

11. William S. Ward sees Lamb's review of *The Excursion* as part of a larger campaign within the *Quarterly* to reward Wordsworth for his increasing conservatism. Ward notes, "The puffing which he received in 1814 and 1815 in the pages of the Tory *Quarterly Review* can hardly have been the result of the *Quarterly*'s turning its back on the conservative tradition in poetry; and the favorable reviews which Wordsworth received in 1814 and 1815, after he had become exciseman in 1813, seem to have been something more than coincidences" (99).

12. For insightful readings of Wordsworth's uneasy relationship with commerce in general and advertising in particular, see Rosenbaum, 25–45, and Bradley, 131–38.

13. While Percy Shelley's review of *Frankenstein* was only published posthumously, his puff of the *Memoirs of Prince Alexy Haimatoff* by his best friend, Thomas Jefferson Hogg, appeared in the *Critical Review* for December 1814, well before his early demise. See Seymour, 125 and 583 (n. 27).

14. Lamb's quip about the "'*Elia*' price" alludes to the rate he usually received for magazine articles appearing under his pseudonym "Elia." For an interesting discussion of Lamb's earlier side-career as a writer of lottery puffs, see Strachan, *Advertising*, 189–95.

15. See Reiman, *The Romantics Reviewed*, Part C, vol. 1 for reprints and attributions of these *Examiner* reviews. Another favorite venue of Cockney School puffery was the *Champion*, John Thelwall's liberal London weekly, which ran glowing reviews of Keats and Hazlitt penned by their close friend Reynolds. Quite remarkably, just a few years after penning these puffs, Reynolds anonymously published *The Press, or Literary Chit-Chat* (1822), a book-length satirical poem on puffery and other journalistic abuses. My thanks to Simon Kövesi for this reference.

16. It apparently wasn't just Scott who received a free pass in the *Quarterly*, as near the end of his life Byron suggested that much of his success had resulted from having a publisher who controlled the content of the *Quarterly*. "Murray has long prevented 'The Quarterly' from abusing me," he reportedly told Thomas Medwin. "Some of its bullies have had their fingers itching to be at me" (qtd. in Medwin, 107). For another discussion of the preferential treatment Murray's books supposedly received in the *Quarterly*, see Lockhart, "Noctes Ambrosianae, No. I," 375.

17. It bears noting that at almost the exact moment when Scott was writing "Of the Living Poets of Great Britain" he was also taking the occasion in an anonymous *Quarterly Review* article on J. W. Croker's *The Battles of Talavera* to claim, "The battle of Talavera is written in that irregular Pindaric measure first applied to serious composition by Mr. Walter Scott" (428). More than just a clever bit of self-promotion,

this is also something of a mistruth, as most scholars believe Scott lifted this unusual metrical form from Coleridge's *Christabel*.

18. Hogg included a slightly embellished version of this quotation in his *Anecdotes of Scott*, altering the latter sentence to read: "It is truly amusing to see how artfully a gentleman can place himself at the head of a school *and one who is his superior perhaps at the tail of it*" (21, addition italicized).

19. "Antipuffado" took to the pages of the *Public Ledger* in the 1770s to "out" any merchants suspected of puffing their wares (McKendrick, "Josiah Wedgwood," 123–25). "Anti-Puff" is the pseudonymous author of the 1849 treatise *The Modern Puff*.

20. This instance of what the *Satirist* dubbed critical "quackery" comes in the opening paragraph of Henry Brougham's anonymous review of Thomas Thornton's *The Present State of Turkey*.

21. William Gifford and Thomas Campbell were, respectively, the editors of Murray's *Quarterly Review* and Colburn's *New Monthly Magazine*. For similarly lighthearted send-ups of puffery from this era, see W. H. Ireland's *Scribbleomania* (1815) (esp. 318ff.), Hazlitt's "On Patronage and Puffing" (1821–22), the opening pages of Lockhart's "*Noctes Ambrosianae*, No. I" (1822), and Horace Smith's "Laus Atramenti" (1824).

22. See Jack, 421–24; Sutherland, "The British Book Trade"; Erickson, *Economy*, 19–48; and Dyer, 139–67. How severe the crash of these years actually was has been a matter of some debate. On one side, Sutherland has suggested that the standard story that several publishers declared bankruptcy and a general paralysis hit the book trade from 1826 forward is largely mythical: "Where, one wonders, are the 'scores' of publishers who were swept away by the 'hurricane' of 1826? Essentially, the field is unchanged: 48 publishers account for 73% (668) of the titles in 1824; 44 of them account for 68% (686) of the titles in 1827" ("British Book Trade," 157–59). Sutherland even goes so far as to suggest that poetry, one of the genres supposedly hit hardest in 1825 and 1826, suffered little during these years, with 110 stand-alone volumes of poetry being published in 1824 and 107 in 1827 (155). Yet, more recent studies, which benefit from J. R. de J. Jackson's comprehensive list of published texts, refute Sutherland's findings and support the traditional history of poetry's suffering badly in the late 1820s and early 1830s. Drawing upon Jackson's survey, Erickson and Dyer have shown that the market for English poetry peaked in 1820, when 321 volumes of verse were published, and bottomed out in 1832, when only 110 volumes of verse appeared (Erickson, *Economy*, 28–29; Dyer, 141).

23. For several other quotations from this era on the decline of poetry, see Felluga, 145–47, and St. Clair, *The Reading Nation*, 413–14.

24. Carlyle repeated these sentiments in a 6 February 1832 letter to Macvey Napier: "The bookselling trade seems on the edge of dissolution; the force of puffing can go no farther, yet bankruptcy clamours at every door: sad fate! to serve the Devil, and get no wages even from *him*! The poor Bookseller Guild, I often predict to myself, will ere long be found unfit for the strange part it now plays in our European world; and give place to new and higher arrangements, of which the coming shadows are already becoming visible" (qtd. in Napier, 119–20).

25. See Southern's "Colburniana," "Mr. Campbell's Universe," "The Man of Refinement," "Lord Normanby's Matilda," and "The Puffs of the Month; or Colburniana."

26. Literally scores of other essays and poems from the late 1820s and 1830s decry the influence of puffery. Among the more noteworthy poems are the anonymous "Colburn's Puff" (1831), George Daniel's "The Conversazione" (1835), Thomas Moore's "Thoughts on Patrons, Puffs, and Other Matters" (1839), and Gerald Griffin's "The Prayer of Dullness" (1820s?). For an insightful reading of Griffin's poem in the context of early-nineteenth-century advertising, see Strachan, *Advertising*, 261–63.

27. In *On the Economy of Machinery and Manufactures* (1832), the Cambridge mathematics professor Charles Babbage voiced similar views on the economic effectiveness of periodical puffs: "Under shelter of [friendly reviewers], a host of ephemeral productions are written into a transitory popularity; and by the aid of this process, the shelves of the booksellers, as well as the pockets of the public, are disencumbered. To such an extent are these means employed, that some of the periodical publications of the day ought to be regarded merely as *advertising machines*" (267–68).

28. One of Montgomery's supporters, Edward Clarkson, deemed the parallels between Macaulay's arguments and those of the *Puffiad* more than coincidental, alleging that Macaulay had plagiarized the work of the very author his article sets out to attack (Clarkson, 157).

29. At various moments in the early nineteenth century, this system of anonymous reviewing was severely challenged in the name of cleaning up criticism. In 1809 Richard Cumberland's *London Review* experimented with printing reviewers' names, and in the late 1830s John Stuart Mill began including reviewers' initials in the *Westminster Review* (Mullan, 188, 200). See also the arguments for signed reviewing in Galt's "Anonymous Publications" and S. C. Hall's "On the Anonymous in Periodicals."

CONCLUSION. THE ART OF ADVERTISING

1. For mid-nineteenth-century journalistic perspectives on the postering-over of London, see Dickens's "Bill-Sticking" and the anonymous articles "The Modern Art of Advertising" and "Thoughts on Puffing." The most extensive critical treatment of this phenomenon comes in Sara Thornton's *Advertising, Subjectivity, and the Nineteenth-Century Novel* (see esp. 21–22, 41–48, and 103–5).

2. In 1712, for instance, Joseph Addison remarked in *Tatler* #224 that "the great Art of writing Advertisements, is the finding out a Proper Method to catch the Reader's Eye" (173); and, in 1740, Henry Fielding introduced readers to Gustavus Puffendorf, a man of "Transcendent Skill in the Art of Puffing" (*Champion*, 1:281). See also *Mirror* #80 (1794), which reads one particular advertisement as "a sort of tragic-comic recital" that "if examined by the rules of Aristotle, will be found to contain all the requisites of the best dramatic composition" (2:123). For additional instances of eighteenth-century spoofs on "literary" ads, see Bradley, 119–26.

3. In this same year, 1825, Hood and Reynolds would collaborate on their landmark collection of literary and social satires, *Odes and Addresses to Great People*. For another *jeu d'esprit* on the literariness of blacking ads, see Horace Smith's 1824 *New Monthly Magazine* poem, "Laus Atramenti; or, The Praise of Blacking" (quoted in part in Chapter 3).

4. Other notable mid-nineteenth-century commentaries on the "art of advertising" come in John Fisher Murray's "The World of London, Part VI" (1841), Nicholas

Wiseman's "The Art of Puffing" (1849), Caroline Alice White's "A Chapter on Puffs and Advertisements" (1849), R. W. Hackwood's "Poetical Advertisements" (1855), the *London Magazine*'s "The Modern Art of Advertising" (1863), Andrew Wynter's "The Art of Advertising" (1868), Tennyson Tupper Thompson Smith's "Poetry and Puffery" (1870), and *All the Year Round*'s "Thoughts on Puffing" (1871). For a list of American equivalents from this era, see Blake, 118–20.

Bibliography

PRIMARY WORKS

Addison, Joseph. "*Tatler* No. 224." 1710. In *Selections from the* Tatler *and* Spectator, ed. Angus Ross, 172–75. London: Penguin, 1982.
"Advertisement." *Monthly Review* 1 (May 1749): n.p.
"Advertisement." *The New American Cyclopedia: A Popular Dictionary of General Knowledge*. Ed. George Ripley and Charles A. Dana. Vol. 1. New York: Appleton, 1868.
"The Advertising Age." *Public Advertiser*, April 13, 1785: 3.
"Advertising Considered as an Art." *Chambers' Edinburgh Journal*, December 28, 1844: 401–3.
"The Anniversary." *Knight's Quarterly Magazine* 3 (August 1824): 178–238.
Anti-Puff. *The Modern Puff: An Exposition on the Modern System of Puffing*. London: Strange, 1849.
Arnold, Matthew. "The Function of Criticism at the Present Time." In *Essays in Criticism*, 1–41. London: Macmillan, 1865.
———. "Stanzas from the Grande Chartreuse." *Fraser's Magazine* 51 (April 1855): 437–40.
The Art of Puffing, An Inaugural Oration. Edinburgh: n.p., 1765.
Babbage, Charles. *On the Economy of Machinery and Manufactures*. London: Knight, 1832.
"Bankruptcies Extraordinary." In *Spirit of the Age Newspaper, for 1828*, ed. Robert Cruikshank, 37. London: A. Durham, 1829.
Barnum, P. T. *The Humbugs of the World: An Account of Humbugs, Delusions, Impositions, Quackeries, Deceits and Deceivers Generally, In All Ages*. New York: Carleton, 1866.
Barrett, Eaton Stannard [Polypus, pseud.]. *All the Talents: A Satirical Poem, in Three Dialogues*. 9th ed. London: Stockdale, 1807.
Barton, Bernard. *The Literary Correspondence of Bernard Barton*. Ed. James E. Barcus. Philadelphia: University of Pennsylvania Press, 1966.
———. "To L.E.L." *Literary Magnet* 2 (July 1824): 167.
———. "To L.E.L. On His or Her Poetic Sketches in the Literary Gazette." *Literary Gazette*, February 9, 1822: 89.
Bates, William. *The Maclise Portrait Gallery of Illustrious Literary Characters*. 2nd ed. London: Chatto and Windus, 1898.

Blanchard, Laman. *Life and Literary Remains of L.E.L.* London: Colburn, 1841.
[———]. "Memoir of Letitia Elizabeth Landon." *New Monthly Magazine* 50 (May 1837): 78–82.
"Book Clubs." *The Anti-Jacobin Review and Magazine; or, Monthly Political and Literary Censor* 1 (October 1798): 473–77.
Boswell, James. *The Life of Samuel Johnson, LL.D.* 2 vols. London: Baldwin, 1791.
[Brougham, Henry]. Review of *Hours of Idleness*, by Lord Byron. *Edinburgh Review* 11 (January 1808): 285–89.
[———]. Review of *The Present State of Turkey*, by Thomas Thornton. *Edinburgh Review* 10 (July 1807): 249–71.
Buchanan, James. *A New Pocket-Book for Young Gentlemen and Ladies: Or, A Spelling Dictionary of the English Language.* London: Baldwin, 1757.
Bulwer-Lytton, Edward. *England and the English.* 2 vols. London: Bentley, 1833.
[———]. Review of *Romance and Reality*, by Letitia Elizabeth Landon. *New Monthly Magazine* 32 (December 1831): 545–51.
Burn, James Dawson. *The Language of the Walls: And a Voice from the Shop Windows.* Manchester: Heywood, 1855.
Burney, Frances. *The Witlings.* 1779. In *The Witlings and The Woman-Hater*, ed. Peter Sabor and Geoffrey Sill, 43–172. London: Pickering and Chatto, 1997.
Byron, Lord. *Byron's Letters and Journals.* Ed. Leslie A. Marchand. 12 vols. London: Murray, 1973. (In text, *BLJ*.)
———. *His Very Self and Voice: Collected Conversations of Lord Byron.* Ed. Ernest J. Lovell, Jr. New York: Macmillan, 1954.
———. *Lord Byron: The Complete Poetical Works.* Ed. Jerome J. McGann. 7 vols. Oxford: Clarendon, 1980–1993. (In text, *CPW*.)
[Campbell, Archibald]. *Lexiphanes, A Dialogue.* London: J. Knox, 1767.
Canning, George. *Some Official Correspondence of George Canning.* Ed. Edward J. Stapleton. 2 vols. London: Longmans, 1887.
Carlyle, Thomas. *Past and Present.* London: Chapman and Hall, 1843.
Carlyle, Thomas, and Jane Welsh Carlyle. *The Collected Letters of Thomas and Jane Welsh Carlyle.* Ed. Charles Richard Sanders et al. 40 vols. to date. Durham: Duke University Press, 1970–.
"A Chapter on Names." *Fraser's Magazine* 35 (May 1847): 566–70.
Chatterton, Thomas. "The Art of Puffing by a Bookseller's Journeyman." In *The Complete Works of Thomas Chatterton*, ed. Donald S. Taylor, 1:650–51. 2 vols. Oxford: Clarendon, 1971.
"Cheap Advertisements." *McLean's Monthly Sheet of Caricatures* 2, no. 15 (March 1831): 1.
"Christian Names in England and Wales." *Cornhill Magazine* 23 (March 1871): 337–53.
Clarkson, Edward. *Robert Montgomery and His Reviewers: With Some Remarks on the Present State of English Poetry and on the Laws of Criticism.* London: James Ridgway, 1830.
[Cleland, John]. Review of *The Case of the Unfortunate Bosavern Penlez*, by John Cleland. *Monthly Review* 2 (November 1749): 60–61.
A Coffee-Man. *The Case of the Coffee-men of London and Westminster.* London: G. Smith, 1728.

"Colburn's Puff." *The National Omnibus*, April 29, 1831.
[Coleridge, John Taylor]. Review of *Remorse*, by Samuel Taylor Coleridge. *Quarterly Review* 11 (April 1814): 177–90.
Coleridge, Samuel Taylor. *Biographia Literaria, or Biographical Sketches of My Literary Life and Opinions*. 1817. Ed. James Engell and W. Jackson Bate. Princeton: Princeton University Press, 1983.
———. "Introductory Essay." *The Watchman*. 1796. Ed. Lewis Patton. Princeton: Princeton University Press, 1970.
———. *Letters of Samuel Taylor Coleridge*. Ed. Earl Leslie Griggs. 6 vols. Oxford: Clarendon, 1956–71.
———. *Poetical Works*. Ed. J. C. C. Mays. 3 vols. Princeton: Princeton University Press, 2001.
"Comparative Criticism." *Satirist* 1 (1807): 91–96.
Constable, Thomas, ed. *Archibald Constable and His Literary Correspondents.*. 3 vols. Edinburgh: Edmonston, 1873.
Coppinger, Miss Arabella Bridget [pseud.]. "The Lament: A Poetical Dialogue between L.E.L. and W. Jerdan, in the Manner of Both." *Royal Lady's Magazine* 3 (June 1832): 265–68.
Crabbe, George. *The News-Paper: A Poem*. London: J. Dodsley, 1785.
Dallas, Robert Charles. *Recollections of the Life of Lord Byron, from the Year 1808 to the End of 1814*. London: Knight, 1824.
[———]. Review of *Childe Harold's Pilgrimage*, by Lord Byron. *Literary Panorama* 11 (March 1812): 417–30.
"Dallas's *Recollections of Lord Byron*." *Gentleman's Magazine* 94 (November 1824): 529–31.
[Daniel, George]. "The Conversazione." In *The Modern Dunciad: Virgil in London and Other Poems*, 217–30. London: Pickering, 1835.
Deacon, William Frederick. *Warreniana*. 1824. Ed. John Strachan. Vol. 4 of *Parodies of the Romantic Age*. London: Pickering and Chatto, 1999.
Defoe, Daniel. *The Complete English Tradesman, in Familiar Letters; Directing Him in All the Several Parts and Progressions of Trade*. London: Rivington, 1725.
———. *A Journal of the Plague Year: Being Observations or Memorials, Of the Most Remarkable Occurrences, As Well Publick as Private, Which Happened in London During the Last Great Visitation in 1665*. London: E. Nutt, 1722.
"Dialogues of the Living. No. IX." *The Repository of Arts, Literature, Fashions, Manufactures, Etc*. 2nd ser. 7 (March 1819): 144–47.
Dickens, Charles. "Bill-Sticking." *Household Words*, March 22, 1851: 601–6.
———. *The Old Curiosity Shop*. London: Chapman, 1841.
[Disraeli, Benjamin]. "The Dunciad of To-Day." *Star Chamber*, May 10, 1826: 75–84.
"The Divan." *Athenaeum*, September 23, 1829: 599.
"Domestic and Literary Intelligence." *Inspector and Literary Review* 1 (1826): 324.
Dudley, Henry Bate. *The Dramatic Puffers, A Prelude*. London: G. Kearsley, 1782.
[Duppa, Richard]. *An Address to the Parliament of Great Britain, on the Claims of Authors to Their Own Copy-Right*. 2nd ed. London: Longman, 1813.
Edgeworth, Maria. *Belinda*. 1801. Ed. Kathryn J. Kirkpatrick. Oxford: Oxford University Press, 1994.

———. *Ennui*. Vol. 1 of *Tales of Fashionable Life*. London: Johnson, 1809.
"The Editor's Room." *Royal Lady's Magazine* 1 (February 1831): 107–9.
[Ellis, George]. Review of *Childe Harold's Pilgrimage*, by Lord Byron. *Quarterly Review* 7 (March 1812): 180–200.
"Euonomy; or, The Art of Novel Writing." *La Belle Assemblée* 2 (September 1825): 97–98.
"Exhibition at Somerset House." *Literary Chronicle and Weekly Review*, May 14, 1825: 317–19.
[Fay, Theodore Sedgwick]. "The Novel." *New-York Mirror*, March 5, 1825: 254–55.
"Female Literature, With a Review of the Poems, by L.E.L." *European Magazine and London Review* 86 (August 1824): 156–60.
Fielding, Henry. *The Champion: Containing a Series of Papers, Humorous, Moral, Political, and Critical*. 2 vols. London: J. Huggonson, 1741.
——— [Conny Keyber, pseud.]. *An Apology for the Life of Mrs. Shamela Andrews*. London: Dodd, 1741.
"Fine Arts." *Literary Gazette*, May 28, 1825: 347–48.
"Fine Arts: Exhibition at Somerset House." *Literary Magnet* 4 (1826): 42–45.
"Fine Arts: Exhibition of the Royal Academy (Seventh and Concluding Notice)." *Literary Gazette*, June 19, 1830: 402–3.
"Fine Arts Exhibitions, &c.: Royal Academy." *Belle Assemblée; or, Court and Fashionable Magazine* 12 (July 1830): 40–41.
The Follies of St. James's Street. 2 vols. London: William Lane, 1789.
[Francis, George Henry]. "The Age of Veneer: The Science of Puffing." *Fraser's Magazine* 45 (January 1852): 87–93.
[Free, John]. *The Monthly Reviewers Reviewed by an Antigallican*. London: E. Owen, 1755.
Frith, W. P. "Artistic Advertising." *The Magazine of Art* 12 (1889): 421–23.
Galt, John. "Anonymous Publications." *Fraser's Magazine* 11 (May 1835): 549–51.
———. *The Autobiography of John Galt*. 2 vols. London: Cochrane, 1833.
Ginsberg, Allen. "Howl." In *Howl and Other Poems*, 9–26. San Francisco: City Lights, 1956.
Gore, Catherine. "Sketches of Modern Character. No. II. Popular People." *New Monthly Magazine* 60 (October 1840): 161–65.
Griffin, Gerald. "The Prayer of Dullness." In *The Poetical Works of Gerald Griffin, Esq.*, 8:263–66. 8 vols. London: Simpkin and Marshall, 1843.
[Griffiths, Ralph]. Review of *The Dictionary of Love*, by John Cleland. *Monthly Review* 9 (December 1753): 464–67.
———. Review of *Felicia to Charlotte*, by Mary Collier. *Monthly Review* 2 (January 1750): 229.
———. Review of *Memoirs of Fanny Hill*, by John Cleland. *Monthly Review* 2 (March 1750): 431–32.
———. Review of *The Oeconomy of a Winter's Day*, by John Cleland. *Monthly Review* 4 (December 1750): 135.
———. Review of *Physical Essay on the Senses*, by Claude Nicolas LeCat. *Monthly Review* 1 (May 1749): 28–38.

Hackwood, R. W. "Poetical Advertisements." *Notes and Queries*, November 3, 1855: 340.

H[all], A[nna] M[aria]. "The Portraits of L.E.L." *Art-Union*, February, 15, 1839: 3–4.

Hall, S[amuel] C[arter]. *A Book of Memories of Great Men and Women of the Age, from Personal Acquaintance*. London: Virtue and Co., 1871.

[———]. "Literature in 1834." *New Monthly Magazine* 40 (1834): 497–505.

[———]. "On the Anonymous in Periodicals." *New Monthly Magazine* 39 (September 1833): 2–6.

[Hayward, Abraham]. "The Advertising System." *Edinburgh Review* 77 (February 1843): 1–43.

Hazlitt, William. "On Patronage and Puffing." In *Table Talk; or, Original Essays on Men and Manners*, 2:303–34. 2nd ed. 2 vols. London: Colburn, 1824.

[Hill, John]. Review of *The Actor*, by John Hill. *Monthly Review* 3 (July 1750): 189–97.

[———]. Review of *The Adventures of Mr. Loveill*, by John Hill. *Monthly Review* 3 (May 1750): 58.

The History of Little Goody Two-Shoes; Otherwise Called, Mrs. Margery Two-Shoes. London: Newbery, 1766.

Hobhouse, John Cam. *Recollections of a Long Life*. Ed. Lady Dorchester. 2 vols. New York: Scribner's, 1909.

[———]. "Review of Dallas and Medwin." *Westminster Review* 3 (January 1825):1–35.

Hogg, James. *Anecdotes of Scott*. 1834. Ed. Jill Rubenstein. Edinburgh: Edinburgh University Press, 2004.

———. *The Spy: A Periodical Paper of Literary Amusement and Instruction Published Weekly in 1810 and 1811*. Ed. Gillian Hughes. Edinburgh: Edinburgh University Press, 2000.

[Hood, Thomas]. "The Advertising Literature of the Age." *New Monthly Magazine* 67 (January 1843): 111–16.

———. [P.A.Z., pseud.]. "The Art of Advertizing Made Easy." *London Magazine*, new series, 1 (February 1825): 246–53.

Hood, Thomas, and John Hamilton Reynolds. *Odes and Addresses to Great People*. London: Baldwin, 1825.

Howitt, William. *Homes and Haunts of the Most Eminent British Poets*. 2nd ed. 2 vols. London: Bentley, 1847.

Huish, Robert. *The Last Voyage of Capt. Sir John Ross, Knt. R.N. to the Arctic Regions; for the Discovery of a North West Passage; Performed in the Years 1829–30–31–32 and 33*. London: Saunders, 1835.

Hunt, Leigh. *Lord Byron and Some of His Contemporaries; With Recollections of the Author's Life, and of His Visit to Italy*. London: Colburn, 1828.

[———]. *Prospectus of The Examiner, A New Sunday Paper, Upon Politics, Domestic Economy, and Theatricals*. London, 1808.

[———]. Review of *Lectures on the English Comic Poets*, by William Hazlitt. *Examiner*, April 18, 1819: 250–51.

[———]. Review of *Lectures on the English Comic Writers* (continued), by William Hazlitt. *Examiner*, June 6, 1819: 362–63.

[———]. Review of *Poems by John Keats. Examiner*, June 1, 1817, 345.

[———]. Review of *Poems by John Keats* (continued). *Examiner*, July 6, 1817: 428–29.
[———]. Review of *Poems by John Keats* (continued). *Examiner*, July 13, 1817, 443–44.
[———]. Review of *Revolt of Islam*, by Percy Bysshe Shelley. *Examiner*, February 1, 1818: 75–76.
[———]. Review of *Revolt of Islam* (continued), by Percy Bysshe Shelley. *Examiner*, February 22, 1818: 121–22.
[———]. Review of *Revolt of Islam* (continued), by Percy Bysshe Shelley. *Examiner*, March 1, 1818: 139–41.
[———]. Review of *Rosalind and Helen*, by Percy Bysshe Shelley. *Examiner*, May 9, 1819: 302–3.
[———]. "Young Poets." *Examiner*, December 1, 1816: 761–62.
[Ireland, William Henry]. *Scribbleomania; or, The Printer's Devil's Polichronicon*. London: Sherwood, 1815.
Jackson, Mason. "Popular Art." *English Illustrated Magazine* 12 (November 1824): 77–83.
James, Robert. *A Dissertation on Fevers and Inflammatory Distempers*. London: Newbery, 1748.
Jerdan, William. *The Autobiography of William Jerdan*. 4 vols. London: Arthur Hall, 1853.
[———]. "The Grand Force!" *Fraser's Magazine* 79 (March 1869): 380–83.
Johnson, Samuel. *A Dictionary of the English Language*. London, 1755.
———. *The Idler and the Adventurer*. Ed. W. J. Bate, John M. Bullitt, and L. F. Powell. New Haven: Yale University Press, 1963.
[J.W.C.]. "Sonnet to L.E.L." *Mirror of Literature, Amusement, and Instruction*, December 4, 1824: 392.
Keats, John. *The Letters of John Keats*. Ed. Maurice Buxton Forman. 4th ed. New York: Oxford University Press, 1952.
[———]. Review of *Peter Bell, A Lyrical Ballad*, by John Hamilton Reynolds. *Examiner*, April 25, 1819: 270.
[Kilgour, Alexander]. *Anecdotes of Lord Byron, From Authentic Sources*. London: Knight and Lacey, 1825.
"Lady's Letter." *Dublin Literary Gazette*, May 15, 1830: 314–15.
Lamb, Charles. *The Letters of Charles Lamb*. 5 vols. Boston: Bibliophile Society, 1905.
[———]. Review of *The Excursion: A Poem*, by William Wordsworth. *Quarterly Review* 12 (October 1814): 100–111.
[———]. Review of *Lamia and Other Poems*, by John Keats. *Examiner*, July 30, 1820: 494–95.
Landon, Letitia Elizabeth. *The Fate of Adelaide, A Swiss Romantic Tale; and Other Poems*. London: Warren, 1821.
———. *The Improvisatrice; and Other Poems*. London: Hurst, 1824.
———. *Letters by Letitia Elizabeth Landon*. Ed. F. J. Sypher. Ann Arbor: Scholars' Facsimiles, 2001.
[———]. "Lines on the Mausoleum of the Princess Charlotte at Claremont." *Gentleman's Magazine* 94 (January 1824): 71–72.
———. *Romance and Reality*. 3 vols. London: Colburn and Bentley, 1831.
[———]. "Rome." *Literary Gazette*, March 11, 1820: 173.

[———]. "Valedictory Lines to a Cadet on Embarking to India." *Gentleman's Magazine* 93 (June 1823): 636.

———. *The Vow of the Peacock, and Other Poems*. London: Saunders, 1835.

"Landon's and Montgomery's Poetry." *Monthly Review*, new series, 13 (February 1830): 159–72.

"Libraries and Catalogues." *Quarterly Review* 72 (May 1843): 1–23.

"List of Those Who Pay to Have Themselves Puffed in the Newspapers." *Telegraph*, February 11, 1797: 2.

"The Literary Gazette." *Athenaeum*, September 4, 1830.

"The Literary Gazette and the Novel 'Truth.'" *Examiner*, August 20, 1826: 532.

"Literary Notes." *The British Controversialist and Literary Magazine*. London: Houlston, 1866. 320.

[Lloyd, Robert]. "The Puff: A Dialogue between the Bookseller and Author." *St. James's Magazine* 1 (September 1762): 1–8.

Lockhart, John Gibson. *Memoirs of the Life of Sir Walter Scott, Baronet*. 7 vols. Philadelphia: Carey, 1837.

[———]. "Noctes Ambrosianae, No. I." *Blackwood's Edinburgh Magazine* 11 (March 1822): 369–71.

[———]. "Noctes Ambrosianae, No. III." *Blackwood's Edinburgh Magazine* 11 (May 1822): 601–18.

[———]. "Noctes Ambrosianae, No. VII." *Blackwood's Edinburgh Magazine* 13 (March 1823): 369–84.

[———]. "Noctes Ambrosianae, No. XVI." *Blackwood's Edinburgh Magazine* 16 (August 1824): 231–50.

[———]. Review of *Lights and Shadows of Scottish Life*, by John Wilson. *Blackwood's Edinburgh Magazine* 11 (June 1822): 669–77.

The London Journal, January 13, 1721: 3.

[Macaulay, Thomas Babington]. "Mr. Robert Montgomery's Poems, and the Modern Practice of Puffing." *Edinburgh Review* 51 (April 1830): 193–210.

[Maginn, William]. "An Apology for a Preface to our Fourth Volume." *Fraser's Magazine*, 4 (1831): 1–7.

[———]. "The Gallery of Illustrious Literary Characters, No. I: William Jerdan, Esq., Editor of the 'Literary Gazette.'" *Fraser's Magazine* 5 (June 1830): 605–6.

[———]. "Miss Landon's Poetry." *Blackwood's Edinburgh Magazine* 16 (August 1824): 189–93.

[———]. "Noctes Ambrosianae, No. IV." *Blackwood's Edinburgh Magazine* 12 (July 1822): 100–114.

[———]. Review of *The Dominie's Legacy*, by Andrew Picken. *Fraser's Magazine* 1 (1830): 318–35.

[Maginn, William, and John Gibson Lockhart]. "Letters of Timothy Tickler, Esq. to Eminent Literary Characters, No. VIII." *Blackwood's Edinburgh Magazine* 14 (August 1823): 212–35.

"Mahogany." *Chambers' Edinburgh Journal*, March 22, 1851: 181–83.

[Mahony, Francis]. "Gallery of Literary Characters. No XLI. Miss Landon." *Fraser's* 8 (October 1833): 433.

Maw-Worm, Richard [pseud.]. *The Trifler, A Periodical Paper.* 2nd ed. Edinburgh: John Elder, 1797.
Medwin, Thomas. *Conversations of Lord Byron.* 1824. Ed. Ernest J. Lovell, Jr. Princeton: Princeton University Press, 1966.
[Merle, Gibbons]. "Provincial Newspaper Press." *Westminster Review* 12 (January 1830): 69–103.
"The Mirror No. 80." *The Mirror*, 2: 119–25. 2 vols. London: J. Parsons, 1794.
"The Mirror of Fashion." *Morning Chronicle*, May 23, 1817: 3.
"The Modern Art of Advertising." *London Society* 4 (August 1863): 188–92.
Moncrieff, W. T. *Wanted a Wife, or, A Checque on my Banker.* London: Lowndes, 1819.
[Montgomery, Robert]. *The Age Reviewed: A Satire.* London: Carpenter, 1827.
——. *The Puffiad: A Satire.* London: Maunder, 1828.
"Monthly Catalogue." *Monthly Review* 1 (July 1749): 238.
"Monumental Advertisements." *Notes and Queries*, 4th series, 2 (July 1868): 33.
Moore, Edward [Adam Fitz-Adam, pseud.]. "The World #115." In *The World, for the Year One Thousand Seven Hundred and Fifty-Five*, 689–94. London: Dodsley, 1755.
Moore, Thomas. *Letters and Journals of Lord Byron: With Notices of His Life.* 2 vols. London: Murray, 1830.
[——]. "Thoughts on Patrons, Puffs, and Other Matters." *Bentley's Miscellany* 3 (March 1839): 326–28.
Morgan, Lady Sydney. *Lady Morgan's Memoirs: Autobiography, Diaries and Correspondence.* 2 vols. London: Allen, 1862.
Murphy, Arthur. *The Gray's-Inn Journal.* 2 vols. Dublin: Sleater, 1756.
Murray, John. *The Letters of John Murray to Lord Byron.* Ed. Andrew Nicholson. Liverpool: Liverpool University Press, 2007.
[Murray, John Fisher]. "The World of London. Part VI." *Blackwood's Edinburgh Magazine* 50 (October 1841): 477–89.
"Names." *Chambers' Edinburgh Journal*, May 4, 1833: 1.
Napier, Macvey. *Selections from the Correspondence of the Late Macvey Napier, Esq.* Ed. Macvey Napier. London: Harrison, 1877.
"New Books." *Ladies' Companion and Monthly Magazine*, 2nd series, 1 (June 1852): 327–29.
Nightingale, Joseph. *The Beauties of England and Wales; or Delineations Topographical, Historical, and Descriptive.* Vol. 13. London: Harris, 1813.
"Notices to and Communications from Correspondents." *Oxberry's Dramatic Biography*, April 2, 1825: 248–50.
Nugent, Thomas. *A New Pocket Dictionary of the French and English Languages.* London: Dilly, 1767.
"Ode to L.E.L. Authoress of the Improvisatrice, and Other Poems." *London Magazine* 12 (August 1825): 582–84.
"On Advertisements; and Advertising, Considered as One of the Fine Arts; in Which the Theory and Practice are Combined." *Tait's Edinburgh Magazine* 2 (September 1835): 575–82.
"On Criticism in General; More Particularly on Theatrical Criticism." *Dublin University Magazine* 37 (June 1851): 727–32.

One Master Trimmer. *The Siege of Pater Noster Row: A Moral Satire*. London: G. Richards, 1826.
"On the Learning of Oxford Tradesmen and College Servants." In *The Student, or, The Oxford Monthly Miscellany*, 1:53–56. 5 vols. London: J. Newbery, 1750.
"Original Correspondence." *Dublin Literary Gazette*, March 6, 1830: 155–56.
Oulton, Walley Chamberlain. *The Busy Body; A Collection of Periodical Essays, Moral, Whimsical, Comic, and Sentimental*. 2 vols. London: C. Stalker, 1789.
[Packwood, George]. "A Dialogue Between a Merchant and His Black Servant." *Morning Post*, November 5, 1794: 3.
———. *Packwood's Whim. The Goldfinch's Nest; or, The Way to Get Money and Be Happy*. London: n.p., 1796.
"A Paper on Puffing." *Ainsworth's Magazine* 2 (1842): 42–47.
"Parody of a Cambridge Examination Paper." *Times*, January 25, 1816: 3.
"Parody of a Cambridge Examination Paper." *Times*, January 17, 1825: 3.
Paulding, James Kirke. *A Sketch of Old England, by a New England Man*. 2 vols. New York: Charles Wiley, 1822.
"Periodical Publications." *Literary Gazette*, December 6, 1823: 781.
Pindar, Peregrine [pseud.]. *Ode to the Hero of Finsbury Square: Congratulatory on His Late Marriage, and Illustrative of His Genius As His Own Biographer*. London: I. Herbert, 1795.
The Poetical March of Humbug! By the Great Unmentionable: Being Burlesque Imitations of the Principal Poets of the Day, After the Manner of "Rejected Addresses." London: James Gilbert, 1832.
"Pompey's Pillar." *The Champion Journal for the Boys of the United Kingdom*, October 13, 1877: 79.
Pope, Alexander. *The Correspondence of Alexander Pope*. Ed. George Sherburn. 5 vols. Oxford: Clarendon, 1956.
———. *An Epistle from Mr. Pope, to Dr. Arbuthnot*. London: J. Wright, 1734 [1735].
[———]. *The Spectator* No. 452, August 8, 1712.
"Prose Postscript." *John Bull Magazine* 1 (July 1824): 37–38.
"Puff Extraordinary." *Satirist* 4 (1809): 588–90.
"Puffing, and *The Puffiad*." *Westminster Review* 9 (1828): 441–50.
Puffs and Mysteries; or, The Romance of Advertising. London: W. Kent, 1855.
[Q. B.]. Letter. *Gentleman's Magazine* 91 (December 1821): 598.
Review of *An Address to Dr. Huddesford*. *Monthly Review* 12 (April–May 1755): 396.
Review of *A Day in Autumn*, by Bernard Barton. *Literary Gazette*, November 4, 1820: 709–10.
Review of *Forget Me Not, A New Christmas and New Year's Present for 1827*. *Atlas*, October 22, 1826: 362–63.
Review of *The Golden Violet, with its Tales of Romance and Chivalry, and Other Poems*, by Letitia Elizabeth Landon. *Gentleman's Magazine* 97 (March 1827): 239–41.
Review of *The Golden Violet, with its Tales of Romance and Chivalry, and Other Poems*, by Letitia Elizabeth Landon. *The Inspector, Literary Magazine, and Review* 2 (1827): 241–48.

Review of *The Golden Violet, with its Tales of Romance and Chivalry, and Other Poems*, by Letitia Elizabeth Landon. *Literary Gazette*, December 16, 1826: 785–87.

Review of *The Golden Violet, with its Tales of Romance and Chivalry, and Other Poems*, by Letitia Elizabeth Landon. *Monthly Review*, new series, 4 (January 1827): 57–65.

Review of *The Happy Release; or, the History of Charles Warton and Sophia Harley*. *Critical Review* 62 (November 1786): 391.

Review of *The Improvisatrice, and Other Poems*, by Letitia Elizabeth Landon. *Attic Miscellany* 1 (October 1824): 150–51.

Review of *The Improvisatrice, and Other Poems*, by Letitia Elizabeth Landon. *Literary Chronicle*, July 10, 1824: 435–36.

Review of *The Improvisatrice, and Other Poems*, by Letitia Elizabeth Landon. *Literary Gazette*, July 3, 1824: 417–20.

Review of *The Improvisatrice, and Other Poems*, by Letitia Elizabeth Landon. *Literary Gazette*, July 10, 1824: 436–37.

Review of *The Improvisatrice, and Other Poems*, by Letitia Elizabeth Landon. *Literary Magnet* 2 (July 1824): 106–9.

Review of *Introduction and Rondo for the Pianoforte, Composed, and Dedicated to Miss Landon*, by John Hopkinson. *Repository of Arts, Literature, Fashion, Manufactures, Etc.*, March 1, 1824: 176–77.

Review of *A Journal of the Heart*. *Athenaeum*, August 21, 1830.

Review of *The Labyrinths of Life*. *Monthly Review*, 2nd series, 5 (July 1791): 337–38.

Review of *Letters from the Aegean*, by James Emerson. *Edinburgh Literary Journal*, February 14, 1829: 189–92.

Review of *The Ligature Preferable to Agaric*. *Monthly Review* 12 (February 1755): 157.

Review of *Memoirs of Celebrated Female Sovereigns*. *Athenaeum*, October 29, 1831: 730–31.

Review of *Memoirs of the Life of Sir Walter Scott, Baronet*, by John Gibson Lockhart. *Knickerbocker* 12 (October 1838): 349–66.

Review of *The Minor; or, the History of George O'Nial, Esq. Critical Review* 63 (April 1787): 307–8.

Review of *Poems*, by Bernard Barton. *Literary Gazette*, April 22, 1820: 260–63.

Review of *The Poetical Album. London Weekly Review*. Reprinted in *Museum of Foreign Literature and Science* 13 (December 1828): 717–19.

Review of *The Poetical March of Humbug! Literary Gazette*, August 11, 1832: 505.

Review of *Poets and Poetry*, by Richard Ryan. *Literary Gazette*, March 31, 1827: 197–98.

Review of *Rob Roy*, by Walter Scott. *Analectic Magazine* 11 (April 1818): 273–311.

Review of *The Royal Lady's Magazine, and Archives of the Court of St. James's. Literary Gazette*, January 8, 1831: 25.

[Reynolds, John Hamilton]. *The Press, or Literary Chit-Chat. A Satire*. London: Relfe, 1822.

[———]. "Professor Wilson's Danciad." *Westminster Review* 2 (July 1824): 213–24.

[———]. Review of *Characters of Shakespear's Plays*, by William Hazlitt. *Champion*, July 16, 1817: 237.

[———]. Review of *Endymion*, by John Keats. *Examiner*, October 11, 1818: 648–49.

[———]. Review of *Poems by John Keats*. *Champion*, March 9, 1817: 78.

"The Rhyming Review." *John Bull Magazine* 1 (August 1824): 76–78.
Rossetti, Dante Gabriel. "Maclise's Character-Portraits." *Academy*, April 15, 1871: 217–18.
Ryan, Richard. *Poets and Poetry: Being a Collection of the Choicest Anecdotes Relative to the Poets of Every Age and Nation*. London: Sherwood, 1826.
[St. Barbe, R. F.]. "Semihorae Biographicae, No. III." *Blackwood's Edinburgh Magazine* 8 (January 1821): 355–58.
Scott, Walter. *Chronicles of the Canongate*. 2 vols. Edinburgh: Cadell, 1827.
[———.]. "Of the Living Poets of Great Britain." *Edinburgh Annual Register* 1 (1810): 417–43.
———. *Periodical Criticism by Sir Walter Scott, Baronet*. Vol. 19 of *The Miscellaneous Prose Works of Sir Walter Scott, Baronet*. Edinburgh: Cadell, 1835.
[———]. Review of *The Battles of Talavera*, by J. W. Croker. *Quarterly Review* 2 (1809): 426–33.
[———]. Review of *Tales of My Landlord*, by Walter Scott. *Quarterly Review* 16 (1817): 430–80.
Scott, William Bell. Introduction. *The Poetical Works of Letitia Elizabeth Landon*. Ed. William Bell Scott. London: Routledge, 1880. xi–xvi.
[Shebbeare, John]. *Lydia, or Filial Piety*. 4 vols. London: J. Scott, 1755.
[Shelley, Mary]. Review of *Cloudesley*, by William Godwin. *Blackwood's Edinburgh Magazine* 27 (May 1830): 711–16.
[Shelley, Percy Bysshe]. Review of *Mandeville*, by William Godwin. *Examiner*, December 28, 1817: 826–27.
Sheridan, Richard Brinsley. *The Critic, or, A Tragedy Rehearsed*. 1779. In *The School for Scandal and Other Plays*, ed. Michael Cordner, 289–337. Oxford: Oxford University Press, 1998.
"A Short Dissertation on Puffs." *Grub-Street Journal*, June 12, 1735: 1.
"A Short Dissertation on Puffs [cont.]." *Grub-Street Journal*, June 19, 1735: 1.
Smart, Christopher. *Hymn to the Supreme Being, on Recovery from a Dangerous Fit of Illness*. London: Newbery, 1756.
[Smith, Horace]. "Laus Atramenti; or, The Praise of Blacking." *New Monthly Magazine* 11 (November 1824): 416.
Smith, Tennyson Tupper Thompson [pseud.]. "Poetry and Puffery." *Punch*, November 19, 1870: 211.
[Smollett, Tobias]. Review of *Treatise on Midwifery*. *Monthly Review* 5 (December 1751): 465–66.
"Song 202: The Innkeeper's Song." In *The Vocal Magazine; or, British Songster's Miscellany*, 54. London: Bew, 1778.
[Southern, Henry]. "Colburniana." *London Magazine*, 2nd series, 1 (1825): 265–69.
[———]. "Lord Normanby's Matilda." *London Magazine*, 2nd series, 4 (1826): 47–48.
[———]. "The Man of Refinement." *London Magazine*, 2nd series, 2 (1825): 128–31.
[———]. "Mr. Campbell's Universe." *London Magazine*, 2nd series, 2 (1825): 36–40.
[———]. "The Puffs of the Month; or Colburniana." *London Magazine*, 2nd series, 5 (1826): 31–32.
Southey, Robert. *Letters from England*. 1807. Ed. Jack Simmons. London: Cresset, 1951.

———. *The Life and Correspondence of Robert Southey.* Ed. Charles Cuthbert Southey. 6 vols. London: Longman, 1850.

"Specimens of Puffing." *Satirist* 6 (1810): 588–90.

Sterne, Laurence. *The Life and Opinions of Tristram Shandy, Gentleman.* 2 vols. York: A. Ward, 1760 [1759].

Sternhold, Thomas. *The Daily Advertiser, In Metre.* 2nd ed. London: Kearsly, 1781.

Stoddard, Richard Henry, ed. *Personal Reminiscences by Chorley, Planché, and Young.* New York: Scribner, 1874.

"Table Talk." *North American Magazine* 3 (March 1834): 356–58.

[Tait, William]. "A Tête à Tête with Mr. Tait." *Tait's Edinburgh Magazine* 1 (1832): 9–16.

Thackeray, William Makepeace. *Notes of A Journey from Cornhill to Grand Cairo: By Way of Lisbon, Athens, Constantinople, and Jerusalem.* 2nd ed. London: Chapman and Hall, 1846.

[———]. "Puffing and Fishing." *The National Standard of Literature, Science, Music, Theatricals, and the Fine Arts,* October 12, 1833: 221.

Thomson, Katherine Byerley. *The Queens of Society.* New York: Harper, 1861.

"Thoughts on Puffing." *All the Year Round,* March 4, 1871: 329–32.

"Titled Authors. *The Keepsake, for 1831.*" *Royal Lady's Magazine* 1 (January 1831): 37–47.

"Titled Authors. *The Keepsake, for 1832.*" *Royal Lady's Magazine* 2 (December 1831): 338–53.

"To Correspondents." *Literary Gazette,* January 1, 1825: 14.

"To Correspondents." *Medical Times and Gazette,* August 18, 1860: 174.

Toupee, S. "To the Author of the *Scots Magazine.*" *Scots Magazine* 1 (1739): 181–82.

The Town, or, A Vindication of Puffing: A Satirical Dialogue. London: Ridgeway, 1785.

Tristan, Flora. *The London Journal of Flora Tristan, 1842, or, The Aristocracy and the Working Class of England.* Trans. Jean Hawkes. London: Virago, 1982.

Trollope, Anthony. *The Struggles of Brown, Jones, and Robinson: By One of the Firm.* 1861–62. Oxford: Oxford University Press, 1992.

[Trusler, John]. *Modern Times, or The Adventures of Gabriel Outcast.* 3 vols. London: J. Walter, 1785.

"Universal Advertiser, No. 50." *The Universal Advertiser.* Dublin, 1754.

"Varieties." *The Preston Chronicle, and Lancashire Advertiser,* September 5, 1840: 2.

Wedgwood, Josiah. *Correspondence of Josiah Wedgwood.* Ed. Katherine Eufemia Farrer. 3 vols. Cambridge: Cambridge University Press, 2011.

The Weekly Register: or, Universal Journal, May 27, 1732: 1.

Whitaker, Edward. "Name Choosing." In *Good Words for 1885,* ed. Donald Macleod, 92–96. London: Isbister, 1885.

White, Caroline Alice. "A Chapter on Puffs and Advertisements." *Ainsworth's Magazine* 16 (July 1849): 42–46.

[Wilson, John]. "*Noctes Ambrosianae,* No. XXVII." *Blackwood's Edinburgh Magazine* 20 (July 1826): 90–109.

[Wiseman, Nicholas]. "The Art of Puffing." *Dublin Review* 27 (September 1849): 146–62.

[W.L.R.]. "To L.E.L." *Literary Gazette,* February 15, 1823: 107.

Wolcot, John [Peter Pindar, pseud.]. *A Poetical, Supplicating, Modest, and Affecting Epistle to Those Literary Colossuses, the Reviewers.* London: Baldwin, 1778.
Wordsworth, William. "Essay, Supplementary to the Preface." 1815. In *Shorter Poems, 1807–1820*, ed. Carl H. Ketcham. Ithaca: Cornell University Press, 1989.
———. *The Prelude: A Parallel Text.* Ed. J. C. Maxwell. London: Penguin, 1971.
Wordsworth, William, and Dorothy Wordsworth. *The Letters of William and Dorothy Wordsworth.* Ed. Ernest de Selincourt. 2nd ed. Revised by Mary Moorman and Alan G. Hill. 8 vols. Oxford: Clarendon, 1967–93.
[Wynter, Andrew]. "Advertisements." *Quarterly Review* 97 (July 1855): 95–117.
[———]. "The Art of Advertising." *Every Saturday*, June 6, 1868: 732–35.
[X]. "To Bernard Barton. On the Publication of His Last Poem, 'A Day in Autumn.'" *Literary Gazette*, December 9, 1820: 795.
Yonge, Charlotte M. *History of Christian Names.* London: Parker, 1863.

SECONDARY WORKS

Adorno, Theodor. *Aesthetic Theory.* Ed. Gretel Adorno and Rolf Tiedemann. Trans. C. Lenhardt. London: Routledge, 1984.
Asquith, Ivon. "Advertising and the Press in the Late Eighteenth and Early Nineteenth Centuries: James Perry and the *Morning Chronicle*, 1790–1821." *The Historical Journal* 18.4 (1975): 703–24.
———. "The Structure, Ownership and Control of the Press, 1780–1855." In Boyce et al., eds., *Newspaper History*, 98–116.
Atkin, Douglas. *The Culting of Brands: Turn Your Customers into True Believers.* New York: Portfolio, 2004.
Baiesi, Serena. *Letitia Elizabeth Landon and Metrical Romance: The Adventures of a Literary Genius.* Bern: Peter Lang, 2010.
Barnard, John, ed. *Pope: The Critical Heritage.* London: Routledge, 1973.
Barthes, Roland. "The Death of the Author." 1968. In *Image-Music-Text*, ed. and trans. Stephen Heath, 142–48. New York: Noonday, 1977.
———. "The New Citroen." 1957. In *Mythologies*, ed. and trans. Annette Lavers, 88–90. New York: Noonday, 1972.
———. "Rhetoric of the Image." 1964. In *Image-Music-Text*, ed. and trans. Stephen Heath, 32–51. New York: Noonday, 1977.
Basker, James. "Criticism and the Rise of Periodical Literature." In Nisbet and Rawson, eds., *The Cambridge History*, 316–32.
———. *Tobias Smollett: Critic and Journalist.* Newark: University of Delaware Press, 1988.
Baudrillard, Jean. "The Ideological Genesis of Needs." 1969. In Schor and Holt, eds., *The Consumer Society Reader*, 57–80.
Belanger, Terry. "Publishers and Writers in Eighteenth-Century England." In *Books and Their Readers in Eighteenth-Century England*, ed. Isabel Rivers, 5–25. New York: St. Martin's, 1982.
Benjamin, Walter. "The Work of Art in the Age of Mechanical Reproduction." 1936. In *Illuminations*, ed. Hannah Arendt, 217–51. New York: Schocken, 1968.
Bennett, Andrew. *The Author.* London: Routledge, 2005.

Bennett, Scott. "John Murray's Family Library and the Cheapening of Books in Early Nineteenth-Century Britain." *Studies in Bibliography* 29 (1976): 139–66.

Benson, John, and Laura Ugolini, eds. *Cultures of Selling: Perspectives on Consumption and Society since 1700*. Aldershot: Ashgate, 2006.

Besterman, Theodore, ed. *The Publishing Firm of Cadell and Davies: Select Correspondence and Accounts, 1793–1836*. Oxford: Oxford University Press, 1938.

Blake, David Haven. *Walt Whitman and the Culture of American Celebrity*. New Haven: Yale University Press, 2006.

Blakey, Dorothy. *The Minerva Press, 1790–1820*. London: Bibliographical Society, 1939.

Bonnell, Thomas F. *The Most Disreputable Trade: Publishing the Classics of English Poetry, 1765–1810*. Oxford: Oxford University Press, 2008.

Boyce, George, et al., eds. *Newspaper History: From the Seventeenth Century to the Present Day*. London: Constable, 1978.

Bracken, James K., and Joel Silver, eds. *The British Literary Book Trade, 1700–1820*. Vol. 154 of *Dictionary of Literary Biography*. Detroit: Gale, 1995.

Bradley, Andrea. "Wanted: Advertising in British Literature, 1700–1830." Ph.D. diss., Vanderbilt University, 2005.

Brake, Laurel, and Marysa Demoor. "Introduction: The Lure of Illustration." In *The Lure of Illustration: Picture and Press*, ed. Laurel Brake and Marysa Demoor, 1–13. Houndsmill: Palgrave, 2009.

Branch, Lori. *Rituals of Spontaneity: Sentiment and Secularism from Free Prayer to Wordsworth*. Waco: Baylor University Press, 2006.

Braudy, Leo. *The Frenzy of Renown: Fame and Its History*. New York: Oxford University Press, 1986.

Brewer, John. *The Pleasures of the Imagination: English Culture in the Eighteenth Century*. New York: Farrar, 1997.

Brewer, John, and Roy Porter, eds. *Consumption and the World of Goods*. London: Routledge, 1993.

Briggs, Peter M. "Laurence Sterne and Literary Celebrity in 1760." *The Age of Johnson* 4 (1991): 251–80.

———. "'News from the little World': A Critical Glance at Eighteenth-Century British Advertising." *Studies in Eighteenth-Century Culture* 23 (1994): 29–45.

Brock, Claire. *The Feminization of Fame, 1750–1830*. New York: Palgrave, 2006.

Brown, Stephen. "Preface: Beanz Meanz Bookz." In Brown, ed., *Consuming Books*, xiii–xv.

———. "Rattles from the Swill Bucket." In Brown, ed., *Consuming Books*, 1–17.

Brown, Stephen, ed. *Consuming Books: The Marketing and Consumption of Literature*. London: Routledge, 2006.

Bruttini, Adriano. "Advertising and Socio-Economic Transformations in England, 1720–1760." *Journal of Advertising History* 5 (1982): 8–26.

Buck, John Dawson Carl. "The Motives of Puffing: John Newbery's Advertisements, 1742–1767." *Studies in Bibliography* 30 (1977): 196–210.

Calkins, Earnest Elmo, and Ralph Holden. *The Art of Modern Advertising*. London: Appleton, 1905.

Campbell, Colin. *The Romantic Ethic and the Spirit of Modern Consumerism.* Oxford: Blackwell, 1987.
Campbell, J. Dykes. "Reviewing Oneself." *Athenaeum*, August 3, 1889: 164.
Campbell, Jill. "Domestic Intelligence: Newspaper Advertising and the Eighteenth-Century Novel." *Yale Journal of Criticism* 15 (2002): 251–91.
Carvajal, Doreen. "For Sale: On-Line Bookstore's Recommendations." *New York Times*, February 8, 1999: A1+.
Chew, Samuel C. *Byron in England: His Fame and After-Fame.* London: Murray, 1924.
Christensen, Jerome. *Lord Byron's Strength: Romantic Writing and Commercial Society.* Baltimore: Johns Hopkins University Press, 1993.
Christie, William. *The* Edinburgh Review *in the Literary Culture of Romantic Britain.* London: Pickering and Chatto, 2009.
Clarke, Bob. *From Grub Street to Fleet Street: An Illustrated History of English Newspapers to 1899.* Burlington: Ashgate, 2004.
Clery, E. J. *The Rise of Supernatural Fiction, 1762–1800.* Cambridge: Cambridge University Press, 1995.
Clery, E. J., Caroline Franklin, and Peter Garside, eds. *Authorship, Commerce, and the Public: Scenes of Writing, 1750–1850.* New York: Palgrave, 2002.
Cooney, Seamus. "Scott's Anonymity—Its Motives and Consequences." *Studies in Scottish Literature* 10 (1973): 207–19.
Corley, T. A. B. "Competition and the Growth of Advertising in the U.S. and Britain, 1800–1914." *Business and Economic History*, 2nd series, 7 (1988): 155–67.
Court, Franklin E. *Institutionalizing English Literature: The Culture and Politics of Literary Study, 1750–1900.* Stanford: Stanford University Press, 1992.
Cox, Jeffrey N. "The Living Pantheon of Poets in 1820: Pantheon or Canon?" In *The Cambridge Companion to British Romantic Poetry*, ed. James Chandler and Maureen N. McLane, 10–34. Cambridge: Cambridge University Press, 2008.
———. *Poetry and Politics in the Cockney School: Keats, Shelley, Hunt and Their Circle.* Cambridge: Cambridge University Press, 1998.
Craciun, Adriana. *Fatal Women of Romanticism.* Cambridge: Cambridge University Press, 2003.
Crane, David. Introduction to *The Critic*, by Richard Brinsley Sheridan, ix–xxv. Ed. David Crane. New York: Norton, 1989.
Crawford, Robert. Introduction. In *The Scottish Invention of English Literature*, ed. Robert Crawford, 1–21. Cambridge: Cambridge University Press, 1998.
Cronin, Richard. *Romantic Victorians: English Literature, 1824–1840.* Houndsmill: Palgrave, 2002.
Curry, Kenneth. *Sir Walter Scott's* Edinburgh Annual Register. Knoxville: University of Tennessee Press, 1977.
Curth, Louise Hill. "The Commercialisation of Medicine in the Popular Press: English Almanacs 1640–1700." *Seventeenth Century* 17.1 (2002): 48–69.
Davis, Alec. *Package and Print: The Development of Container and Label Design.* New York: Potter, 1967.
De Brouwer, Walter. "Joshua Toulmin in *The Analytical Review.*" *Notes and Queries* 30 (June 1983): 209–12.

Demata, Massimiliano, and Duncan Wu. *British Romanticism and the* Edinburgh Review: *Bicentenary Essays*. New York: Palgrave Macmillan, 2002.

De Vries, January. "Between Purchasing Power and the World of Goods: Understanding the Household Economy in Early Modern Europe." In Brewer and Porter, eds., *Consumption and the World of Goods*, 85–132.

Dobson, Austin. *Eighteenth-Century Vignettes*. New York: Dodd, 1892.

Doherty, Francis. *A Study in Eighteenth-Century Advertising Methods*. Lewiston, N.Y.: Edwin Mellen, 1992.

Donoghue, Frank. *The Fame Machine: Book Reviewing and Eighteenth-Century Literary Careers*. Stanford: Stanford University Press, 1996.

Draper, Roger. "The Faithless Shepherd." *New York Review of Books*, June 26, 1986: 14.

Dunbar, David S. "The Agency Commission System in Britain: A First Sketch of its History to 1941." *Journal of Advertising History* 2 (1979): 19–21.

Dyer, Gary. *British Satire and the Politics of Style, 1789–1832*. Cambridge: Cambridge University Press, 1997.

Eagleton, Terry. *The Function of Criticism: From* The Spectator *to Post-Structuralism*. London: Verso, 1984.

——. *Literary Theory: An Introduction*. Minneapolis: University of Minnesota Press, 1983.

Eaves, T. C. Duncan, and Ben D. Kimpel. *Samuel Richardson: A Biography*. Oxford: Clarendon, 1971.

Eisenstein, Elizabeth L. *The Printing Press as an Agent of Change*. Cambridge: Cambridge University Press, 1979.

Eisler, Benita. *Byron: Child of Passion, Fool of Fame*. New York: Knopf, 1999.

Eisner, Eric. *Nineteenth-Century Poetry and Literary Celebrity*. New York: Palgrave, 2009.

Elfenbein, Andrew. *Byron and the Victorians*. Cambridge: Cambridge University Press, 1995.

Elliott, Blanche B. *A History of English Advertising*. London: Business Publications, 1962.

Elmhirst, Edward Mars. *Merchants' Marks*. Ed. Leslie Dow. London: Harleian Society, 1959.

Engell, James, and W. Jackson Bate. Introduction and notes to *Biographia Literaria, or Biographical Sketches of My Literary Life and Opinions*, by Samuel Taylor Coleridge. Princeton: Princeton University Press, 1983.

Erickson, Lee. *The Economy of Literary Form: English Literature and the Industrialization of Publishing, 1800–1850*. Baltimore: Johns Hopkins University Press, 1996.

——. "'Unboastful Bard': Originally Anonymous English Romantic Poetry Book Publication, 1770–1835." *New Literary History* 33.2 (2002): 247–78.

Fader, Daniel, and George Bornstein. *Two Centuries of British Periodicals*. Ann Arbor: Xerox University Microfilms, 1974.

Fay, Elizabeth. "Framing Romantic Dress: Mary Robinson, Princess Caroline and the Sex/Text." In *Historicizing Romantic Sexuality*, ed. Richard Sha. *Romantic Circles Praxis Series*, January 2006. Web.

Feather, John. *English Book Prospectuses: An Illustrated History*. Minneapolis: Daedulus, 1984.

---. *A History of British Publishing*. London: Croom Helm, 1988.
---. *The Provincial Book Trade in Eighteenth-Century England*. Cambridge: Cambridge University Press, 1985.
Feldman, Paula C. "The Poet and the Profits: Felicia Hemans and the Literary Marketplace." In *Women's Poetry, Late Romantic to Late Victorian*, ed. Isobel Armstrong and Virginia Blain, 71–101. New York: St. Martin's, 1999.
---. "Women Poets and Anonymity in the Romantic Era." In Clery, Franklin, and Garside, eds., *Authorship, Commerce, and the Public*, 44–53.
Felluga, Dino Franco. *The Perversity of Poetry: Romantic Ideology and the Popular Male Poet of Genius*. Albany: State University of New York Press, 2005.
Ferdinand, C. Y. "Selling it to the Provinces: News and Commerce Round Eighteenth-Century Salisbury." In Brewer and Porter, eds., *Consumption and the World of Goods*, 393–411.
Ferry, Anne. "Anonymity: The Literary History of a Word." *New Literary History* 33.2 (2002): 193–214.
Fine, Ben. *The World of Consumption: The Material and Cultural Revisited*. London: Routledge, 2002.
Finkelstein, David. Introduction. In *Print Culture and the Blackwood Tradition, 1805–1930*, ed. David Finkelstein, 3–17. Toronto: University of Toronto Press, 2006.
Forbes, Margaret. *Beattie and His Friends*. Westminster: Constable, 1904.
Forster, Antonia. "Avarice or Interest: The Secrets of Eighteenth-Century Reviewing." *Yale University Library Gazette* 81.3–4 (2007): 167–76.
---. *Index to Book Reviews in England 1749–1774*. Carbondale: Southern Illinois University Press, 1990.
---. "Ralph Griffiths." In Bracken and Silvers, eds., *The British Literary Book Trade, 1700–1820*, 150–58.
---. "Ralph Griffiths." *Oxford Dictionary of National Biography*. 2004. Web.
---. "Review Journals and the Reading Public." In *Books and Their Readers in Eighteenth-century England: New Essays*, ed. Isabel Rivers, 171–90. London: Continuum, 2003.
Forster, John. *The Life of Charles Dickens*. Ed. A. J. Hoppe. 2 vols. London: Dent, 1966.
Foucault, Michel. "What Is an Author?" 1969. In *Language, Counter-Memory, Practice: Selected Essays and Interviews*, ed. Donald F. Bouchard, 113–38. Ithaca: Cornell University Press, 1977.
Fox, Stephen. *The Mirror Makers: A History of American Advertising*. London: Heinemann, 1984.
Fulcher, James. *Capitalism: A Very Short Introduction*. Oxford: Oxford University Press, 2004.
Galbi, Douglas A. "Long-Term Trends in Personal Given Name Frequencies in the UK." www.galbithink.org. 2002. Web.
Galbraith, John Kenneth. *The Affluent Society*. New York: Houghton-Mifflin, 1958.
Galperin, William H. *The Return of the Visible in British Romanticism*. Baltimore: Johns Hopkins University Press, 1993.
Garside, Peter. "Essay on the Text." In *Waverley; or, 'Tis Sixty Years Since*, ed. Peter Garside, 367–456. Edinburgh: Edinburgh University Press, 2007.

Genette, Gerard. *Paratexts: Thresholds of Interpretation*. 1987. Trans. Jane E. Lewin. Cambridge: Cambridge University Press, 1997.

Giles, Jeff. "See More about Me." *Newsweek*, November 5, 2001:14.

Gloag, John. *Advertising in Modern Life*. London: Heinemann, 1959.

Goldsmith, Jason N. "The Promiscuity of Print: John Clare's 'Don Juan' and the Culture of Romantic Celebrity." *Studies in English Literature* 46.4 (2006): 803–32.

Graham, Walter. *English Literary Periodicals*. New York: Thomas Nelson and Sons, 1930.

Green, Hardy. "Selling Books Like Bacon: Horrors! The Industry is Taking a Leaf from Supermarkets." *Business Week*, June 16, 2003: 80.

Greer, Germaine. "The Tulsa Center for Women's Literature: What We Are Doing and Why We Are Doing It." *Tulsa Studies in Women's Literature* 1.1 (1982): 5–26.

Griffin, Robert. Introduction. In Griffin, ed., *The Faces of Anonymity*, 1–17.

Griffin, Robert, ed. *The Faces of Anonymity: Anonymous and Pseudonymous Publication from the Sixteenth to the Twentieth Century*. New York: Palgrave, 2003.

Guillory, John. *Cultural Capital: The Problem of Literary Canon Formation*. Chicago: University of Chicago Press, 1993.

Habermas, Jürgen. *The Structural Transformation of the Public Sphere: An Inquiry into a Category of Bourgeois Society*. 1962. Trans. Thomas Burger. Cambridge: MIT Press, 1991.

Harmon, Amy. "Amazon Glitch Unmasks War of Reviewers." *New York Times*, February 14, 2004: A1+.

Harris, Michael. "The Structure, Ownership, and Control of the Press, 1620–1780." In Boyce et al., eds., *Newspaper History*, 82–97.

Hayden, John O. "Hazlitt Reviews Hazlitt?" *Modern Language Review* 64 (1969): 20–26.

——. *The Romantic Reviewers, 1802–1824*. Chicago: University of Chicago Press, 1969.

Haynes, Christine. "Reassessing 'Genius' in Studies of Authorship." *Book History* 8 (2005): 287–320.

Hebdige, Dick. "Object as Image: The Italian Scooter Cycle." In *Hiding in the Light: On Images and Things*, 77–115. London: Routledge, 1988.

Higgins, David. *Romantic Genius and the Literary Magazine: Biography, Celebrity, Politics*. New York: Routledge, 2005.

Hoagwood, Terence, and Kathryn Ledbetter. *"Colour'd Shadows": Contexts in Publishing, Printing, and Reading Nineteenth-Century British Women Writers*. New York: Palgrave, 2005.

Hoagwood, Terence, Kathryn Ledbetter, and Martin M. Jacobsen. "Introduction to the *Keepsake*." *L.E.L.'s "Verses" and the Keepsake for 1829*. Romantic Circles. Fall 1998. Web.

Hodnett, Edward. *Five Centuries of English Book Illustration*. Brookfield, Vt.: Scolar, 1988.

Hogan, Charles Beecher. *The London Stage, 1776–1800*. Carbondale: Southern Illinois University Press, 1968.

Holbrook, Morris B. "On the Commercial Exaltation of Mediocrity: Books, Bread, Postmodern Statistics, Surprising Success Stories, and the Doomed Magnificence of Way Too Many Big Words." In Brown, ed., *Consuming Books*, 96–113.

Holden, Anthony. *The Wit in the Dungeon: The Remarkable Life of Leigh Hunt, Poet, Revolutionary, and the Last of the Romantics*. New York: Little Brown, 2005.
Horn, John. "The Reviewer Who Wasn't There," *Newsweek*, June 11, 2001: 8.
Jack, Ian. *English Literature, 1815–1832*. Oxford: Clarendon Press, 1963.
Jackson, H. J. *Romantic Readers: The Evidence of Marginalia*. New Haven: Yale University Press, 2005.
Jackson, J. R. de J. *Annals of English Verse, 1770–1835: A Preliminary Survey of the Volumes Published*. New York: Garland, 1985.
Jacobs, Edward H. *Accidental Migrations: An Archaeology of Gothic Discourse*. Lewisburg: Bucknell University Press, 2000.
Jager, Colin. *The Book of God: Secularization and Design in the Romantic Age*. Philadelphia: University of Pennsylvania Press, 2007.
Jerrold, Walter. *Thomas Hood: His Life and Times*. London: Rivers, 1907.
Jones, Christine Kenyon. Introduction. In *Byron: The Image of the Poet*, ed. Christine Kenyon Jones, 17–28. Newark: University of Delaware Press, 2008.
Jordan, John O., and Robert L. Patten, eds. *Literature in the Marketplace: Nineteenth-Century British Publishing and Reading Practices*. Cambridge: Cambridge University Press, 1995.
Joseph, Gerhard. "Commodifying Tennyson: The Historical Transformation of 'Brand Loyalty.'" *Victorian Poetry* 34 (1996): 133–47.
Kernan, Alvin. "The Idea of Literature." *New Literary History* 5 (1973): 31–40.
———. *Samuel Johnson and the Impact of Print*. Princeton: Princeton University Press, 1987.
Keymer, Thomas, and Peter Sabor. *Pamela in the Marketplace*. Cambridge: Cambridge University Press, 2006.
Keymer, Thomas, and Peter Sabor, eds. *The Pamela Controversy: Criticism and Adaptations of Samuel Richardson's* Pamela, *1740–1750*. 6 vols. London: Pickering and Chatto, 2001.
Klancher, Jon P. *The Making of English Reading Audiences, 1790–1832*. Madison: University of Wisconsin Press, 1987.
Knapp, Lewis Mansfield. "Ralph Griffiths, Author and Publisher, 1746–1750," *The Library*, 4th series, 20 (1939): 197–213.
———. *Tobias Smollett: Doctor of Men and Manners*. New York: Russell, 1963.
Knowles, Claire. *Sensibility and the Female Poetic Tradition, 1780–1860: The Legacy of Charlotte Smith*. Burlington: Ashgate, 2009.
Knowles, Owen. "Veneering and the Age of Veneer: A Source and Background for *Our Mutual Friend*." *The Dickensian* 81.2 (1985): 88–96.
Kramnick, Jonathan Brody. *Making the English Canon: Print-Capitalism and the Cultural Past, 1700–1770*. Cambridge: Cambridge University Press, 1999.
Labbe, Jacqueline M. "Selling One's Sorrows: Charlotte Smith, Mary Robinson, and the Marketing of Poetry." *Wordsworth Circle* 25.2 (1994): 68–71.
Latané, David E. "Alaric 'Attila' Watts, the *Fraser's* Portrait Gallery, and William Maginn." In *The Lure of Illustration: Picture and Press*, ed. Laurel Brake and Marysa Demoor, 60–75. Houndsmill: Palgrave, 2009.
Lawford, Cynthia. "Diary." *London Review of Books*. September 21, 2000: 36–37.

———. "'Thou shalt bid thy fair hands rove': L.E.L.'s Wooing of Sex, Pain, Death and the Editor." *Romanticism on the Net*, 29–30 (February–May 2003). Web.
Leasor, James. *The Plague and the Fire*. New York: McGraw-Hill, 1961.
Leibenstein, Harvey. "Bandwagon, Snob, and Veblen Effects in the Theory of Consumers' Demand." *Quarterly Journal of Economics* 64 (1950): 183–207.
Leighton, Angela. *Victorian Women Poets: Writing Against the Heart*. Charlottesville: University Press of Virginia, 1992.
Lewis, Lawrence. *The Advertisements of the* Spectator. Boston: Houghton-Mifflin, 1909.
Lightfoot, Martin. "Scott's Self-Reviewal: Manuscript and Other Evidence." *Nineteenth-Century Fiction* 23 (1968): 150–60.
Loeb, Lori Anne. *Consuming Angels: Advertising and Victorian Women*. Oxford: Oxford University Press, 1994.
Lootens, Tricia. "Receiving the Legend, Rethinking the Writer: Letitia Landon and the Poetess Tradition." In *Romanticism and Women Poets: Opening the Doors of Reception*, ed. Harriet Kramer Linkin and Stephen C. Behrendt, 242–59. Lexington: University Press of Kentucky, 1999.
Luckhurst, Mary, and Jane Moody, eds. *Theatre and Celebrity in Britain, 1660–2000*. Basingstoke: Palgrave, 2005.
"The Mammoth Mirror." *Time*, October 12, 1962. Web.
Manning, Peter J. "Childe Harold in the Marketplace: From Romaunt to Handbook." *Modern Language Quarterly* 52 (1991): 170–90.
Marchand, Leslie A. *The Athenaeum: A Mirror of Victorian Culture*. Chapel Hill: University of North Carolina Press, 1941.
———. *Byron: A Biography*. 3 vols. New York: Knopf, 1957.
Marcus, James. *Amazonia: Five Years at the Epicenter of the Dot.com Juggernaut*. New York: New Press, 2004.
Marcus, Sharon. "The Profession of the Author: Abstraction, Advertising, and *Jane Eyre*." *PMLA* 110 (1995): 206–19.
Mason, Nicholas. General Introduction. In vol. 1 of *Blackwood's Magazine, 1817–25: Selections from Maga's Infancy*, ed. Nicholas Mason, ix–xxiv. 6 vols. London: Pickering and Chatto, 2006.
Matoff, Susan. *Conflicted Life: William Jerdan, 1782–1869, London Editor, Author and Critic*. Brighton: Sussex, 2011.
Mazzeo, Tilar J. *Plagiarism and Literary Property in the Romantic Period*. Philadelphia: University of Pennsylvania Press, 2007.
McCalman, Iain. *Radical Underworld: Prophets, Revolutionaries and Pornographers in London, 1795–1840*. Cambridge: Cambridge University Press, 1988.
McDayter, Ghislaine. *Byromania and the Birth of Celebrity Culture*. Albany: SUNY Press, 2009.
McGann, Jerome, and Daniel Riess. Introduction. In *Letitia Elizabeth Landon: Selected Writings*, ed. Jerome McGann and Daniel Riess, 11–31. Peterborough, Ont.: Broadview, 1997.
McKendrick, Neil. "The Commercialization of Fashion." In McKendrick, Brewer, and Plumb, eds., *The Birth of a Consumer Society*, 34–99.
———. "The Consumer Revolution of Eighteenth-century England." In McKendrick, Brewer, and Plumb, eds., *The Birth of a Consumer Society*, 9–33.

———. "George Packwood and the Commercialization of Shaving: The Art of Eighteenth-century Advertising, or 'The Way to Get Money and Be Happy.'" In McKendrick, Brewer, and Plumb, eds., *The Birth of a Consumer Society*, 146–94.
———. Introduction. In McKendrick, Brewer, and Plumb, eds., *The Birth of a Consumer Society*, 1–8.
———. "Josiah Wedgwood and the Commercialization of the Potteries." In McKendrick, Brewer, and Plumb, eds., *The Birth of a Consumer Society*. 100–145.
McKendrick, Neil, John Brewer, and J. H. Plumb, eds. *The Birth of a Consumer Society: The Commercialization of Eighteenth-century England*. Bloomington: Indiana University Press, 1982.
McLuhan, Marshall. *The Gutenberg Galaxy: The Making of Typographic Man*. Toronto: University of Toronto Press, 1962.
Mellor, Anne K. *Romanticism and Gender*. New York: Routledge, 1993.
Merriam, Harold G. *Edward Moxon: Publisher of Poets*. New York: Columbia University Press, 1939.
Miller, Laura J. *Reluctant Capitalists: Bookselling and the Culture of Consumption*. Chicago: University of Chicago Press, 2006.
Mole, Tom. "Byron's 'Ode to the Framers of the Frame Bill': The Embarrassment of Industrial Culture." *Keats-Shelley Journal* 52 (2003): 111–29.
———. *Byron's Romantic Celebrity: Industrial Culture and the Hermeneutic of Intimacy*. New York: Palgrave, 2007.
———. "Mary Robinson's Conflicted Celebrity." In Mole, ed., *Romanticism and Celebrity Culture*, 186–205.
Mole, Tom, ed. *Romanticism and Celebrity Culture, 1750–1850*. Cambridge: Cambridge University Press, 2009.
Moore, Doris Langley. *Lord Byron: Accounts Rendered*. New York: Harper, 1974.
Morgan, Marjorie. *Manners, Morals, and Class in England, 1774–1858*. New York: St. Martin's, 1994.
Mounsey, Christopher. *Christopher Smart: Clown of God*. Lewisburg: Bucknell University Press, 2001.
Mozer, Hadley J. "*Don Juan* and the Advertising and Advertised Lord Byron." Ph.D. diss., Baylor University, 2003.
———. "'I WANT a hero': Advertising for an Epic Hero in *Don Juan*." *Studies in Romanticism* 44.2 (2005): 239–60.
Mudge, Bradford. "Romanticism, Materialism, and the Origins of Modern Pornography." *Romanticism on the Net* 23 (August 2001). Web.
Mui, Hoh-Cheung, and Lorna H. Mui. *Shops and Shopkeeping in Eighteenth-Century England*. Kingston: McGill-Queen's University Press, 1989.
Mullan, John. *Anonymity: A Secret History of English Literature*. London: Faber, 2007.
Mulrooney, Jonathan. "Reading the Romantic-period Daily News." *Nineteenth-Century Contexts* 24 (2002): 351–77.
Murray, Brian. "The Authorship of Some Unidentified or Disputed Articles in *Blackwood's Magazine*." *Studies in Scottish Literature* 4 (1966–67): 144–54.
Nangle, Benjamin Christie. *The Monthly Review, First Series, 1749–1789: Indexes of Contributors and Articles*. Oxford: Clarendon, 1934.

Nevett, Terry. *Advertising in Britain: A History.* North Pomfret, Vt.: Heinemann, 1982.
——. "London's Early Advertising Agents." *Journal of Advertising History* 1 (1977): 15–17.
Newlyn, Lucy. *Reading, Writing, and Romanticism: The Anxiety of Reception.* Oxford: Oxford University Press, 2000.
Nicholson, Andrew, ed. *The Letters of John Murray to Lord Byron.* Liverpool: Liverpool University Press, 2007.
Nisbet, H. B., and Claude Rawson. "Editor's Preface" In Nisbet and Rawson, eds., *The Cambridge History of Literary Criticism*, xiv–xviii.
Nisbet, H. B., and Claude Rawson, eds. *The Cambridge History of Literary Criticism, Volume IV: The Eighteenth Century.* Cambridge: Cambridge University Press, 1997.
O'Guinn, Thomas C. "Touching Greatness: The Central Midwest Barry Manilow Fan Club." 1991. In Schor and Holt, eds., *The Consumer Society Reader*, 155–68.
Ohmann, Richard. *Selling Culture: Magazines, Markets, and Class at the Turn of the Century.* London: Verso, 1996.
Oliphant, Margaret. *Annals of a Publishing House: William Blackwood and His Sons, Their Magazine and Friends.* 2 vols. New York: Scribner's, 1897.
Ong, Walter J. *Orality and Literacy: The Technologizing of the Word.* London: Methuen, 1982.
Parker, Mark. *Literary Magazines and British Romanticism.* Cambridge: Cambridge University Press, 2000.
Partington, Wilfred. *The Identity of Mr. Slum: Charles Dickens and the Blacking Laureate.* London, 1937.
Pascoe, Judith. *Romantic Theatricality: Gender, Poetry, and Spectatorship.* Ithaca: Cornell University Press, 1997.
Patey, Douglas Lane. "The Eighteenth Century Invents the Canon." *Modern Language Studies* 18 (1988): 17–37.
——. "The Institution of Criticism in the Eighteenth Century," in Nisbet and Rawson, eds., *The Cambridge History of Literary Criticism*, 3–31.
Peterson, Linda H. *Becoming a Woman of Letters: Myths of Authorship and Facts of the Victorian Market.* Princeton: Princeton University Press, 2009.
——. "Rewriting A *History of the Lyre*: Letitia Landon, Elizabeth Barrett Browning and the (Re)Construction of the Nineteenth-Century Woman Poet." In *Women's Poetry: Late Romantic to Late Victorian: Gender and Genre, 1830–1900*, ed. Isobel Armstrong and Virginia Blain, 115–32. New York: St. Martin's, 1999.
Pincas, Stephane, and Marc Loiseau. *Born in 1842: A History of Advertising.* Paris: Mundocom, 2006.
Plant, Marjorie. *The English Book Trade: An Economic History of the Making and Sale of Books.* 1939. London: Allen, 1965.
Plumb, J. H. "The Commercialization of Leisure in Eighteenth-century England." In McKendrick, Brewer, and Plumb, eds., *The Birth of a Consumer Society*, 265–85.
Porter, Roy. *Health for Sale: Quackery in England, 1660–1850.* Manchester: Manchester University Press, 1989.
Presbrey, Frank. *The History and Development of Advertising.* 1929. New York: Greenwood, 1968.

Price, F. G. Hilton. "Coronation Advertisement of 1685." *Notes and Queries*, 9th series, 10 (August 30, 1902): 166.

Price, Leah. *The Anthology and the Rise of the Novel*. Cambridge: Cambridge University Press, 2000.

Radin, Margaret Jane. *Contested Commodities: The Trouble with Trade in Sex, Children, Body Parts, and Other Things*. Cambridge: Harvard University Press, 1996.

Raven, James. "The Anonymous Novel in Britain and Ireland, 1750–1830." In Griffin, ed., *The Faces of Anonymity*, 141–66.

———. *The Business of Books: Booksellers and the English Book Trade*. New Haven: Yale University Press, 2007.

———. *Judging New Wealth: Popular Publishing and Responses to Commerce in England, 1750–1800*. Oxford: Clarendon, 1992.

———. "Publishing and Bookselling, 1660–1780." In *The Cambridge History of English Literature, 1660–1780*, ed. John Richetti, 13–36. Cambridge: Cambridge University Press, 2005.

Reilly, Robin. *Wedgwood*. 2 vols. New York: Stockton Press, 1989.

Reiman, Donald H., ed. *The Romantics Reviewed: Contemporary Reviews of British Romantic Writers*. 3 vols. in 9. New York: Garland, 1972.

Richards, Thomas. *The Commodity Culture of Victorian England: Advertising and Spectacle, 1851–1914*. Stanford: Stanford University Press, 1990.

Ries, Al, and Laura Ries. *The Twenty-Two Immutable Laws of Branding: How to Build a Product or Service into a World-Class Brand*. New York: Harper Business, 1998.

Rollins, Hyder Edward. *The Keats Circle: Letters and Papers, and More Letters and Poems of the Keats Circle*. 2nd ed. 2 vols. Cambridge: Harvard University Press, 1965.

Roper, Derek. *Reviewing Before the Edinburgh: 1788–1802*. Newark: University of Delaware Press, 1978.

Rosa, Matthew Whiting. *The Silver-Fork School: Novels of Fashion Preceding "Vanity Fair."* New York: Columbia University Press, 1936.

Rose, Mark. "The Author as Proprietor: *Donaldson v. Becket* and the Genealogy of Modern Authorship." *Representations* 23 (1988): 51–85.

———. *Authors and Owners: The Invention of Copyright*. Cambridge: Harvard University Press, 1993.

———. "The Development of the Author's Copyright in Britain." In Bracken and Silvers, eds., *The British Literary Book Trade*, 293–96.

Rosenbaum, Susan B. *Professing Sincerity: Modern Lyric Poetry, Commercial Culture, and the Crisis in Reading*. Charlottesville: University Press of Virginia, 2007.

Ross, Trevor. *The Making of the English Literary Canon from the Middle Ages to the Late Eighteenth Century*. Montreal: McGill-Queen's University Press, 1998.

Rovee, Christopher. *Imagining the Gallery: The Social Body of British Romanticism*. Stanford: Stanford University Press, 2006.

Rowton, Frederic. *The Female Poets of Great Britain, Chronologically Arranged*. Philadelphia: Carey, 1849.

Sabor, Peter. Introduction to *Memoirs of a Woman of Pleasure*, by John Cleland, vii–xxvi. Ed. Peter Sabor. Oxford: Oxford University Press, 1985.

Sadleir, Michael. *"Minerva Press" Publicity*. London: Bibliographical Society, 1940.

Saenger, Michael Baird. "The Birth of Advertising." In *Printing and Parenting in Early Modern England*, ed. Douglas A. Brooks, 197–219. Burlington: Ashgate, 2005.

St. Clair, William. "The Impact of Byron's Writings: An Evaluative Approach." In *Byron: Augustan and Romantic*, ed. Andrew Rutherford, 1–25. New York: St. Martin's, 1990.

———. *The Reading Nation in the Romantic Period*. Cambridge: Cambridge University Press, 2004.

Sampson, Henry. *A History of Advertising*. London: Chatto and Windus, 1874.

Schmidt, Barbara Quinn. "John Murray." In Bracken and Silver, eds., *The British Literary Book Trade*, 203–15.

Schoenfield, Mark. *British Periodicals and Romantic Identity: The "Literary Lower Empire."* New York: Palgrave, 2009.

Schor, Juliet B., and Douglas B. Holt, eds. *The Consumer Society Reader*. New York: New Press, 2000.

Schuwer, Philippe. *History of Advertising*. London: Leisure Arts, 1966.

Seymour, Miranda. *Mary Shelley*. New York: Grove, 2000.

Shattock, Joanne. *Politics and Reviewers: The "Edinburgh" and the "Quarterly" in the Early Victorian Age*. Leicester: Leicester University Press, 1989.

Sher, Richard B. *The Enlightenment and the Book: Scottish Authors and Their Publishers in Eighteenth-Century Britain, Ireland, and America*. Chicago: University of Chicago Press, 2006.

Simonsen, Peter. *Wordsworth and Word-Preserving Arts: Typographic Inscription, Ekphrasis, and Posterity in the Later Work*. New York: Palgrave, 2007.

Siskin, Clifford. *The Work of Writing: Literature and Social Change in Britain, 1700–1830*. Baltimore: Johns Hopkins University Press, 1998.

Smith-Banister, Scott. *Names and Naming Practices in England, 1538–1700*. Oxford: Oxford University Press, 1997.

Sommerville, C. John. *The News Revolution in England: Cultural Dynamics of Daily Information*. New York: Oxford University Press, 1996.

Stead, William, Jr. *The Art of Advertising: Its Theory and Practice Fully Described*. London: T. B. Browne, 1899.

Stephenson, Glennis. *Letitia Landon: The Woman Behind L.E.L*. Manchester: Manchester University Press, 1995.

Stobart, Paul. Introduction. In *Brand Power*, ed. Paul Stobart, 1–16. New York: New York University Press, 1994.

Strachan, John. *Advertising and Satirical Culture in the Romantic Period*. Cambridge: Cambridge University Press, 2007.

———. Introduction. In Deacon, *Warreniana*, vii–xl.

Strasser, Susan. *Satisfaction Guaranteed: The Making of the American Mass Market*. New York: Pantheon, 1989.

Strout, Alan Lang. *A Bibliography of Articles in Blackwood's Magazine, 1817–1825*. Lubbock: Texas Technological College Press, 1959.

Styles, John. "Product Innovation in Early Modern London." *Past and Present* 168 (2000): 124–69.

Sutherland, John. "The British Book Trade and the Crash of 1826." *The Library*, 6th series, 9 (1987): 148–61.

———. "Henry Colburn, Publisher." *Publishing History* 19 (1986): 59–84.
———. *How to Read a Novel: A User's Guide*. New York: St. Martin's, 2006.
———. *The Life of Walter Scott: A Critical Biography*. Oxford: Blackwell, 1995.
Sypher, F. J. *Letitia Elizabeth Landon: A Biography*. 2nd ed. Ann Arbor: Scholars' Facsimiles, 2009.
Terry, Richard. *Poetry and the Making of the English Literary Past*. Oxford: Oxford University Press, 2001.
Thomas, Sophie. "Poetry and Illustration: 'Amicable Strife.'" In *A Companion to Romantic Poetry*, ed. Charles Mahoney, 354–73. Chichester: Blackwell, 2011.
Thornton, Sara. *Advertising, Subjectivity, and the Nineteenth-Century Novel: Dickens, Balzac, and the Language of the Walls*. New York: Palgrave, 2009.
Thrall, Miriam M. H. *Rebellious Fraser's: Nol Yorke's Magazine in the Days of Maginn, Thackeray, and Carlyle*. New York: Columbia University Press, 1934.
Tierney, James. "Book Advertisements in Mid-18th-century Newspapers: The Example of Robert Dodsley." In *A Genius for Letters: Booksellers and Bookselling from the 16th to the 20th Century*, ed. Robin Myers and Michael Harris, 103–22. New Castle, Del.: Oak Knell, 1995.
Trumpener, Katie. *Bardic Nationalism: The Romantic Novel and the British Empire*. Princeton: Princeton University Press, 1997.
Tucker, Jennifer. *Nature Exposed: Photography as Eyewitness in Victorian Science*. Baltimore: Johns Hopkins University Press, 2005.
Turner, E. S. *The Shocking History of Advertising!* London: Michael Joseph, 1952.
Turner, J. R. "Alfred Bird." *Oxford Dictionary of National Biography*. 2004–9. Web.
Veblen, Thorstein. *The Theory of the Leisure Class*. 1899. Ed. Martha Banta. Oxford: Oxford University Press, 2008.
Vincent, David. *Literacy and Popular Culture: England, 1750–1914*. Cambridge: Cambridge University Press, 1989.
Vincent, Patrick H. *The Romantic Poetess: European Culture, Politics and Gender, 1820–1840*. Durham: University of New Hampshire Press, 2004.
Wall, Cynthia Sundberg. *The Prose of Things: Transformations of Description in the Eighteenth Century*. Chicago: University of Chicago Press, 2006.
Waller, Philip. *Writers, Readers, and Reputations: Literary Life in Britain, 1870–1918*. Oxford: Oxford University Press, 2006.
Ward, William S. "Wordsworth, the 'Lake' Poets, and Their Contemporary Magazine Critics." *Studies in Philology* 42 (1945): 87–113.
Warner, William B. *Licensing Entertainment: The Elevation of Novel Reading in Britain, 1684–1750*. Berkeley: University of California Press, 1998.
Watt, James. "Robert Charles Dallas." *Oxford Dictionary of National Biography*. 2004. Web.
Watt, Julie. *Poisoned Lives: The Regency Poet Letitia Elizabeth Landon (L.E.L.) and British Gold Coast Administrator George Maclean*. Eastbourne: Sussex, 2010.
Weilbacher, William M. *Brand Marketing: Building Winning Brand Strategies That Deliver Value and Customer Satisfaction*. Lincolnwood, Ill.: NTC Contemporary Publishing, 1993.
Wellek, René. "What Is Literature?" In *What Is Literature?* ed. Paul Hernadi, 16–23. Bloomington: Indiana University Press, 1978.

Welsh, Charles. "A Bookseller of the Last Century." 1855. In *John Newbery and His Books: Trade and Plumb-Cake for Ever, Huzza!*, ed. John Rowe Townsend, 29–113. New York: Scarecrow, 1994.

Whitley, William T. *Art in England, 1821–1837*. Cambridge: Cambridge University Press, 1830.

Wicke, Jennifer. *Advertising Fictions: Literature, Advertisement, and Social Reading*. New York: Columbia University Press, 1988.

Widdowson, Peter. *Literature*. London: Routledge, 1999.

Williams, Franklin B., Jr. "Commendatory Verses: The Rise of the Art of Puffing," *Studies in Bibliography* 19 (1966): 1–14.

Williams, Raymond. "Advertising: The Magic System." *Problems in Materialism and Culture*. London: Verso, 1980: 170–95.

———. *Keywords: A Vocabulary of Culture and Society*. London: Fontana, 1976.

———. *Marxism and Literature*. Oxford: Oxford University Press, 1977.

Wood, Ellen Meiksins. *The Origin of Capitalism: A Longer View*. London: Verso, 2002.

Wood, Gillen D'Arcy. *The Shock of the Real: Romanticism and Visual Culture, 1760–1860*. New York: Palgrave, 2001.

Wood, Marcus. *Radical Satire and Print Culture, 1790–1822*. Oxford: Clarendon, 1994.

Yoon, Carol Kaesuk. *Naming Nature: The Clash between Instinct and Science*. New York: Norton, 2009.

Zachs, William. *The First John Murray and the Late Eighteenth-Century London Book Trade*. Oxford: British Academy, 1998.

Index

Addison, Joseph, 18, 38, 164n2
Adorno, Theodor, 4
advertising, art of, 144, 146–48
advertising, general: fortunes made from, 17, 58, 121, 122; as literature, 11–12, 144, 146–48; rise of literary criticism and, 37–49; rise of novel and, 34–37; as science, 11–12; stigmas against, 13, 26–28, 39, 57–58, 130; as system, 11–12, 49, 146; term's origins and development, 18, 25
advertising, historiography of: American biases in, 6, 8; Romantic-era scholarship and, 8–9, 119; Victorian biases in, 6–8, 12, 20, 21, 22, 143, 151n6
advertising, history of: pre-1700, 13, 23, 25–26, 56–57, 153n10, 155n4; 1700–1800, 17–26, 50–51; 1800–1850, 11–12, 24, 51, 62, 118–44; post-1850, 143; illustration in, 102–3, 114, 160n23; preconditions for modern advertising, 13–17; professionalization of, 21–22, 48–49, 52. See also puffery entries; quack medicine
advertising agents, 21–22, 52
advertising techniques: front matter in books, 23, 35; gifts and special offers, 29, 30, 153n7; handbills, 20; horse-drawn billboards, 20; illustrated ads, 62–63, 102–3, 114, 160n23; lies, 29, 48, 120; loss leaders, 21; manufactured scandal, 36, 48, 70; money-back guarantees, 21; narrative advertisements, 58–60; outdoor advertising, 13, 20, 31, 62, 143, 145, 148, 164n1; posters, 13, 62, 143, 145, 148, 164n1; product families, 30; product placement, 21, 30, 58, 75, 122; sandwich-board carriers, 20; sex appeal, 99–117; slogans and jingles, 20, 62–63;

street criers, 13; trade cards, 20, 32–33; trade catalogues, 23; veiled authorship, 87–92; word-of-mouth marketing, 36, 65. *See also* bandwagon marketing; branding; portraits; publicity; puffery *entries*; quack medicine
Age, 126
"Age of Veneer, The" (Francis), 11–13, 151n1 (chap. 1)
Ainsworth's Magazine, 123
Allison, Archibald, 126
amazon.com, 3–5, 151n3
America. *See* United States of America
Analectic Magazine, 89
Annual Register, 132
annuals, 100–102, 103
anonymity: Byron and, 68, 72, 86; Landon and, 89–93; and literary criticism, 142, 164n29; mitigated, 87; as promotional device, 87–92; before Romantic Century, 158n7; during Romantic Century, 86–90, 158n8; Scott and, 85–89, 158n9
Antijacobin Review, 45
"Anti-Puff," 136, 163n19
"Antipuffado," 136, 163n19
Arnold, Matthew, 11, 142
Athenaeum, 125, 138–39, 142
Atkinson, James, 146
Atlas, 100–101
Attic Miscellany, 99–100
Austen, Henry, 88
Austen, Jane, 87, 88
Austen, Mary, 88
authorship: anonymity and, 85–92; branding and, 69; false attributions and, 29–30, 159n20; modern forms of, 22, 28; puffery's sullying of, 139

INDEX

Babbage, Charles, 164n27
Baiesi, Serena, 90
Bailey, Benjamin, 131
Ballantyne, James, 88, 137
Ballot, 126
bandwagon marketing, 94–99
Barker, Charles, 21
Barnes and Noble, 3, 5
Barnum, P. T., 6, 62
Barrett, Eaton Stannard, 59
Barthes, Roland, 6
Barton, Bernard, 2, 91, 92–95, 159n19
Basker, James, 39, 41
Bates, William, 82
Bayley, William, 58
Bayley's blacking cakes, 58–60
Beattie, James, 46
Beckford, William, 119
Belle Assemblée, 107
Benbow, William, 136
Bennett, Andrew, 87
Bentley's Miscellany, 106–7
bestsellers, 35, 65, 97–98, 101
Bezos, Jeff, 3
Bird, Alfred, 161n6
blacking: branding and, 58–63, 123, 155n5, 156n10; literature and, 52–53, 130, 138–39, 144; "poet laureate" of, 52–53
Blacklock, Thomas, 46
Blackwood, William, 1–2, 157n2. *See also Blackwood's Edinburgh Magazine*
Blackwood's Edinburgh Magazine: on anonymity, 90–91, 135, 158n8, 158n9; on blacking poetry, 52–53; on Cockney School, 1, 131, 136, 142; on Landon, 83, 99, 108, 159n14; puffery assailed in, 1–2, 126, 131, 136–39; puffery practiced in, 2–3, 129, 157n2
Blair, Hugh, 69, 126
Blake, David Haven, 162n9
Blakey, Dorothy, 120
Blanchard, Laman, 89–91
book clubs, 45
book reviewing. *See* criticism
book trade: advertising innovation in, 24–31; in America today, 3–5; branding in, 75–76; competition in, 28; corruption in, 29, 78, 104–6, 118–19, 135–41

Boot, Jesse, 155n2
Borders bookstores, 3, 5
Borington, Lady, 88
Boswell, James, 154n23
Boulton, Matthew, 21
Braithwaite, Kent, 4
branding: Byron and, 53–54, 62–80; early practitioners of, 57–62, 144, 146–47; Landon and, 101–2; nationwide trade and, 12, 21, 57; preconditions for, 56; of publishers, 75; quack medicines and, 57; theory, logic, and efficacy of, 57–58, 69, 76, 77
Brewer, John, 7, 14, 15
Briggs, Peter M., 7
British Critic, 2
Brock, Claire, 69
Brougham, Henry, 163n20
Brown, Stephen, 23
Bruttini, Adriano, 17
Bulwer-Lytton, Edward, 64, 89–91, 125
Burdett, Sir Francis, 73
Burn, James Dawson, 147
Burney, Charles, 154n23
Burney, Frances (Fanny), 37, 87–88
Busy Body, 46
Byron, Catherine Gordon, 67, 68, 70
Byron, Lord: ambition of, 66–69; anonymity and, 68, 72, 86; blacking poetry and, 52–53; branding of, 53–54, 64–80; celebrity and, 64–74; Cockney School and, 129, 131; Dallas and, 74–80; insincerity of, 65; Landon and, 84–85, 90; Murray and, 74–80; portraits of, 70–71, 75, 113; publicity and, 69–73; puffery and, 78, 79–80, 162n16; on reviews' influence, 124
Byron, Lord, works of: *Childe Harold's Pilgrimage* (cantos 1 and 2), 52, 53, 54, 64–65, 69–80; *The Corsair*, 68, 74, 75, 97; *Don Juan*, 75; *English Bards and Scotch Reviewers*, 67–68, 70, 72, 76, 78, 80; *Fugitive Pieces*, 66, 68; *Hints from Horace*, 70; *Hours of Idleness*, 66–68, 70, 78; "Ode to the Framers of the Frame Bill," 73; *Poems on Several Occasions*, 66, 68

INDEX 195

Cadell, Thomas, 139
Caledonian Mercury, 133
Calkins, Earnest Elmo, 6–7
Campbell, Archibald, 45
Campbell, Colin, 15–17, 146
Campbell, Jill, 7, 37
Campbell, Thomas, 72, 126, 134, 136
Canning, George, 81–82
capitalism: and advertising's rise, 14–15, 25; and literature, 4; origins of, 22
Carlyle, Thomas, 136, 137–38, 163n24
Cawthorn, James, 68, 69–70, 78
Caxton, William, 13, 23
celebrity: advertising culture and, 144, 146, 147; Byron and, 64–73; Landon and, 89–111; Pope and, 68, 69
Chambers' Edinburgh Journal, 85–86, 147
Champion, 34, 131, 162n15
Charles II, 25
Chatterton, Thomas, 46
Childe Harold's Pilgrimage. *See* Byron, Lord, works of
child naming practices. *See* onomastic revolution
Chorley, Henry Fothergill, 157n2
Christensen, Jerome, 64
Christie, William, 45
circulating libraries, 45
Clarkson, Edward, 164n28
Cleland, John, 42, 44
Clery, E. J., 120
Cockney School, 129–32
coffeehouses, 18
Colburn, Henry, 82, 92, 124–25, 136, 138–39, 162n8
Coleridge, John Taylor, 128
Coleridge, Samuel Taylor: anonymity and, 86, 124; as object of criticism and satire, 1, 62, 115, 124; poetic theory and practice of, 147, 162n17; puffery and, 118–19, 123, 126–28, 134, 136
Collier, John Payne, 125
commendatory verses and dedications, 35–36, 153n10
commodification: of art, 4–5, 148–49; in contemporary economic theory, 5; of Landon, 100–101, 158n11; of literature, 4–5, 65, 80, 118–19, 138–42, 148–49

Constable, Archibald: on anonymity, 86–87; Crash of 1826 and, 137; *Edinburgh Review* and, 1; Murray and, 74–75; Scott and, 88, 89, 97, 132
consumer society, 14–17, 22, 25–26, 51
Cooney, Seamus, 88
copyright, 22, 28
Corley, T. A. B., 122
Cornhill Magazine, 148
Cornwall, Barry (Bryan Waller Procter), 2, 91, 157n2
Court Journal, 125, 126
Cox, Jeffrey N., 129, 131
Craciun, Adriana, 84
Crash of 1826, 102, 137, 163n22
Critic, The (Sheridan), 46–49, 50, 147
Critical Review, 40, 120, 129
criticism: advertising and the rise of, 37–49; corruption in, 31–49, 79–80, 118–42; *The Critic* on, 47–49; history of, 37–38; *Monthly Review* and the rise of, 38–40; power of, over readers, 45–46, 124–25; reform of, 142; scholarship on, 119
Croker, John Wilson, 125, 162n17
Croly, George, 126
Cronin, Richard, 99, 158n11
Crose, Jean de la, 38
Cruikshank, George, 8, 62, 103
Cumberland, Richard, 164n29
Cunningham, Allan, 2
Curran, John Philpot, 65

Daily Advertiser, In Metre, The (Sternhold), 50–51
Daily Post (London), 18
Dallas, Robert Charles, 70, 72–80
Day and Martin's blacking, 52–53, 62, 147, 155n2
Deacon, William Frederick, 53, 115
Defoe, Daniel, 26–27, 57
De Quincey, Thomas, 91
Desoer, John, 58–60
Dickens, Charles, 20, 61, 151n1 (chap. 1), 155n9, 164n1
Disraeli, Benjamin, 99
Dodsley, Robert, 28
Donoghue, Frank, 41

Dorset, Catherine, 88
Dr. James's Fever Powders, 31, 57
Dublin Literary Gazette, 107
Dublin University Magazine, 46
Dunton, John, 153n10
Duppa, Richard, 76
Dyer, Gary, 163n22

Eagleton, Terry, 38
Edgeworth, Maria, 37, 52, 59
Edinburgh Annual Register, 134
Edinburgh Monthly Review, 2
Edinburgh Review: on advertising, 123, 140; Byron and, 52, 67, 68, 79; failings of, 126, 136, 163n20; independence of, 142; influence of, 1, 124; scholarship on, 119; Scott and, 132
editions: misnumbering of, 29; rarity of second, 68, 156n19; time required to produce new, 97
Eggers, Dave, 4
Eisner, Eric, 69, 84
Ellis, George, 79
English Bards and Scotch Reviewers. *See* Byron, Lord, works of
Englishman's Magazine, 129
engraving, 102–3
Erickson, Lee, 163n22
Erskine, William, 133
European Magazine, 160n26
Examiner: Cockney School of puffery in, 129–31, 142; contributors to, 135; Jerdan and, 82

fame. *See* celebrity
Fanny Hill (Cleland), 42, 44
Feather, John, 23
Ferdinand, C. Y., 25
Fielding, Henry: on advertising, 18; on corruption in book trade, 29–30; on puffery, 34–36, 136, 164n2
Fine, Ben, 17
Forster, Antonia, 46
Forster, John, 160n28
Foucault, Michel, 75
Fox, Stephen, 6
Francis, George Henry, 11–13, 151n1 (chap. 1)

Franzen, Jonathan, 4
Fraser's Magazine: on advertising's power, 116, 143; "Age of Veneer" series, 11–12; "Gallery of Illustrious Literary Characters," 82, 108–9, 111; on puffery, 124, 125–26, 138, 142; "Regina's Maids of Honour," 161n32
Frith, W. P., 160n23
Fuseli, Henry, 154n23

"Gallery of Illustrious Literary Characters." *See Fraser's Magazine*
Garrick, David, 46
Garrick, Eva, 46
Genette, Gérard, 6, 159n12
Gentleman's Magazine, 38, 92, 96
Gifford, William, 78–79, 128, 133, 136
Ginsberg, Allen, 4–5
Gladstone, William, 161n6
Godbold, Nathaniel, 18–19
Godwin, William, 129, 130
Goldsmith, Oliver, 40, 46
Gore, Catherine (Mrs. Charles), 126, 141
Gray's-Inn Journal, 40
Great Exhibition of 1851, 7, 11, 22
Greenfield, William, 89
Griffiths, Ralph, 38–45
Grub-Street Journal, 34
Gunning, Susannah, 120–21

Hall, Anna Maria, 161n32
Hall, Basil, 126
Hall, S. C., 107, 110
Hamilton, Elizabeth, 88
Hayden, John O., 119, 132, 161n2
Hayward, Abraham, 123, 146
Hazlitt, William, 123, 124, 129–31, 162n15
Hebdige, Dick, 6
Hemans, Felicia, 2, 86
Hill, Aaron, 36
Hill, John, 44–45
History of the Works of the Learned, 38
Hobhouse, John Cam, 64, 74
Hodnett, Edward, 103
Hogg, James, 109–10, 126, 134–35, 163n18
Hogg, Thomas Jefferson, 162n13
Holden, Anthony, 130

Holden, Ralph, 6–7
Holland, Lord, 72–73
Hone, William, 8
Hood, Thomas, 62, 99, 125, 144, 146
Hopkinson, John, 92
Hunt, John, 129, 130
Hunt, Leigh, 1, 129–31
Hurst and Robinson (publishers), 96–97

Illustrated London News, 103
illustration, 102–3
imagination, 146–48
Improvisatrice, The. See Landon, Letita Elizabeth (L.E.L.), works of
initials: as signing strategy, 89–92, 99, 159n20, 159n21
Inspector and Literary Review, 84, 101

James II, 25
James, Robert, 31
Jeffrey, Francis, 78, 79
Jerdan, William: on advertising's power, 116–17; affair with Landon, 110–17; bandwagon marketing and, 94–99; Barton and, 93–94; influence and reputation of, 81–85; marketing of Landon, 91–111, 157n2, 159n18
John Bull Magazine, 97–98, 125, 136, 159n14
Johnson, Samuel, 18, 24, 50, 69, 147
Jones, Christine Kenyon, 70
Jonson, Ben, 29
Journal des Scavans, 38

Kean, Edmund, 46
Keats, John, 129–32, 136, 142, 162n15
Kemble, John, 130
Kemp, Alexander, 155n2
Keymer, Thomas, 35–37
Klancher, Jon P., 119
Knickerbocker, 134
Knight, George, 102–3
Knowles, Claire, 84
Kövesi, Simon, 162n15

Lackington, James, 28, 120–21
Ladies' Companion, 82
Lake Poets, 127

Lamb, Charles, 103, 128, 129, 130, 162n14
Lancet, 126
Landon, Letitia Elizabeth (L.E.L.): bandwagon marketing and, 94–99; celebrity and, 98–111; as "female Byron," 84–85, 90, 101; insincerity of, 84; on Jerdan, 158n4; as "L.E.L.," 89–92, 159n14; portraits of, 104–17, 160n26, 161n32; professional acumen of, 83–84, 90, 101–2, 113–14, 158n11; puffery and, 83, 92–101; scandals surrounding, 108, 110–17, 160n28; sex appeal of, 99–117; visual culture and, 103–17
Landon, Letitia Elizabeth (L.E.L.), works of: *Fate of Adelaide*, 91, 97; gift books and annuals, 100, 101–2; *Golden Violet*, 100–1; *Improvisatrice*, 83, 91–92, 95–100, 108; novels, 102, 160n29; *Troubadour*, 100; *Vow of the Peacock*, 111–12
Lane, William, 120, 122, 161n4
Lawford, Cynthia, 110
LeCat, Claude Nicolas, 41
Leighton, Angela, 90
L.E.L. See Landon, Letitia Elizabeth
Liberal, 129
Lightfoot, Martin, 132
Linnaeus, Carl, 54, 155n3
literacy rates, 13–14
Literary Chronicle, 98, 104
literary criticism. See criticism
Literary Gazette: Jerdan and, 81, 82, 125, 157n2; marketing of Landon in, 90–101, 104–5, 107–8, 115–117
Literary Magnet, 98, 104, 159n18
Literary Panorama, 79
literature: commerce and, 4–5; "death" of, 137–41; as invention of Romantic Century, 22, 28, 152n8
Lockhart, John Gibson, 1–3, 90–91, 133
Loeb, Lori Anne, 7
London Magazine: initials in, 91; on Landon, 99; puffery and, 1, 93, 138, 144
London Society, 143–44
London Weekly Review, 137
Longman, Thomas, 86, 92
Lootens, Tricia, 158n11

INDEX

Macaulay, Thomas Babington, 136, 140–41, 161n6, 164n28
Mackenzie, Henry, 2, 66
Mackintosh, Sir James, 126
Maclise, Daniel, 106–9, 111–15, 160n28
Magazine de Londres, 41–42
magazines. *See* periodicals
Maginn, William: on blacking poetry, 53; Landon and, 99, 107–8; on puffery, 124, 126, 138–39
Mahony, Francis, 108
Manning, Peter J., 64
Marchand, Leslie, 138
Marcus, James, 3
Martin, John, 146–47
Matoff, Susan, 90
McGann, Jerome, 84, 103, 158n11, 159n16
McKendrick, Neil, 7, 15–17
medical advertisements. *See* quack medicine
Medwin, Thomas, 68
Mellor, Anne, 99, 158n11
Memoirs of a Woman of Pleasure (Cleland), 42, 44
Metropolitan Magazine, 126
Mill, John Stuart, 138, 164n29
Miller, William, 70, 76
Milman, Henry, 2
Minerva Press, 120, 122, 161n4
Mirror, 164n2
Moir, David Macbeth, 91
Mole, Tom, 73, 86, 157n21
Moncrieff, W. T., 22
Montgomery, Robert, 101, 116, 139–41, 164n28
Monthly Magazine, 126
Monthly Review: contributors to, 135, 142; on *Fanny Hill*, 44; on Landon, 101; as pioneer in literary criticism, 39–40; puffery in, 38–45
Moore, Thomas, 64–65, 72, 131
Morgan, Marjorie, 161n3
Morning Chronicle (London), 17, 48, 77, 125, 133
Motteaux, Peter Anthony, 38
Moxon, Edward, 124, 129
Mui, Hoh-Cheung, 7

Mui, Lorna, 7
Mulrooney, Jonathan, 152n4
Murray, John (the elder), 74
Murray, John (the younger): advertising genius of, 64, 85, 97; Crash of 1826 and, 137; Byron and, 70, 72–80, 86, 162n16; Landon and, 85, 86, 92; puffery and, 136; Scott and, 132

names and naming. *See* anonymity; initials; onomastic revolution; onymity; pseudonymity
Nangle, Benjamin Christie, 40
National Standard, 82–83
Nevett, T. R., 21
Newbery, John, 28, 30–31, 120
New Monthly Magazine, 2, 112, 114, 125, 137
News (London), 129–30
newspapers: column and layout restrictions in, 20, 114; early advertising in, 13, 23–25; emergence of, in Britain, 14; proliferation of advertisements in, 20, 24–25, 152n4
Nicholson, Andrew, 78
Nisbet, H. B., 38
Norton, Caroline, 115
Nouveau Magasin Francois, Le, 41
novels: advertising's role in rise of, 37; anonymity in, 86

"One Master Trimmer," 119, 139
onomastic revolution: anonymity and, 85–92; in biology, 54; branding of products and, 56–62; in infant naming, 54–56
onymity, 91, 159n12
Opie, Amelia, 86–87
Oxberry's Dramatic Biography, 159n20

packaging, 52, 56
Packwood, George: in branding history and popular culture, 59, 61; *Packwood's Whim*, 59; poetry and, 52
Packwood's razor strops, 12, 59, 61
Pamela (Richardson), 34–37
Pamela Censured, 36–37
papermaking, 56, 137

Parker, Mark, 119
Parry, John Orlando, 143, 145
Pascoe, Judith, 69, 159n13
patent medicines. *See* quack medicine
Patmore, Peter George, 125
Paulding, James Kirke, 118
Pears' Soap, 114
Penny Magazine, 103
periodicals: booksellers' acquisition of, 124–25; in coffeehouses, 18; earliest in Britain, 14; illustrations in, 102–3; reliance of, on advertising revenue, 17, 25. *See also* newspapers; print culture
Perry, James, 17
Peterson, Linda H., 158n11
Pickersgill, H. W., 104–5, 106–7, 160n26
Pillars of Priestcraft and Orthodoxy Shaken, The, 42–43
Plumb, J. H., 7, 15
Poetical March of Humbug!, The, 115–17, 127, 155n2, 161n33
poetry: advertising and, 50–53, 62–63, 144, 146–48; anonymity in, 86–87; Crash of 1826 and, 102, 137, 140, 163n22; Landon's reinvigoration of, 101
Pope, Alexander: advertising and, 27–28, 34; celebrity of, 68, 69; on *Pamela*, 36
pornography, 36–37, 42, 44, 102
Porter, Roy, 24
portraits: of Byron, 70–71, 75, 113; of Landon, 103–17, 160n26, 161n32
press secretaries, 81, 157n1
prices: of books, 65, 137, 156n16; of literary advertising campaigns, 76
print culture: credibility of printed materials, 49, 124, 140; eighteenth-century expansion of, 28; as precondition of modern advertising, 13–14; rise of criticism and, 49
Procter, Bryan Waller. *See* Cornwall, Barry
pseudonymity, 87–92
Public Advertiser, 50
Publicis, 7
publicity: Byron's flair for, 65, 69–73, 157n23; for *Childe Harold's Pilgrimage*, 76–80; for Landon, 92–98, 159n18;

Lane's flair for, 120, 122; via manufactured scandal, 36, 48, 70; Murray's faith in, 75
publishers. *See* Blackwood, William; book trade; Colburn, Henry; Constable, Archibald; Griffiths, Ralph; Jerdan, William; Lackington, James; Lane, William; Murray, John (elder and younger); Newbery, John
puffery, attacks on: by *Blackwood's*, 1–2, 131; by Carlyle, 137–38, 163n24; by Coleridge, 126–28, 136; by Fielding, 34–36, 136; by Hunt, 129–30, 136; by Macaulay, 140–41; by Montgomery, 139–41; by reform-era consortium, 136–42, 143–44; by Sheridan, 47–49, 136; by travelers in Britain, 118, 123
puffery, history of: pre-1730, 153n10; 1730–1800, 31–49; 1800–1850, 118–42; contemporary, 3–4, 151n3; scholarly neglect of, 119, 132, 135–36, 161n1, 161n2; taxonomies of, 48–49, 154n26, 154n27; term's origins and definition, 31, 34, 153n11, 153n12
puffery, impact of: on canon formation, 141; on literature's "demise," 137–41
puffery, insider reviews as: Beckford and, 119; in *Blackwood's*, 1–3, 126; Blair and, 126; Byron and, 78–80, 162n16; Cockney School and, 129–32; Colburn and, 124–25, 138–39; Jerdan and Landon and, 83–84, 92–101, 157n2; Lake Poets and, 125–29; in *Literary Gazette*, 82–83, 92–101; Montgomery and, 139–41; in *Monthly Review*, 38–45; Pope and, 27; Richardson and, 34–37; Robinson and, 119, 126; in theater world, 47–49, 129–30, 154n25
puffery, self-reviews as: on amazon.com, 4; by Barton, 93; in *Blackwood's*, 2–3; by Boswell, 154n23; by Charles Burney, 154n23; by Coleridge, 128, 134; by Fuseli, 154n23; by Garrick, 46; by Hazlitt, 129; by Lamb, 129; by minor writers, 125–26; in *Monthly Review*, 44–45; by Scott, 132–35, 162n17; by

puffery (*continued*)
  Smollett, 154n23; by Whitman, 125; by Wollstonecraft, 126
Puffiad, The (Montgomery), 139–40, 164n28
Puffs and Mysteries, 147

quack medicine: advertisements for, 18–19, 20, 21, 24, 26, 162n7; early branding and, 57; ties of, to book trade, 30–33, 118, 123, 138
Quarterly Review: on advertising, 123, 146–47; Byron and, 78, 79; Coleridge and, 127–28; contributors to, 135; influence of, 1, 74, 78, 124; on Keats, 131; puffery and, 2, 93, 126, 128, 132–34, 162n11, 162n16, 162n17; scholarship on, 119; Scott and, 132–34

Radin, Margaret Jane, 5
Raven, James, 7, 21
Rawson, Claude, 38
Reade, Edmund, 91
Rechy, John, 4
Reiman, Donald, 161n1
Repository of the Arts (Ackermann), 89
reviews. *See* criticism; puffery *entries*
Reynolds, John Hamilton, 99, 130–31, 144, 162n15
Richards, Thomas, 7
Richardson, Samuel, 34–37, 45, 69
Riess, Daniel, 84, 103, 158n11, 159n16
Riggio, Len, 5
Robert, James, 36
Robins, George, 146–47
Robinson, Henry, 104–5
Robinson, Jacob, 38–39
Robinson, Mary, 69, 119, 126
Rogers, Samuel, 72, 157n23
Romantic Century, 5, 151n4
Roper, Derek, 41
Ross, John, 111, 160n30
Rossetti, Dante Gabriel, 108
Rowland, Alexander, 146
Rowton, Frederic, 84
Royal Lady's Magazine, 110–11, 160n29
Ryan, Richard, 104–6

Sabor, Peter, 35–37
Saenger, Michael Baird, 23
Sanders, George, 70–71
satire: in advertisements, 8–9, 52; on advertising, 47–49, 50–53, 122–23, 136, 144, 146–48, 163n21, 164n26, 164n2; anonymity and, 86
Satirist, 136
Scots Magazine, 34
Scott, Sir Walter: anonymity and, 85–89, 91, 102, 158n6, 158n8, 158n9; blacking poetry and, 62, 155n2; Byron and, 68; celebrity of, 69, 97, 104, 147; self-reviews by, 132–35, 162n17
Scott, William Bell, 83
self-reviews. *See* puffery, self-reviews as
sermons, 36–37
Seymour, Robert, 51, 116–17, 161n33
Shakespeare, William, 13, 29, 59
Shamela (Fielding), 34–36
Shelley, Mary, 129–31
Shelley, Percy Bysshe, 129–31, 147, 162n13
Sher, Richard B., 75, 87
Sheridan, Richard Brinsley, 47–49, 50, 136, 147
Shoberl, Frederic, 125
Sinclair, Sir John, 89
Slocock, Benjamin, 36
Smart, Christopher, 31
Smellie, William, 44
Smith, Charlotte, 88
Smith, Horace, 53
Smollett, Tobias, 40, 44, 154n23
Sommerville, C. John, 25
Southern, Henry, 138
Southey, Robert: on advertising culture, 21, 126; anonymity and, 86; Barton and, 93; on illustrated books, 103; puffery and, 126, 129; satires on, 68, 115; Scott and 134, 135
Spectator, 38
Spy, 135
Stapleton, A. G., 81
Star (London), 120, 122
Star Chamber, 99
St. Clair, William, 156n19
Stead, William, Jr., 148, 151n6

Steele, Richard, 38
Stephenson, Glennis, 90
Sterne, Laurence, 55
Sternhold, Thomas, 50–51
Strachan, John, 8–9, 52, 130, 155n8, 161n5, 162n14, 164n26
Strasser, Susan, 57–58
Struggles of Brown, Jones, and Robinson, The (Trollope), 147–48
Sunday Times, 110, 125
Sutherland, John, 88, 163n22
Swift, Jonathan, 30, 156n10
Sypher, F. J., 160n25

Tait's Edinburgh Magazine, 137, 146
Tatler, 38, 164n2
taxes: on advertisements, 17, 18–20, 31; attempts to circumvent, 19–20; on paper (stamp tax), 19, 31; repeal of, 114
Tayler, Charles Benjamin, 91
Tayler, William, 21
Taylor and Hessey (publishers), 2, 93
Telegraph, 119
Tennyson, Lord Alfred, 11
Thackeray, William Makepeace, 65, 82–83
theater, puffery in the, 47–49, 129–30, 154n25
Thelwall, John, 162n15
Thornton, Sara, 6, 51, 164n1
Thrall, Miriam M. H., 138
Tighe, Mary, 104
Time magazine, 6
Times (London), 77, 122, 125–26, 161n5
title pages, 23, 29, 46
transportation, advances in, 12, 15, 57
Trifler, 162n7
Tristan, Flora, 123
Tristram Shandy (Sterne), 55
Trollope, Anthony, 147–48
Trusler, John, 29, 120
Tytler, Alexander Fraser, 66

United Service Journal, 125
United States of America, 161n6, 164n4: advertising in contemporary book trade, 3–5; birth of advertising and, 5–6; literary nationalism and, 118; and Scott, 133–34; visual advertising in, 114
Universal Advertiser, 40

Veblen, Thorstein, 15
Victorian period: advertising in, 6–8, 12, 20, 21, 114, 147–48; as "Age of Veneer," 11–12; as transitional age, 11; visual culture in, 85, 114
Vincent, Patrick, 99
visual culture: and marketing of Landon, 103–17; in Romantic-era Britain, 102–4

Wakley, Thomas, 126
Walker, Henry, 153n10
Wall, Cynthia, 7
Ward, William S., 162n11
Warner, William B., 35
Warren, Robert: advertising campaigns of, 62, 156n12; blacking of, 12, 51, 52–53, 61–63; commercial poetry and, 52–53, 62–63, 103, 144, 146, 155n2; in Dickensian lore, 61, 155n9; as object of satires, 62, 115–16
Warreniana (Deacon), 53, 115
Warren's blacking. *See* Warren, Robert
Wasp, 110
Watt, Julie, 90
Waugh, John, 2
Weber, Max, 15
Webster, William, 36
Wedgwood, Josiah, 15, 21, 58, 120
Weekes, Henry, 111–13
Weekly Register, 34
Wellek, René, 152n8
Wellesley Index to Victorian Periodicals, 142
Westmacott, Charles Malloy, 126
Westminster Review, 114, 124, 144, 164n29
White, Caroline Alice, 143
White, James, 21
Whitman, Walt, 125, 162n9
Wicke, Jennifer, 8
Williams, D. E., 125–26
Williams, Raymond, 6, 7, 148–49, 152n8

Williams, Robert Folkestone, 125
Wilson, Effingham, 138
Wilson, John, 1–3, 139
Wolfson, Susan, 84
Wollstonecraft, Mary, 126
Wood, Marcus, 8–9, 52
woodcuts, 102–3
Wordsworth, Dorothy, 128–29

Wordsworth, William: on advertising and visual culture, 20, 103, 162n12; anonymity and, 86; on influence of reviews, 124, 141; Keats and, 131; Landon on, 100; as object of satire, 62, 68, 115; *Prelude*, 11, 20, 103; puffery and, 127–29, 162n11
Wright, John William, 112, 114
Wynter, Andrew, 103